CATALYST
LEADERSHIP

Proven Tools to Drive
Innovation, Empower People,
and Crush The Competition

Rich Gee

Published by HMDPublishing.com

ISBN: 978-1-83556-464-6   eBook
ISBN: 978-1-83556-465-3   Paperback
ISBN: 978-1-83556-466-0   Hardback

First Edition
First printing, 2025

Legal Disclaimer:
The information in this book is provided for general informational purposes only and is not intended as professional advice. The author and publisher make no warranties or representations regarding the accuracy, applicability, or completeness of the contents. Readers are encouraged to consult with qualified professionals before making business decisions based on this material. Any reliance on the information is at the reader's own risk. Names, companies, and examples mentioned may be based on real entities or events but are used illustratively; any resemblance to specific outcomes or situations is coincidental and not a guarantee of similar results.

Credits:
Cover design by Rich Gee
Illustrations by Rich Gee

Cataloging-in-Publication Data:
Gee, Rich.
Catalyst Leadership / Rich Gee.
Description: First edition. | Stamford : Brentwood Farm Press, 2025.
Identifiers: ISBN 000-0-000000-00-0

Subjects: LCSH: Leadership. | Organizational change. | Business planning. | BISAC: BUSINESS & ECONOMICS / Leadership | BUSINESS & ECONOMICS / Management | BUSINESS & ECONOMICS / Organizational Development

Classification: LCC HD57.7 .D64 2023 | DDC 658.4/092--dc23

Printer's Key:
10 9 8 7 6 5 4 3 2 1

Printed in the United States of America

ACKNOWLEDGMENTS

To Silvia, Chris, and Andrew
who believe in me every day.

CONTENTS

VISIONARY LEADERSHIP & INNOVATION

EMPOWERING TEAMS

NAVIGATING TECHNOLOGICAL & CULTURAL SHIFTS

CATALYST

CAT-uh-list - /ˈkæt.ə.lɪst/

A catalyst is something or someone that accelerates or triggers change, growth, or a reaction without being consumed or fundamentally altered in the process.

In chemistry, a catalyst speeds up a chemical reaction by lowering the activation energy required yet remains unchanged at the end.

In a broader, non-scientific context, **a catalyst can be an event, individual, or factor that sparks significant transformation or inspires others to act.**

"Leaders who avoid bold moves don't get remembered - they get forgotten. Playing it safe doesn't protect you; it buries you."

WHY I WROTE THIS BOOK
(READ THIS FIRST)

THE REASONS WHY LEADERS NEED THIS BOOK AND WHY I STRUCTURED IT THIS WAY.

WHY THIS BOOK?

Let's cut through the noise: too many leaders are terrified of rocking the boat. They're scared of making their bosses angry, uncovering mismanagement, or drawing attention to their own ideas. It's a leadership epidemic - companies prioritizing smooth sailing over bold, meaningful change.

Here's the dirty little secret: for most executives, their career, bonus, and reputation are tied to one thing - *not screwing up*. Boards and shareholders want predictability, quarterly targets hit, and no drama. Change is scary, and rocking the boat risks everything, even when the ship is heading straight for an iceberg.

This book is for the leaders who don't want to coast. It's for the catalysts - the ones who are ready to step up, push boundaries, and make a lasting impact.

WHY LEADERS FAIL TO LEAD

The truth is, most leaders don't embrace change until they're staring into the abyss. Think about it: when do companies finally act? When they're bleeding cash. When the future looks murky. When survival is on the line. Only then do they start asking the big questions, taking risks, and fighting to innovate.

But why wait until the walls are closing in? Jeff Bezos didn't wait. Reed Hastings didn't wait. Steve Jobs? He got kicked out of his own company, came back, and still didn't wait. These leaders knew that *complacency is a slow death sentence*.

Now, contrast them with the cautionary tale of Kodak.

THE KODAK LEADERSHIP PHILOSOPHY: HOW COMFORT KILLED A GIANT

Once upon a time, Kodak wasn't just a company - it was *the* company. They didn't just dominate the film industry; they *invented* it. And here's the kicker: Kodak also invented the digital camera. That's right. The very technology that ultimately destroyed their business was created in-house by their own engineers in 1975.

So what went wrong?

Kodak's leadership. The company's executives saw digital as a threat to their cash cow - the film business. Instead of adapting and doubling down on innovation, they shelved the digital camera for fear it would cannibalize their core product.

They played it safe.

By the time Kodak decided to take digital seriously, it was too late. Competitors like Sony and Canon had captured the market. Startups with nothing to lose disrupted the status quo. Kodak's leaders were so obsessed with protecting their existing business that they failed to see where the future was headed.

And here's the kicker: can you name a single Kodak executive who was responsible for these decisions? Of course not. That's the point. Leaders who avoid bold moves don't get remembered - they get forgotten.

The lesson? Playing it safe doesn't protect you; it buries you.

WHY I WROTE THIS BOOK

Because this kind of thinking - the "Kodak Leadership Philosophy" - is everywhere. It's in companies big and small, where CEOs are handcuffed by boards and Wall Street analysts. Their sole mission? Hit targets. Stay the course. Don't take risks. And God forbid they suggest launching a new product line or pivoting in a different direction - they'll be out the door before they can finish their pitch.

But the world doesn't wait. Markets don't pause. Innovation doesn't slow down. Companies that don't adapt, grow, and innovate, they die. Period.

The problem is, real change doesn't come from the top. Catalyst Leadership starts from the bottom and builds upward. It's a grassroots movement. It's getting buy-in from your team, creating momentum, and finding your evangelists. You're not just pitching a new idea - you're starting a revolution within your organization.

Every company needs catalysts. Without them, businesses stagnate, merge with other bloated dinosaurs, and wait for the next disruptor to blow up their world. Think about Motorola, Nokia, Blackberry. They didn't die because the market wasn't there - they died because they failed to change.

HOW THIS BOOK WORKS

Let's get one thing straight: most business books suck.

They're too fluffy, too philosophical, and way too long. I used to be that guy with a massive bookshelf full of "business classics." You know the type. But here's the dirty little secret: I barely finished any of them. Most of those books were more about padding pages than delivering value.

I'm not here to waste your time.

The best book I ever read? *How to Win Friends and Influence People* by Dale Carnegie. Short. Practical. Powerful. It didn't drown you in theory; it gave you real stories and actionable steps to apply immediately.

That's the formula I'm borrowing for this book. Each chapter is structured to give you precisely what you need:

1. **Story**: Real-world examples of Catalyst Leadership in action.

2. **Key Takeaways:** Learnings from the real-life example.

3. **Theory**: Breaking down the "why" behind the story.

4. **Take Action**: What can you do today to lead like a catalyst?

5. **Final Thoughts:** Wrapping it all up.

EXTRA CREDIT: Tools: Every chapter, I'll throw in a powerful resource tool that I use in my workshops.

This isn't a book - it's a toolbox.

DON'T READ THIS BOOK (NOT THE WAY YOU THINK)

Let me say something most authors won't: PLEASE . . . *don't read this book.*

At least, please don't read it cover to cover like a novel. That's not the point. This isn't a story with characters and arcs. It's a resource. Skip around. Dive into the chapters that resonate with you. Ignore the ones that don't. Tear out pages. Highlight the hell out of it. Make it your own.

This is a book for leaders who want to **DO**. It's for those ready to spark change, ignite innovation, and build teams that thrive in uncertainty. It's for the leaders who refuse to settle for the status quo and are hungry to create something meaningful.

So grab your tool belt. Flip to the chapter that hits you in the gut. And let's go build something that matters.

INTRODUCTION: IGNITE THE SPARK OF CATALYST LEADERSHIP

"DO YOU BELIEVE YOUR ORGANIZATION HAS UNTAPPED POTENTIAL WAITING TO BE UNLEASHED?"

"The question isn't whether change is coming; it's whether you'll lead it - or be left in its wake."

INTRODUCTION:
IGNITE THE SPARK OF CATALYST LEADERSHIP

Imagine standing on the edge of a precipice, staring into the abyss of irrelevance.

That's precisely where LEGO found itself in 2004 - teetering on the brink of bankruptcy, $800 million in debt, and questioning its very existence. A brand that had once been synonymous with creativity and endless possibilities was now a bloated giant, lost in a maze of its own making. But here's the kicker: LEGO didn't just survive; it roared back to life, becoming the world's most powerful brand by 2015. This is a testament to the potential for growth and success, even in the face of adversity. How? By embracing a catalyst leadership mindset that reignited its core purpose and sparked a revolution from within.

Now, let me ask you: Are you ready to ignite that same spark in your organization? Because here's the brutal truth - standing still is the fastest way to move backward in today's hyper-competitive, ever-evolving business landscape. The game has changed, and the old playbook is obsolete. It's not enough to be a caretaker of the status quo; you need to be the catalyst that drives innovation, inspires your team, and leads transformational change. The time for change is now, and the urgency is palpable.

This book is your blueprint for becoming that catalyst leader. We're diving deep into what it takes to keep up with change and be the force that propels it. We're talking about visionary thinking, embracing disruption, fostering innovation, and empowering your team to reach heights they've only dreamed of. This isn't some theoretical mumbo jumbo; this is actionable, no-nonsense guidance forged in the trenches of real-world business challenges.

So buckle up. It's time to ditch the complacency, shatter the barriers holding you back, and skate to where the puck is going - not where it's been. Let's get into it.

THE BURNING PLATFORM: WHY CATALYST LEADERSHIP IS NON-NEGOTIABLE

Let's cut to the chase. Globalization isn't just a buzzword; it's the reality that your next competitor could emerge from any corner of the world. Technological disruption isn't looming on the horizon; it's knocking on your front door, ready to upend everything you thought you knew about your industry. AI and automation aren't future considerations; they're current game-changers reshaping job roles and market dynamics as we speak.

Look at Sony. Once a titan in consumer electronics, they found themselves blindsided by nimble competitors who embraced digital transformation faster and more effectively. Or take Blockbuster, a company that had every opportunity to adapt to technological shifts but chose to cling to outdated models until Netflix ate their lunch and left them in the dust.

The writing is on the wall: Adapt or become obsolete.

JOBBERS VS. CATALYSTS: THE CHOICE IS YOURS

You might be thinking, "We've been doing fine so far. Why rock the boat?" Well, let me be brutally honest - being a jobber who does the job and maintains the status quo is a one-way ticket to irrelevance. Kodak learned this the hard way. They invented the digital camera but shelved it to protect their film business. The result? They became a footnote in the very industry they once dominated.

Catalyst leaders, on the other hand, drive progress. They're the Jeff Bezoses and Steve Jobses of the world - visionaries who don't just anticipate the future but actively shape it. They understand that complacency is the enemy and continuous innovation is the lifeblood of sustained success.

SKATING TO WHERE THE PUCK IS GOING

Wayne Gretzky, one of the greatest hockey players of all time, famously said, "I skate to where the puck is going to be, not where it has been." This philosophy is pure gold for leadership. It's about anticipation, foresight, and being proactive rather than reactive.

In leadership terms, this means you need to:

- **Anticipate Future Trends:** Stay on top of emerging technologies, market shifts, and consumer behaviors.

- **Embrace Change:** View disruption not as a threat but as an opportunity to innovate and grow.

- **Implement Proactive Strategies:** Don't wait for change to force your hand. Lead the charge. Being proactive is not just a choice; it's necessary in today's fast-paced business environment. It's about taking control of the situation and shaping the future rather than being at the mercy of external forces.

THE CATALYST MINDSET: WHAT SETS YOU APART

Being a catalyst leader is about something other than having a fancy title or a corner office. It's about embodying specific characteristics that set you apart:

- **Visionary Thinking:** You see beyond the immediate horizon. You're not content with incremental improvements; you aim for transformational change.

- **Embracing Change:** You understand that change is the only constant and that adaptability is non-negotiable.

- **Innovative Problem-Solving:** You're not stuck in traditional ways of thinking. You encourage creativity and are open to unconventional solutions.

LEGO'S RESURRECTION: A MASTERCLASS IN PURPOSE-DRIVEN LEADERSHIP

Let's check back in with LEGO because their story is a masterclass in catalyst leadership. When Jørgen Vig Knudstorp took over as CEO, he didn't just trim the fat; he reignited the company's core purpose: "To inspire and develop the builders of tomorrow." This wasn't some hollow mission statement slapped on a wall; it was a rallying cry that permeated every facet of the organization.

They simplified operations, focusing on what they did best - creating bricks that unlocked children's creativity. They sold off non-core ventures, honed in on their primary audience, and even harnessed the power of their user community for co-creation. They didn't just adapt; they transformed, leading to profits that quadrupled between 2008 and 2010.

FROM PURPOSE TO ACTION: TURNING VISION INTO REALITY

A compelling purpose is fantastic but isn't very helpful without action. LEGO didn't just talk the talk; they walked the walk by:

- **Simplifying Operations:** They cut down on unnecessary complexity to focus on their core product.

- **Focusing on Customers:** They re-engaged with their primary audience - children - and listened intently to what they wanted.

- **Harnessing Community Power:** They involved their users in innovation, turning customers into co-creators.

- **Cultural Realignment:** They built a culture mirrored the creativity and innovation they wanted to inspire in children.

THE CATALYST LEADERSHIP FRAMEWORK: YOUR ROADMAP TO TRANSFORMATION

This book is structured to equip you with the tools, insights, and strategies to become a catalyst leader who can drive similar transformational change in your organization. Here's what we're diving into:

1. **Lead Like Bezos** - Igniting Transformation – Lead Like a Catalyst.

2. **The Imperative for Catalyst Leadership** - Understanding why traditional leadership models fail and why catalyst leadership is the future.

3. **Understanding the Catalyst Mindset** - Exploring the characteristics that define catalyst leaders and how to cultivate a growth mindset.

4. **Developing Visionary Leadership** - Crafting a compelling vision and leading with purpose, just like LEGO did.

5. **Fostering Innovation and Creativity** - Building an innovative culture that encourages experimentation and rewards creativity.

6. **Empowering and Engaging Your Team** - Strategies for developing your team members and enhancing collaboration.

7. **Navigating Technological Transformations** - Understanding AI's impact and preparing your team for technological change.

8. **Cultivating Emotional Intelligence** - The importance of self-awareness, empathy, and social skills in effective leadership.

9. **Leading Through Change** - Mastering change management to overcome resistance and sustain momentum.

10. **Shaping Industry Futures** - Becoming a thought leader who drives industry standards and collaborates across sectors.

11. **The Path Forward** - Personal leadership development and sustaining the catalyst leadership model for long-term success.

12. **Ignite Your Catalyst** - Next Steps

YOUR CALL TO ACTION: IGNITE THE CHANGE

Look, reading this book isn't going to transform you into a catalyst leader overnight. It will challenge you, push you out of your comfort zone, and force you to confront the hard truths about your leadership style and your organization's culture. But that's the point. Growth doesn't happen in the comfort zone; it occurs when you stretch your capabilities, take calculated risks, and push the envelope.

So here's your call to action:

- **Be Proactive:** Don't wait for the market to force your hand. Take the initiative to drive change.

- **Embrace Disruption:** See technological advancements like AI not as threats but as tools to propel your organization forward.

- **Invest in Your Team:** Empower your people to think creatively, take risks, and contribute to the vision.

- **Lead with Purpose:** Align every action, every strategy, every initiative with a clear and compelling purpose.

THE STAKES HAVE NEVER BEEN HIGHER

We live in a world where the pace of change accelerates exponentially. Industries are being upended overnight, and consumer expectations are evolving quickly. The question isn't whether change is coming; it's whether you'll lead it or be left in its wake.

Just like LEGO faced its moment of truth, so too will you. Will you be the leader who navigates your team through the storm to calmer waters and new horizons? Or will you cling to outdated models until the market renders you obsolete?

FINAL THOUGHTS: THE JOURNEY AHEAD

This isn't just a book; it's a manifesto for leaders who refuse to accept mediocrity and who are committed to unlocking the full potential of their teams and organizations. It's for those who understand that authentic leadership isn't about maintaining the status quo; it's about being the catalyst for positive, meaningful change.

As we embark on this journey together, remember that every great leader starts somewhere. They faced challenges, doubts, and setbacks, but what set them apart was their unwavering commitment to their vision and their relentless pursuit of innovation.

So, are you ready to step up? Are you prepared to become the catalyst leader your team needs, your organization deserves, and the future demands?

"The best way to predict the future is to create it." – Peter Drucker

It's time to create the future - your future, your team's future, and your organization's future.

Welcome to the Catalyst Leadership journey.

Let's get to work.

FOUNDATIONS OF CATALYST LEADERSHIP

1

"ARE YOU READY TO STOP BEING JUST A MANAGER AND START BEING A CATALYST LEADER WHO TRANSFORMS YOUR ORGANIZATION?"

LEAD LIKE BEZOS

"In a world where change is constant and the stakes are high, playing it safe isn't just a mistake - it's the riskiest move of all."

CHAPTER 1
LEAD LIKE BEZOS

In 2001, Amazon faced what should have been a death sentence. With a staggering $1.4 billion lost, the company was hemorrhaging cash, firing thousands of employees, and weeks away from financial ruin. Amazon was a name whispered as a cautionary tale on Wall Street, nicknamed "Amazon.bomb."

They were burning through $1 million a day, and everyone in the business world believed Jeff Bezos was on the edge of failure. The reality? He was about to make the game-changing decision to turn Amazon from a sinking ship into a $2 trillion empire.

As a leader, you've been there. Maybe not at Amazon's scale, but you know the pressure mounting, expectations crashing down, and every voice around you saying, "It's over." But here's what separates a Catalyst Leader from the rest: vision and grit.

When Bezos faced a wall of doubters, he didn't play it safe or revert to a standard business model. No - he did the exact opposite. In an era where brand loyalty was sacred, he made the seemingly crazy decision to open Amazon's platform to competitors, allowing other retailers to sell directly on Amazon's site.

He tore down the walls, welcoming rivals with open arms. At first, the decision was seen as an unmitigated disaster, but Bezos saw what others didn't: that the future of retail wasn't in owning the product but in owning the customer relationship.

THE VISION BEYOND THE HORIZON

A Catalyst Leader doesn't just have a plan for tomorrow; they're thinking years down the line, understanding that today's actions will resonate in ways others can't even imagine. Bezos didn't see Amazon as an online bookstore or a retail store. He saw Amazon as the ultimate customer-centric company, built around the idea of providing everything a customer might want in one convenient place. To get there, he had to sacrifice short-term gains, endure public criticism, and hold onto his vision while navigating immense turmoil.

For you, this means adopting a mindset of relentless foresight. No more playing it safe. You must be willing to chart a new course for your team or organization, making decisions that might initially look like failures. Here's the truth: real innovation is uncomfortable. Your team might feel the burn of every risk you take, but if you want to ignite change, if you want to truly be a catalyst, you have to be willing to shoulder the weight of what others can't see yet.

BUILDING THE FRAMEWORK FOR TRANSFORMATION

Catalyst Leaders thrive on three pillars: audacity, adaptability, and accountability. Let's break it down:

1. **Audacity** – Bezos took an audacious leap by inviting competitors onto Amazon's platform. He wasn't playing for short-term comfort; he was building an empire. In your world, audacity might look different, but the principle remains: take bold action. Quit worrying about what others think or what's been done before. Think about what you can create that has never existed.

2. **Adaptability** – Amazon didn't just add competitors and hope for the best. Bezos overhauled operations, aggressively slashing costs and re-negotiating supplier contracts to ensure the strategy was sustainable. When you lead through change, you'll need to pivot and adjust, adapting to each new challenge while staying grounded in the mission. Adaptability means refining your methods without sacrificing your purpose.

3. **Accountability** – Catalyst Leaders hold themselves to a higher standard. Bezos didn't make these bold changes and leave it to luck; he held himself accountable to Amazon's mission and kept moving toward his vision, no matter how steep the path. As a leader, you must set the bar high and hold yourself and your team accountable to that

standard, no matter how challenging it becomes. Accountability isn't just about meeting expectations - it's about pushing through when everyone else would quit.

CREATING A CULTURE OF INNOVATION

Amazon's transformation wasn't solely Bezos's doing. He had a team that shared his commitment, a culture that rewarded innovation and resilience. A Catalyst Leader knows that the key to igniting change isn't only in the strategy; it's in building a team that believes in the mission. You can't be the only one with the fire in your belly - you need everyone on board.

To foster this, you must cultivate a space where creativity and risk are not just encouraged but expected. Let's be real - change is uncomfortable, and people don't like leaving their comfort zones. But if you want your team to create breakthroughs, they have to trust that they can experiment, even fail, without fear of retribution. This isn't about indulging sloppy work but creating a safe space for smart risks and calculated bets. The payoff? A team that's not afraid to bring their best, boldest ideas to the table.

Bezos did this by setting Amazon apart as a place where failure wasn't just tolerated - it was a stepping stone. He told his people that it was okay to fall, as long as they learned and came back stronger. He encouraged them to think of failure not as the end, but as a beginning. And this was critical to Amazon's growth. You, too, can create an environment where your team feels empowered to think big, move fast, and learn continuously. When they understand that their leader values growth over perfection, they'll push harder, dream bigger, and strive to innovate.

UNITING STRATEGY AND EXECUTION

Big ideas are worthless without execution. Amazon's survival and eventual domination didn't happen simply because Bezos thought up a novel concept; it worked because he followed through with ruthless focus. He and his team meticulously executed every part of the plan: cutting costs, renegotiating contracts, optimizing customer experience, and investing in operational efficiency.

Execution is where Catalyst Leaders shine. You don't just throw ideas out there; you work on them every day, adapting as needed to bring them to life. Your team needs to see you in the trenches, making it happen. When they see that you're not just the visionary but the executor, they'll follow suit. They'll become problem-solvers, adapters, and, ultimately, catalysts for change within your organization.

MASTERING PATIENCE IN THE FACE OF DOUBT

In the early days of Amazon's transformation, Bezos faced backlash from every angle. Wall Street criticized him. The media questioned his sanity. Yet he had a powerful guiding principle: "We are willing to be misunderstood for long periods of time."

Here's the thing: Catalyst Leaders don't need everyone to get on board immediately. When you're driving real, transformative change, there will be skeptics, naysayers, and critics. People will question your decisions, push back against your strategies, and maybe even label you as reckless. But the true strength of a leader lies in the patience to endure that criticism without swerving off course.

This patience doesn't mean passivity. Instead, it's the resilience to withstand external pressure and the confidence to let your results speak for themselves. Bezos didn't try to win over his critics with words - he let Amazon's eventual success prove them wrong. As a Catalyst Leader, you, too, must hold your ground. Trust your vision, stay the course, and focus on the results.

THE ART OF SUSTAINING MOMENTUM

After the first glimpse of success, many leaders get complacent. They bask in the achievement and let their foot off the gas. Catalyst Leaders, though, understand that success is merely a checkpoint, not the destination. Bezos didn't celebrate Amazon's first profitable quarter as the endgame - he reinvested, improved, and continued to build, using each win as a springboard for further growth.

To keep your team's momentum, celebrate the wins, but keep the vision alive. Recognize their achievements but remind them that the journey is far from over. A Catalyst Leader knows that motivation is sustained through a shared purpose and a commitment to continual improvement.

EMBRACING THE POWER OF CUSTOMER-CENTRIC INNOVATION

At the core of Amazon's reinvention was a focus on the customer. Bezos knew that if he could win over the customer, everything else would fall into place. That's the essence of Catalyst Leadership - making decisions with the customer (or end user) at the center of every strategy. As a leader, you must consistently ask, "How does this improve the experience for those we serve?" When you stay customer-focused, you set a foundation for long-term loyalty and trust that outlasts any market trend.

For your team, this means constantly refining their understanding of the customer's needs, pain points, and desires. When they see you obsessed with delivering unparalleled value, they will adopt the same mindset, fueling a culture where customer-centricity isn't just a strategy - it's the core of everything you do.

THE RISK OF PLAYING IT SAFE

In a world where change is constant and the stakes are high, playing it safe isn't just a mistake - it's the riskiest move of all. By 2001 standards, Bezos should have trimmed Amazon down, cut innovation costs, and focused on surviving another quarter. But he knew that such short-sighted thinking would keep Amazon small. Instead, he bet everything on his vision and fundamentally changed how the world views e-commerce.

As a Catalyst Leader, you're not here to keep the lights on - you're here to set the place on fire with ideas and action. Stop worrying about the status quo. Embrace the unknown, take bold steps, and push your team to think beyond their comfort zones. The greatest opportunities are found outside the boundaries of what's known, so dare to step beyond them.

YOUR CATALYST MINDSET

Becoming a Catalyst Leader isn't about a single big move; it's about the mindset that every action you take can drive change, inspire innovation, and unlock potential. It's about refusing to accept "good enough" and pushing yourself and your team to levels you never thought possible.

Lead Like Bezos.

CULTIVATE AN UNSHAKEABLE BELIEF IN YOUR VISION

As a Catalyst Leader, every decision, every action, and every challenge is an opportunity to reshape the future. Bezos didn't waver in his vision when everything seemed destined to fall apart. Instead, he stayed relentlessly focused, knowing that temporary setbacks were just the price of lasting impact. To be a Catalyst Leader, you must cultivate this unshakeable belief - not just in the goals of today, but in the broader vision of what your organization could become.

Believe in your ability to see the future, and know that every step you take, no matter how small or seemingly insignificant, is moving your team and organization closer to that vision. When you lead with this kind of clarity and conviction, your team will follow, embodying the mindset and determination needed to turn challenges into achievements.

INSPIRE RELENTLESS DRIVE AND OWNERSHIP

True leadership is not about pushing people from behind; it's about igniting a drive so fierce that your team wants to run through walls to reach the goal. Cultivate a sense of ownership among your team members. Empower them to make decisions, take risks, and learn from mistakes. Let them feel the weight and pride of responsibility, knowing they're not just working for a paycheck but contributing to a mission far greater than themselves. When you empower your team to own their roles and results, they won't need micromanagement - they'll be unstoppable.

THE POWER OF PURPOSE OVER PROFIT

Bezos's decision to open Amazon to competitors wasn't about boosting short-term profits; it was about aligning with Amazon's purpose: to be the most customer-centric company in the world. And that alignment drove everything else. As a Catalyst Leader, don't chase profit as the primary goal; chase purpose. If your organization has a clear, customer-focused mission, the profit will follow. This kind of focus creates loyalty, drives innovation, and fosters resilience.

Let your team see that their work has a purpose beyond numbers. Remind them who they're serving, why it matters, and how their contributions make a difference. When you inspire a purpose-driven culture, you tap into a source of motivation that can weather any storm.

BE BOLD, BE RESILIENT, BE THE CATALYST

Catalyst Leaders aren't just managers - they're trailblazers, risk-takers, and relentless drivers of change. When everyone else is playing it safe, you're challenging the status quo. When others hesitate, you're charging forward. It's this kind of leadership that transforms companies, reinvents industries, and ultimately, changes the world.

So step up. Embrace your role as a Catalyst Leader with boldness, resilience, and unrelenting focus. Rally your team, inspire their best work, and lead with conviction. Because in the end, it's the leaders who dare to dream bigger, act bolder, and stay true to their vision that spark the fires of change and turn aspirations into empires.

Go out there and make it happen. Be the catalyst.

2

"DO YOU WANT TO EMBRACE CATALYST LEADERSHIP TO THRIVE IN A RAPIDLY CHANGING WORLD?"

THE IMPERATIVE FOR CATALYST LEADERSHIP

Part One:
The Changing Business Landscape

Part Two:
The Limitations of Traditional Leadership

Part Three:
Skating to Where the Puck Is Going

"Complacency is a death sentence - no matter how dominant you are today, consumer habits and technological advances can flip the script overnight."

PART ONE:
THE CHANGING BUSINESS LANDSCAPE

BLOCKBUSTER: THEY WERE RENTING MOVIES, BUT THEY RENTED OUT THEIR FUTURE

When Blockbuster was riding high in the late 1990s, it practically owned the home video rental market. Stores popped up on every corner, raking in profits from VHS and DVD rentals. People spent Friday nights scouring aisles for the latest new release and those late fees - everyone hated them, but they kept Blockbuster's cash flow roaring. Executives felt unstoppable: they were the kings of home entertainment, seemingly too big and entrenched to fail.

But then the world started to shift. DVDs gave way to mail-order rental services and then streaming technology. A smaller company, Netflix, offered DVD-by-mail subscriptions, slashing the need for customers to drive to a store. Blockbuster's leadership scoffed at the concept, dismissing it as a mere fad that would never replace the tangible experience of visiting a rental store.

They had countless opportunities to pivot - one being a chance to buy Netflix for a relatively small sum. But they stuck to their old model of physically stocked shelves and an over-reliance on those hefty late fees. Executives made short-term decisions - focusing on quarterly profits and ignoring the emerging threat of digital distribution.

Soon, Netflix innovated again, launching an online streaming service that transformed how people consumed entertainment. Blockbuster attempted a late pivot into streaming, but it was too little, too late. Stores bled revenue, customers abandoned the brand in droves for the convenience of digital streaming, and new competition like Redbox ate into their already thinning margins. The final blow came quickly: Blockbuster filed for bankruptcy, shuttering nearly all its locations, left as a cautionary tale of how refusing to adapt can decimate a once-thriving empire.

This saga underscores the brutal lesson: complacency is a death sentence no matter how dominant you are today. Consumer habits, technological advances, and global competition can flip the script overnight. If you're not scanning the horizon - prepared to pivot, evolve, and disrupt your comfortable status quo - you risk going the way of Blockbuster: from market leader to relic, almost nobody remembers, all in a handful of years.

KEY TAKEAWAYS

Complacency and Failure to Adapt: The Blockbuster story is a classic example of how complacency and a failure to adapt to changing market conditions can lead to the downfall of even the most dominant companies.

Disruption and Innovation: Netflix's success demonstrates the power of disruptive innovation. They identified a changing consumer need and developed a new business model that completely transformed the industry.

Short-Term vs. Long-Term Thinking: Blockbuster's focus on short-term profits and failure to anticipate long-term trends contributed to its demise.

Introducing the New Reality: Global Markets, Technological Upheaval, and AI

The modern business landscape isn't just shifting - it's quaking under the force of globalization, rapid technological disruption, and the AI-driven revolution in automation. Ignoring these tremors is as reckless as burying your head in the sand while a tsunami approaches. If you want to be a catalyst leader, you need to be crystal clear about what's happening around you and act decisively before the next disruptive wave hits.

SECTION 1: GLOBALIZATION AND COMPETITION

First, let's dissect globalization: it's not just about shipping products to a few extra countries or outsourcing mundane tasks to cheaper labor markets. Globalization has flattened the competitive playing field. A small startup in Estonia or Kenya can now take advantage of e-commerce, digital marketing, and advanced logistics networks to challenge giant incumbents that once seemed untouchable. Consumer expectations have soared - they demand better quality, faster shipping, frictionless online experiences, and local personalization, whether you're based in Seoul, São Paulo, or San Francisco.

It means that your competition isn't just the rival down the street - it's someone halfway across the globe, hustling in a bedroom office, who might code a new app or build a new product that outclasses yours within a year. Everything is connected: currency fluctuations in Asia can affect your sales in Europe, or a trending hashtag in Latin America can influence brand perceptions in North America. The pace is relentless, and that's exactly why you need to think bigger, faster, and more globally than ever before.

Being a catalyst leader in a global arena requires intense cultural awareness. You can't assume your marketing campaign that works in one country will automatically resonate elsewhere. You need teams that reflect the global audience you serve - people who understand local contexts, speak local languages, and have the cultural fluency to navigate complexities on the ground. And all that must be woven into your strategic planning, not treated like an afterthought.

SECTION 2: TECHNOLOGICAL DISRUPTION

Meanwhile, technology is rewriting the rules of every industry, from finance to farming. The internet let Netflix dethrone Blockbuster. Smartphones crushed the flip-phone market in just a few years. E-commerce decimated countless brick-and-mortar businesses. But it goes deeper. Emerging tech - like blockchain, 3D printing, bio-engineering - continues to spawn whole new markets and warp consumer expectations about speed, choice, and personalization.

This means your old processes - maybe they worked fine when you only had a local customer base - are now antiquated in a new digital-first world. Consumers want frictionless experiences: one-click buying, real-time updates, instant customer support. If your technology can't keep up, your brand looks prehistoric.

What's crucial to understand is that disruptive technology doesn't always arrive with a big neon sign announcing itself. Sometimes it creeps up, quietly transforming a niche or overlooked part of the market until, suddenly, it goes mainstream and topples established giants. Catalyst leaders have their antennae up, scanning for hints of emerging tech that could revolutionize operations, open new business lines, or blindside your existing product offerings.

But it's not just about adopting new gadgets or software - it's about rethinking your entire value chain. Are there manual processes that could be automated? Is there data you're collecting but not analyzing for strategic insights? Technology can be your rocket fuel, but only if you harness it with a visionary approach.

SECTION 3: AI AND AUTOMATION

And now we come to the juggernaut: Artificial Intelligence (AI) and automation. AI isn't just another piece of software or an IT project - it's a seismic shift in how work is done. Machine learning algorithms can process massive amounts of data at lightning speed, revealing patterns humans might never see. Automation can handle repetitive tasks with near-zero error rates, freeing up humans for more creative or high-level strategic work.

But don't be naive - AI will also displace certain job roles that rely on routine. This is no longer science fiction; it's happening in real time, from chatbots taking over basic customer service tasks to advanced AI diagnosing medical images more accurately than seasoned specialists. If you're not planning for AI's profound impact on labor, productivity, and competition, you're already behind.

For a catalyst leader, AI offers an unparalleled opportunity to accelerate innovation. Imagine drastically cutting time spent on manual analyses, redirecting that energy into product R&D, strategic alliances, or new market experiments. The challenge is to manage the transition responsibly - how do you retrain or up-skill employees whose jobs are threatened by AI? How do you ensure you maintain a human touch where it counts, like brand authenticity and empathetic customer relations?

The bottom line: AI is reshaping job roles, but it's also giving companies tools to outmaneuver the competition at scale. If you can adapt your workforce and processes, you'll stand out in an overcrowded marketplace. If not, you risk becoming the next cautionary tale - like Blockbuster - overrun by more nimble, tech-savvy players.

TAKE ACTION

1. **Global Audit**

- Gather a cross-functional team to conduct a "Global Audit" of your business. Map out current markets, potential new markets, and how local cultural factors might shift product positioning. Ask: "Where are we failing to resonate?" "Which regions do we overlook?" "Could we localize marketing or user experiences more effectively?"

- Based on these findings, define at least one pilot project to target a foreign market with a tailored approach. This might mean local-language content, a region-specific feature, or forging a local partnership. The goal: break free of your home-market bubble.

2. **Tech and AI Readiness Workshop**

- Host a one-day internal workshop on emerging tech and AI. Invite experts or watch curated talks on cutting-edge developments. Split teams into breakout sessions, brainstorming ways your org could leverage AI - automating a slow internal process or tapping into machine learning for advanced analytics.

- Have each breakout group present a proposal. Pick one or two that show real promise. Give them a small budget and a rapid timeline (a month or two) to build a minimum viable product or a tangible test. This approach seeds a culture of proactive tech experimentation rather than passive adoption.

FINAL THOUGHTS

You hold the blueprint for a new era of leadership - one that's not paralyzed by global pressures, overwhelmed by tech disruption, or intimidated by AI's rise. Now use it. Go beyond cautionary tales and show your team, your market, and yourself what real catalysts do. They spot the future, seize it, and carry everyone across the finish line.

As Mahatma Gandhi said, "The future depends on what you do today." Don't wait for disruptions to corner you - drive forward, experiment fearlessly, and turn your nightmares of obsolescence into a legacy of forward momentum. Your move.

"Complacency is the ultimate silent assassin - it soothes you with short-term comfort while quietly poisoning your long-term viability."

PART TWO:
THE LIMITATIONS OF TRADITIONAL LEADERSHIP

DON'T JUST COMPETE, DOMINATE:
THE RAY KROC STORY OF AMBITION AND EXECUTION

Ray Kroc was a traveling milkshake machine salesman, roaming the United States in the 1950s, pushing equipment to small-time diners and mom-and-pop eateries. His sales routes were filled with polite rejections and occasionally mild enthusiasm, but nothing game-changing. Then, during a stop in California, he discovered a small hamburger restaurant owned by the McDonald brothers.

Their system for delivering quick, no-frills meals at rock-bottom prices dazzled him. He recognized that these men had stumbled on something extraordinary - something that could revolutionize the fast-food industry - yet they seemed content to remain local heroes, sticking to what they knew.

Kroc saw far more potential. He envisioned a nationwide chain, identical in efficiency and quality, flipping burgers and fries at record speed, appealing to busy American families who wanted convenience without sacrificing taste. While the McDonald brothers were satisfied with modest growth, Kroc pitched them an ambitious plan to franchise their operation across the country.

They were cautious, rooted in tradition, and reluctant to scale aggressively. But Kroc, undeterred, struck a deal to manage franchising. He systematically built out a training program, established consistent operational standards, and demanded the highest levels of cleanliness and customer service from every new location.

The result was a game-changer. McDonald's expanded at a pace that made other burger joints look prehistoric. Soon, the Golden Arches became synonymous with fast, dependable, family-friendly meals in suburban strip malls and busy city corners alike.

Customers flocked for the consistency - identical Big Macs from Boston to Boise - and Ray Kroc's leadership style turned the operation into a machine of replicable success. By the time the McDonald brothers realized the scope of Kroc's ambition, McDonald's was morphing into an international juggernaut.

Their reluctance to break from tradition might have kept them local legends, but Kroc's relentless drive to adapt and scale changed global eating habits forever. He wasn't just a "jobber" running a burger stand; he was a catalyst, orchestrating a shift in how Americans - and eventually the world - dined out.

KEY TAKEAWAYS

Kroc's Vision and Drive: Kroc's vision, persistence, and business acumen were essential to McDonald's becoming the global fast-food giant it is today. He saw the potential where the McDonald brothers did not.

Systematization and Replication: Kroc's focus on systematizing the McDonald brothers' operational model and replicating it through franchising was crucial to the company's rapid growth and consistent quality.

The Tension Between the Brothers and Kroc: The story highlights the tension between the McDonald brothers' desire to maintain a small, family-run business and Kroc's ambition to create a massive corporation. This tension ultimately led to Kroc buying them out.

TRADITIONAL LEADERSHIP VS. CATALYST LEADERSHIP

The story of Ray Kroc and the McDonald brothers shines a glaring light on the difference between leaders who settle for what's comfortable and those who see the bigger picture - the catalysts who rewrite the rules. This distinction isn't trivial. It's at the core of whether your organization remains a local footnote or evolves into a globally recognized force.

JOBBERS VS. CATALYSTS: DEFINING THE DIFFERENCE

In many organizations, you've got "jobbers." These are leaders who maintain the status quo, manage the day-to-day, push for incremental changes, and avoid rocking the boat. They might be efficient, dependable, and great at stabilizing operations. But their primary aim? Keep the machine running as is. They measure success by whether the quarter's numbers are stable, turnover remains low, or no major scandal erupts. In short, they're caretakers - doing the job, fulfilling requirements, preserving tradition. And that's where the problem starts.

Enter the catalysts - leaders who push beyond maintaining. Catalysts are all about forward motion. They question every assumption, scanning the horizon for opportunities and disruptions that others gloss over. Where a jobber sees an established practice, a catalyst sees an outdated routine begging for an upgrade. While jobbers rely on what has historically worked, catalysts chase the next frontier. They measure success not just by stability but by growth, innovation, transformation, and potential breakthroughs.

This difference matters because the modern marketplace moves fast. New players, new technologies, new consumer expectations spring up almost overnight. If your leadership style is locked in tradition or incremental improvement, you can't keep pace with a world that demands agility, creativity, and risk-taking. Jobbers might keep your ship afloat in calm waters, but catalysts chart new courses and sail into unknown territory - where real growth, differentiation, and longevity reside.

THE RISKS OF BEING A JOBBER

1. **Stagnation** - Jobbers love routine. They find comfort in repeating what's worked in the past. But the risk is obvious: when consumer behavior shifts or new competitors emerge (like Netflix or Blockbuster), your proven methods can become your downfall. Stagnation is a stealthy killer - it creeps up, numbing you with the lull of familiarity until the market blindsides you.

2. **Talent Drain** - High-performing, ambitious employees crave challenges and growth. If jobbers run your organization, star performers may become bored or disillusioned. They'll jump to competitor com-

panies where they can make a bigger splash. Your top talent eventually leaks away to more dynamic workplaces that champion bold initiatives.

3. **Short-Termism** - Many jobbers fixate on next quarter's metrics, ignoring long-term strategies that might require higher initial investment or risk. This short-term view can lead to missed opportunities and a slow bleed of market relevance. Before you know it, rivals have leaped ahead with new products or global expansions while you tinkered with minor optimizations.

THE IMPORTANCE OF CATALYST LEADERSHIP

Catalyst leaders, in contrast, stay hungry. They see complacency as a threat, not a comfort. They systematically challenge their teams: "What if we tried this new approach?" "What are we not seeing that a competitor might exploit?" Instead of punishing failure, catalysts expect it as part of the learning process. They set audacious goals that terrify jobbers, yet energize the dreamers within the company who want more than just a paycheck.

Consider what that means in a broader sense. A catalyst leader:

- **Positions the company for future markets,** not just the ones currently served.

- **Attracts top-tier talent** who want to make a meaningful impact.

- **Drives a culture of constant improvement** - not settling for "good enough" but aiming for "breakthrough."

- **Builds organizational resilience** because innovation becomes a collective habit rather than a one-off campaign.

THE RISK OF COMPLACENCY: STAYING THE SAME LEADS TO OBSOLESCENCE

Complacency is the ultimate silent assassin. It can set in when business is "fine" and no immediate crisis looms. Leaders or entire teams slip into autopilot, doing what they've always done, feeling safe assuming that because it worked yesterday, it'll work tomorrow. But the business graveyard is littered with companies that once dominated their fields - Xerox, Sears, Yahoo - only to be overshadowed by more agile rivals. Their legacy? Proof that refusing to evolve invites a slow death, especially in an age of warp-speed tech advances and shifting consumer tastes.

A hallmark of complacency is ignoring signals: dropping customer satisfaction, new market entrants, or tech that drastically lowers barriers to entry. People might see these signs but assume they're "outliers." If you're comfortable, you won't do the uncomfortable tasks: investing in a new vertical, reorganizing your team, pivoting from your bread-and-butter product line. Complacency soothes you with short-term comfort while quietly poisoning your long-term viability.

In contrast, catalysts remain paranoid in a constructive way. They always ask: "If I started a rival company tomorrow, how would I beat the business I run today?" That question keeps them from falling asleep at the wheel. They tear down their own walls before the competition can do it for them.

TAKE ACTION

1. Conduct a Complacency Audit

- Gather your executive or leadership team and map out all current processes, product lines, and revenue streams. Ask the uncomfortable questions: "Which areas have we not updated in over a year?" "Which assumptions do we treat as sacred?" "What are we ignoring because it's 'too risky 'or 'too different?'"

- Next, identify at least two areas that seem overdue for a shake-up. Don't just note them - commit to scheduling a deep-dive session within the next month. The goal is to spark conversation about revamping or scrapping outdated practices that hold your organization back.

2. Launch a Catalyst Council

- Pick a diverse group of employees - some from leadership, some from frontline roles, maybe an intern or two. The only requirement: they're forward-thinking, not afraid to challenge norms.

- Have them meet monthly and produce short briefs on emerging industry trends, new technologies, or consumer shifts. They also propose potential experiments to address these shifts.

- Make sure their recommendations don't go into a black hole. Assign resources - budget, staff time - for a couple of pilot projects each quarter. This keeps the company from slumping into jobber territory.

FINAL THOUGHTS

Most leaders are jobbers. They keep the lights on, tally a mild profit, and celebrate hitting modest benchmarks. But if you crave something bigger - an audacious legacy, market-shaking moves, insane loyalty from a team on fire - then accept no substitute for catalyst leadership. You challenge assumptions. You obliterate complacency. You set the bar so high it scares you - and then you blow past it anyway.

As Pablo Picasso once said, "I am always doing that which I cannot do, in order that I may learn how to do it." Go do the impossible, and don't look back. Your revolution starts now.

"If you're still thinking about how to optimize your local DVD rental store, the puck is a thousand miles down the ice already."

PART THREE:
SKATING TO WHERE THE PUCK IS GOING

CRUSHING IT BEFORE THEY KNEW IT: HOW HENRY FORD HUSTLED AND FLIPPED THE AUTO GAME FOREVER

In the early 1900s, the automobile industry was a patchwork of tiny manufacturers building custom cars for the wealthy. Most assumed mass ownership was impossible; cars were too expensive, roads were poor, and horse-drawn carriages had served society just fine for centuries. Initially dismissed by big-name industrialists, Henry Ford envisioned a completely different future. He realized that if automobiles were standardized, simpler to produce, and priced so average families could afford them, the entire world would transform - people could travel farther for work, trade might flourish, and rural isolation would shrink.

He didn't have the technology, labor force, or social acceptance just to flip a switch. But Ford was adamant about "skating to where the puck is going," anticipating that future mass consumption demanded radical efficiency. He introduced the moving assembly line at his Highland Park plant, dividing complex tasks into smaller, specialized jobs. Skeptics scoffed, calling it robotic and demeaning to skilled artisans, or claiming he was chasing a pipe dream - who but the wealthy even wanted these mechanical beasts?

Yet he pushed forward, ignoring naysayers. Worker hours and pay were restructured to accommodate the new system - famously doubling daily wages at one point - to stabilize his labor force and cut turnover. As production soared and unit costs plummeted, the Model T became wildly accessible, changing the automotive game forever.

The outcome was staggering. By the time other carmakers woke up, Ford had standardized parts, hammered down costs, and built a distribution network that blanketed the country. Once-average families bought their first automobile for a fraction of earlier prices. Towns and cities reconfigured themselves around roads, highways multiplied, and an entire culture of personal mobility sprang up. Henry Ford didn't just build a car - he orchestrated a global shift in transportation and commerce. All because he anticipated where consumer demand would be, rather than clinging to old ways of doing business.

Ford's story underscores the power of forward thinking. By setting his sights on an evolving landscape (even one that didn't fully exist yet), he single-handedly shaped how people lived and worked for decades. That's the essence of skating to where the puck is going: seeing tomorrow's opportunities and acting decisively to seize them before everyone else.

KEY TAKEAWAYS

Vision and Innovation: Ford's vision of mass production and his innovative manufacturing techniques were crucial to his success.

Affordability and Mass Market: Ford's focus on making cars affordable for the average person created a mass market for automobiles.

Impact on Infrastructure and Society: The widespread adoption of the automobile had a transformative impact on infrastructure, urban planning, and social life.

EMBRACING GRETZKY'S PHILOSOPHY AND PROACTIVE LEADERSHIP

The famous quote from hockey legend Wayne Gretzky is a touchstone for visionary leadership: "I skate to where the puck is going, not where it has been." It sounds deceptively simple, yet it holds a powerful truth: if you direct all your energy to what's currently happening, you're reacting to a trailing edge. By the time you move, the opportunity may have zipped past you. That can be lethal in business, especially in an era where markets flip in a blink. Leaders who only respond to current demands or who pivot after the market has signaled a shift are perpetually behind. Catalyst leaders, on the other hand, anticipate the next shift and prime their teams to capitalize on it.

SECTION 1: ANTICIPATING FUTURE TRENDS – EMBRACING GRETZKY'S PHILOSOPHY IN LEADERSHIP

Let's break down why this idea is crucial. Our world is hyper-connected: new technologies, social movements, or consumer preferences can explode globally in days or weeks. Consider how streaming services disrupted cable TV nearly overnight, how electric vehicles jumped from fringe eco projects to mainstream status in a few short years, or how remote work soared from a niche perk to a global norm. If you're still thinking about how to optimize your local DVD rental store, the puck is a thousand miles down the ice already.

THE ANATOMY OF "SKATING WHERE THE PUCK IS GOING"

1. **Market Foresight** - You need a structured way to scan for emerging trends - tech, cultural, regulatory, etc. Maybe that's monthly "future trend" meetings or a dedicated R&D team that tracks how consumer data is changing. Or you glean signals from big conferences, academic research, or edge-case startups launching intriguing pilots. The point is to constantly gather intel about where consumer behavior or technology might be in a year or five.

2. **Flexible Strategy** - Knowing a trend might be coming is one thing; positioning your organization to capitalize on it is another. **You must stay nimble to truly move to where the puck will be.** That could mean setting aside a portion of your budget for experimental products or acquisitions that look irrelevant now but become vital tomorrow. It also means giving your teams the psychological safety to propose big changes without fear of immediate pushback.

3. **Cultural Acceptance of Change** - If your organizational culture resists stepping outside current success, you'll never chase future opportunities. People **must feel safe** exploring unknown markets or pivoting away from what's comfortable. If your team hears, "But we've always done it this way," you're condemning yourself to chasing the puck long after it's gone. Catalyst leaders actively stamp out that complacent mindset, replacing it with a hunger for the next play.

WHY THE "PUCK" IS RAPIDLY MOVING

Human behavior, technology, and information flow are accelerating. Social media alone can spark global trends within hours. AI breakthroughs can annihilate entire industries or birth new markets within months. Geopolitical shifts can reorder supply chains in ways you never planned for. The puck isn't just moving fast - it's also weaving unpredictably. A single piece of data can spin it in a new direction, meaning your approach must be both forward-leaning and adaptive.

Leaders used to have the luxury of reacting every few years. Today, if you're not scanning the next 12 to 18 months actively, you're dinosaur bait. That's why Gretzky's philosophy resonates so hard: success belongs to those who see the future's shape while others are still celebrating or lamenting yesterday's scoreboard.

SECTION 2: PROACTIVE VS. REACTIVE STRATEGIES – THE BENEFITS OF FORWARD-THINKING LEADERSHIP

What happens when you focus your energy on skating ahead? First, let's define proactive vs. reactive in a leadership context:

- **Reactive Leadership**: You wait for problems or opportunities to become so obvious that ignoring them is impossible. Only then do you mobilize resources to respond. Sure, you might handle crises decently, but you're often behind, letting external events dictate your timeline.

- **Proactive Leadership**: You track early indicators of emerging opportunities or threats. You adjust your plans before issues balloon or while opportunities are still ripe. That might mean pivoting product lines, re-skilling staff, or forging strategic partnerships that preempt competitors.

THE EDGE OF PROACTIVE LEADERSHIP

1. **Capitalizing on Early Mover Advantage** - By engaging a new market or tech early, you lock in branding, build customer loyalty, and set industry benchmarks. You define the rules, while competitors scramble to play catch-up.

2. **Minimizing Crisis Impact** - If you sense an economic downturn brewing, you can streamline costs, build cash reserves, or adjust your supply chain in time. Reactors get blindsided, forcing panic layoffs, rushed restructuring, or suboptimal deals just to stay afloat.

3. **Employee Morale and Culture** - Teams prefer working under leaders who have a sense of direction. A forward-thinking approach fosters excitement: "We're building the future." Contrast that with the dreariness of always firefighting or blaming externalities for every slump.

4. **Innovation Becomes Habitual** - Proactive leadership normalizes risk-taking and encourages employees to propose new angles. Over time, you build a culture where innovation isn't an event - it's second nature.

THE DANGER OF CONSTANTLY REACTING

Reactive strategies leave you drained, pivoting wildly without a coherent plan. It's an endless cycle of playing defense. This can create morale issues: employees feel stressed, disempowered, and always late to the party. You also waste resources because reactive measures often cost more. Think of last-minute inventory changes or expensive emergency consultants. Meanwhile, proactive leaders did more minor experiments months ago, gleaned their insights, and scaled calmly.

Of course, you can't foresee everything. Even the best forward-thinker gets blindsided sometimes. However, a track record of proactive planning means you typically have contingency plans or a cultural readiness to adapt fast. The result? Crisis moments become accelerators rather than train wrecks.

TAKE ACTION

1. **Year-Plus Lens Planning**

• Establish a recurring "Year-Plus Lens" session - quarterly or biannually - where top leadership and key creative thinkers gather. The rule: no immediate, short-term topics allowed. This session strictly brainstorms what could happen 12 to 24 months out. Maybe that's exploring new demographic segments, global expansions, or technology shifts like advanced AI tools.

- Assign a small team to produce a short "Future Landscape" brief. They'll gather data on emerging consumer behaviors, competitor pivots, or brand-new startups with disruptive ideas. The group then debates how these trends could reshape your business. From there, pick one or two strategic experiments to run with a mid-level budget and a quick timeline.

2. **Proactive Culture Kickstart**

- Host a company-wide challenge: ask employees to propose one idea that positions your organization ahead of a future trend - be it an upcoming cultural shift or a technology wave. Encourage them to think big, even if the idea seems outlandish.

- Have your leadership team select the top three ideas. Grant those teams time and resources for a 60-day pilot or prototype. At the end, they present findings to the entire company. Whether the pilot succeeds or fails, you've signaled that forward-thinking innovation is everyone's responsibility, not just an executive whim.

FINAL THOUGHTS

Sometimes, the puck shifts direction on a dime. If you're a step behind, you'll never catch it before the shot's fired. Authentic leadership isn't about analyzing last week's stats; it's about glimpsing where the game is heading - and then staking your claim.

As Wayne Gretzky put it, you don't chase the puck of present-day success; you skate to where tomorrow's opportunity will appear. Don't stand around, blindsided by unstoppable market forces. Get out there first, shape the ice, and direct the flow.

One more for good luck: As Leonardo da Vinci once said, "Simplicity is the ultimate sophistication." Aim for clarity on tomorrow's horizon, and bolt for it.

The Catalyst Radar

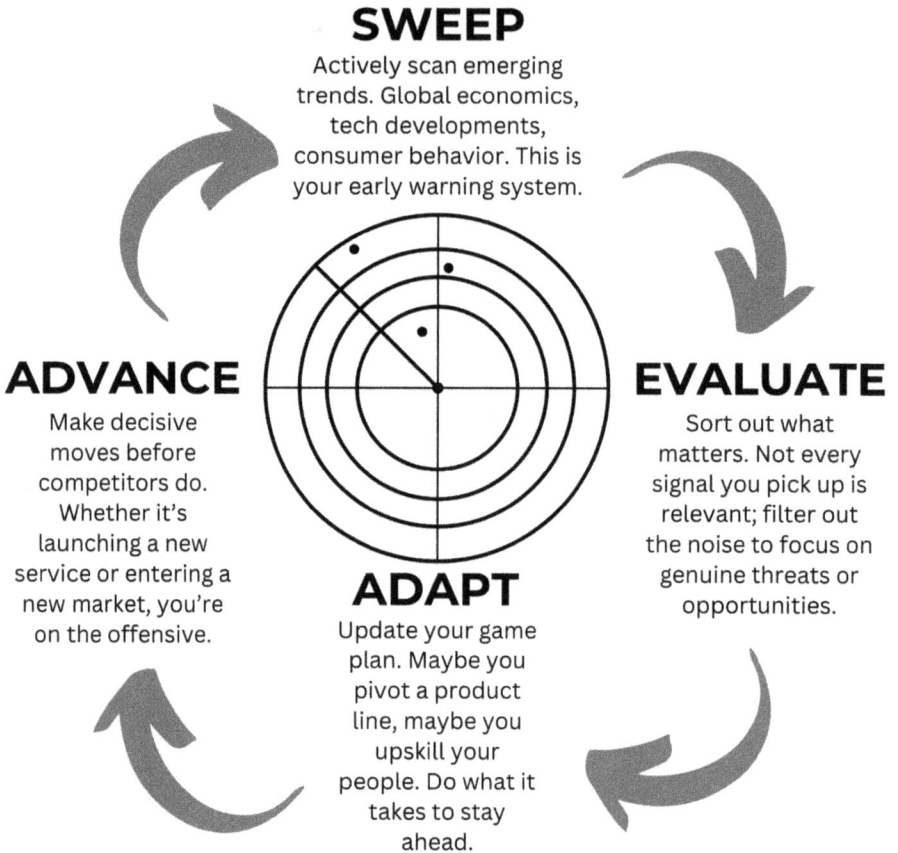

SWEEP
Actively scan emerging trends. Global economics, tech developments, consumer behavior. This is your early warning system.

EVALUATE
Sort out what matters. Not every signal you pick up is relevant; filter out the noise to focus on genuine threats or opportunities.

ADAPT
Update your game plan. Maybe you pivot a product line, maybe you upskill your people. Do what it takes to stay ahead.

ADVANCE
Make decisive moves before competitors do. Whether it's launching a new service or entering a new market, you're on the offensive.

TOOL:
THE CATALYST RADAR

This is a no-BS method for scanning market shifts, sidestepping outdated leadership, and positioning yourself where the action is headed.

Let's be honest: The market is changing faster than you can blink. You're already behind if you're only reacting to what happened yesterday.

My Catalyst Radar Tool is your go-to playbook for spotting shifts on the horizon - global, technological, or AI-driven - and pivoting before the competition even knows what hit them. Ready to future-proof your leadership?

WHY IT WORKS WHEN POSITIONING YOUR COMPANY FOR A CHANGE:

The Changing Business Landscape

- Globalization and Competition: The Radar method forces you to keep scanning for global opportunities and threats, so you're never surprised by a competitor from the other side of the world.

- Technological Disruption: By actively monitoring tech signals, you won't get blindsided when entire business models shift overnight.

- AI and Automation: Spot where AI can elevate your team's potential - or replace it - long before it becomes a crisis.

The Limitations of Traditional Leadership

- Jobbers vs. Catalysts: Traditional "jobbers" wait for change to happen and then scramble. With the Catalyst Radar, you're making moves before the shift hits.

- The Risk of Complacency: Complacency is the silent killer of great organizations. The Radar keeps you on your toes, so you're always ready to pivot instead of being stuck in yesterday's success.

Skating to Where the Puck Is Going

- Anticipating Future Trends: The Radar's constant scanning forces you to see beyond the present and aim for where the marketplace is heading next.

- Proactive vs. Reactive Strategies: Instead of firefighting once disruption arrives, you're already leading the pack in developing tomorrow's solutions.

WHAT IS IT?

The Catalyst Radar consists of four straightforward steps to stay ahead of any shift:

1. **Sweep - Actively scan emerging trends.** Global economics, tech developments, consumer behavior. This is your early warning system.

2. **Evaluate - Sort out what matters.** Not every signal you pick up is relevant; filter out the noise to focus on genuine threats or opportunities.

3. **Adapt - Update your game plan.** Maybe you pivot a product line, maybe you up-skill your people. Do what it takes to stay ahead.

4. **Advance - Make decisive moves before competitors do.** Whether it's launching a new service or entering a new market, you're on the offensive.

Each step naturally leads to the next - ensuring a continuous cycle of scanning, refining, and acting.

HOW TO USE IT

In the Office

- Sweep: Assign someone to report weekly on fresh market trends or disruptive technologies.

- Evaluate: In monthly strategy sessions, categorize each trend by impact and relevance.

With Your Team

- Adapt: Encourage a "pivot mindset." If a new tool or tactic pops up, run a quick test project with a small team to gauge feasibility.

- Advance: Reward teams that move quickly on promising ideas - sprint first, refine later.

With Yourself

- Sweep: Read, watch, or listen to one thought-leadership piece daily - on tech, leadership, or market shifts.

- Evaluate: Once a week, jot down potential actions from your reading. Only pick the ones that align with your bigger vision and ignore the rest.

Here's the bottom line: If you're playing catch-up, you're losing. The Catalyst Radar keeps you scanning the environment, filtering out the noise, and making proactive decisions.

Embrace this tool, and you won't just keep pace with an evolving world - you'll define the pace for everyone else. Time to lead like a catalyst!

3

"DO YOU WANT TO
EMBRACE A NEW
LEADERSHIP STYLE TO
THRIVE IN A RAPIDLY
CHANGING WORLD?"

UNDERSTANDING THE CATALYST MINDSET

Part One:
Characteristics of Catalyst Leaders

Part Two:
Cultivating a Growth Mindset

"Catalyst leaders don't wait for disruption - they disrupt themselves before the market can do it for them."

PART ONE: CHARACTERISTICS OF CATALYST LEADERS

HOW REED HASTINGS PUNK'D BLOCKBUSTER AND TURNED RED ENVELOPES INTO A STREAMING EMPIRE

When Reed Hastings co-founded Netflix in 1997, it was a modest DVD-by-mail rental service taking on the behemoth that was Blockbuster (as we covered in Chapter Two). Nobody in the industry believed a company sending discs in red envelopes could topple an entrenched multi-billion-dollar empire with thousands of physical locations. Skeptics sneered that Netflix would remain a "niche novelty," a passing trend that serious movie buffs or mainstream consumers wouldn't stick with. But Hastings spotted deep inefficiencies in the traditional rental model - late fees, limited inventory, and a painful in-store experience. He saw a better way: deliver entertainment by mail, eradicate late fees, and eventually harness the power of the internet to stream directly into people's homes.

Many doubted Netflix's ability to pivot into streaming. The tech infrastructure was still clunky; broadband hadn't fully penetrated households, and licensing content for digital distribution presented a legal labyrinth. Yet Hastings stayed a step ahead. He poured resources into building robust recommendation algorithms - something no competitor had done at scale - turning user data into a personalized goldmine. He also hammered out deals with studios for streaming rights before they realized just how big the digital wave would be.

In the end, Blockbuster's late pivot to online rentals and streaming was far too little, too late. Netflix seized the future of on-demand entertainment. Meanwhile, Hastings continued to push boundaries - betting big on original content like "House of Cards" when the world hadn't fully grasped the potential of streaming exclusive shows. Today, Netflix stands as a global entertainment powerhouse, having reshaped how we consume media and forced an entire industry to revamp distribution models. All because Reed Hastings refused to coast on current successes. He envisioned a world beyond plastic discs and store visits, embraced change as an opportunity, and fostered a culture where innovative problem-solving is not just allowed but expected. Netflix's meteoric rise offers a masterclass in catalyst leadership - seeing beyond the immediate horizon, welcoming disruption, and turning bold ideas into unstoppable momentum.

KEY TAKEAWAYS

Hastings' Vision and Leadership: Reed Hastings's vision, strategic thinking, and ability to anticipate future trends were crucial to Netflix's success.

Adaptability and Innovation: Netflix's willingness to adapt and innovate, particularly its transition from DVD-by-mail to streaming, was essential to its survival and growth.

Focus on User Experience: Netflix's focus on providing a convenient and personalized user experience, through features like recommendation algorithms, was a key differentiator.

INTRODUCING THE CATALYST MINDSET

Catalyst leaders operate under a fundamentally different ethos than conventional managers. They don't ask, "How do we maintain the status quo?" They ask, "How do we reinvent, disrupt, and transform before the market forces us to?" Where traditional leaders might see adversity as a threat, catalysts see an opportunity to evolve. And in a world that flips on a dime - due to digital innovation, globalization, consumer fickleness - waiting to adapt is basically signing your brand's death warrant.

This chapter zeroes in on **three** defining characteristics of catalyst leaders:

1. **Visionary Thinking** – The ability to see beyond the immediate horizon and imagine possibilities others deem unrealistic.

2. **Embracing Change** – The discipline to treat change not as an unwelcome intruder but as a fresh wave to ride.

3. **Innovative Problem-Solving** – The knack for galvanizing teams to propose radical ideas, iterate fast, and refine solutions that set the pace for an entire industry.

Your job, if you want to be a catalyst leader, is not to memorize bullet points but to fundamentally shift how you approach challenges. You look at adversity and see a path to iteration. You look at a new technology and ask, "How can this amplify my impact?" You stare down disruption and respond, "We'll disrupt ourselves before anyone else does." Let's dive deeper into these hallmark traits.

SECTION 1: VISIONARY THINKING – SEEING BEYOND THE IMMEDIATE HORIZON

Catalyst leaders operate with a wide-angle lens. They don't just observe today's profits or this quarter's metrics; they obsess about tomorrow's marketplace, tomorrow's consumer preferences, tomorrow's technologies. Look at Reed Hastings: he didn't wait for streaming infrastructure to be perfect. He laid the groundwork early, investing in digital capabilities even as Netflix was still shipping DVDs. That's visionary thinking: positioning your organization in front of emerging waves so you can ride them - maybe even shape them.

Why does it matter? Because in an economy swarming with new apps, social movements, and fleeting consumer loyalties, playing catch-up is a losing proposition. If you're only pivoting when a shift is painfully obvious, you're arriving late. Visionary thinking also energizes your teams. People don't flock to safe, incremental plans. They get fired up about audacious missions - like "We're going to revolutionize how the world watches TV," or "We'll be the first to commercialize self-driving grocery deliveries."

So what holds leaders back from visionary thinking? Often, it's fear. Fear of being wrong. Fear of cannibalizing existing cash cows. Fear of looking foolish. But catalysts accept that fear is part of the process. They factor in risk, build prototypes, test quickly, and see failure as part of the route to bigger successes.

SECTION 2: EMBRACING CHANGE – VIEWING CHANGE AS AN OPPORTUNITY, NOT A THREAT

Change is inevitable, whether it's technological (AI replacing routine tasks), societal (a new generation's preferences shaking up entire product categories), or global crises (supply chain upheavals). Traditional leaders might react to these shifts by defending the status quo, building walls to keep external factors at bay. But catalyst leaders fling open the doors, letting fresh air blow through every department. They see change as a springboard to new opportunities.

Why is this so critical? Because markets and consumer tastes are fluid. What's hot now could be ice-cold next year. If you cling too tightly to your old methods or big brand legacy, you risk turning into the next cautionary tale. Blockbuster, ironically, had the resources to pivot early to streaming, but they remained fixated on in-store revenues and late fees. They saw change as an intrusion, not a signpost for the future. Catalyst leaders do the opposite: when they spot a shift, they realign resources, slash bureaucracy, and empower squads or task forces to experiment. If something fails, they glean the lessons and move on fast.

Embracing change also fosters loyalty. Your staff sees you're not just reacting but actively inventing tomorrow's business model. That sense of urgency and creative freedom draws in top-tier talent who want to be part of shaping the next big thing, not simply maintaining legacy systems.

SECTION 3: INNOVATIVE PROBLEM-SOLVING – ENCOURAGING CREATIVITY AND NEW IDEAS

Finally, catalyst leaders champion an environment where innovative problem-solving thrives. This isn't a once-a-year hackathon or an "innovation day" scheduled on a slow Friday. It's a daily mindset. People feel safe proposing wild solutions or contrarian perspectives, because the culture celebrates invention and forgives constructive mistakes.

Why is innovation so central? Because routine problems can be solved with routine solutions. But new frontiers require creative leaps - like how Netflix reimagined content delivery, or how Tesla rethought car distribution without dealerships. Catalyst leaders don't wait for their R&D department to come up with breakthroughs in secrecy. They embed a problem-solving ethos in every role. A frontline warehouse employee could spark the next operational breakthrough if they're encouraged to pitch ideas. A marketing assistant might dream up a viral campaign if they see that their voice is valued.

Yes, not every idea will pan out. But if you kill ideas prematurely, you kill momentum. Catalyst leaders set up small "test labs" or pilot programs that quickly vet feasibility. If an idea bombs, you pull the plug and let everyone glean the lessons. If it shows promise, you scale up. This approach short-circuits the bureaucratic gridlock that dooms many large organizations, letting them remain agile despite their size.

ACTION ITEMS

Now that you grasp these traits - visionary thinking, embracing change, innovative problem-solving - how do you infuse them into your leadership style and organization?

1. Map Future Opportunities

•   Gather your top thinkers and doers in a monthly "Future Radar" session. Pick one to three areas where you foresee major shifts - maybe AI, new consumer demographics, or shifts in social media. Brainstorm how these forces could reshape your business. End each session with at least one experiment you'll test in the upcoming quarter.

•   This keeps your vision forward-focused and ingrains the habit of scanning horizons rather than clinging to the immediate.

2. Empower Cross-Functional "Change Teams"

•   Pick a pressing challenge - say, an outdated inventory process or a lagging product line. Form a cross-functional team with authority to overhaul it. Make it clear they can break from standard procedures, so long as they keep you updated. Provide seed resources (budget, time) and ask for quick prototypes within weeks.

•   By baking in autonomy and speed, you're telling everyone that fresh ideas are a top priority, not an afterthought. This also hammers home that change is welcomed, even demanded.

FINAL THOUGHTS

You've got a choice: embody the spark of a catalyst leader or stay tethered to an outdated model that dies the moment markets shift. Visionaries don't hoard the stage; they see beyond the horizon. Change-embracers don't cower in storms; they surf the waves to new shores. Creative problem-solvers don't ask permission to innovate; they unleash breakthroughs daily. As Walt Whitman wrote, "Dismiss whatever insults your own soul." Dismiss complacency. Dismiss fear. Charge forward with audacious vision, fierce adaptability, and a relentless quest for innovative solutions. That's the catalyst mindset. Step into it, and watch your team light the path forward.

"Cultivating a growth mindset at scale isn't just a motivational poster slogan - it can revive an entire tech empire."

PART TWO:
CULTIVATING A GROWTH MINDSET

HOW SATYA NADELLA SMACKED MICROSOFT AWAKE, DITCHED THE EGO, AND BUILT A LEARN-IT-ALL BEAST

When Satya Nadella stepped in as CEO of Microsoft in 2014, the tech giant struggled to remain relevant in an ever-shifting digital landscape. Long hailed for its Windows operating system and Office suite, Microsoft lost its edge to nimbler competitors specializing in cloud, mobile, and open-source platforms. Executives were split on how to adapt, bureaucratic silos weighed down employees, and the company's once-legendary competitiveness was fading fast. Investors and analysts cast doubt on whether Microsoft could ever reclaim its standing among the new tech titans capturing the world's imagination.

Nadella refused to accept that narrative. He saw that the real challenge wasn't just about launching better products and transforming Microsoft's very culture. He famously pivoted the company from a "know-it-all" to a "learn-it-all" mentality, championing curiosity, empathy, and humility as core corporate values. Teams were encouraged to break free of old departmental fiefdoms, collaborating across engineering, marketing, and sales to rapidly develop cloud services, AI solutions, and cross-platform tools. Nadella also steered resources into acquisitions like LinkedIn and GitHub, not for quick wins but to expand Microsoft's ecosystem in the talent, social, and developer spaces.

In a few short years, Microsoft's cloud service, Azure, vaulted into a leading position, Office 365 reinvented how people collaborate online, and Windows integrated more seamlessly with open-source platforms. The once-cynical developer community began to see Microsoft as a partner, not a dinosaur, especially after the company open-sourced core technologies and welcomed Linux with open arms. The cultural shift manifested in skyrocketing employee morale, surging stock prices, and a wave of new product releases that hammered home the message: Microsoft was back, more agile than ever, determined to learn and adapt on the fly.

That transformation hinged on Nadella's decision to cultivate a **growth mindset** across the enterprise. By tearing down bureaucratic walls, rewarding learning over entrenched expertise, and embracing new alliances, Microsoft turned its brand from borderline irrelevance to an unstoppable market force. This story underscores a crucial lesson: adopting a growth mindset at scale isn't just a motivational poster slogan - it can revive an entire tech empire.

KEY TAKEAWAYS

Cultural Transformation as the Primary Driver: The narrative correctly emphasizes that cultural transformation was the key driver of Microsoft's resurgence. It wasn't just about new products or strategies but changing how the company operated.

Growth Mindset at Scale: The text accurately points out that implementing a growth mindset at the scale of a large enterprise like Microsoft is a significant achievement and can have a profound impact.

INTRODUCTION TO THE GROWTH MINDSET

The idea of a "growth mindset" exploded in business circles over the last decade, with countless leaders touting its power to spark innovation and resilience. But let's be clear: a growth mindset isn't just about "believing you can improve" - it's about structurally embedding the expectation that **everyone** in your organization has the capacity to learn, adapt, and iterate. You're not coddling people with empty positivity; you're challenging them to push beyond complacency, to see failures and setbacks as data points rather than dead ends, and to treat every day as a fresh opportunity to level up.

SECTION 1: CONTINUOUS LEARNING – FOSTERING AN ENVIRONMENT OF PERPETUAL DEVELOPMENT

A growth mindset starts with the premise that the status quo is never enough. The second you accept "We're good the way we are," you've already begun sliding toward irrelevance. By contrast, continuous learning sets a cultural norm where employees at all levels are expected - and empowered - to expand their skills, cross-train in new domains, and stay abreast of industry shifts.

WHY CONTINUOUS LEARNING MATTERS

1. **Market Shifts**: In a world of hyper-fast disruption, a skill set that was state-of-the-art two years ago might now be borderline obsolete. Continuous learning isn't a luxury; it's how you survive the next wave of AI, cloud computing, or quantum leaps in biology.

2. **Employee Engagement**: When people feel they're growing, they stay more engaged and loyal. They sense that the company invests in their future, not just in their output. This stokes intrinsic motivation - people want to excel because they see a clear path for personal and professional expansion.

3. **Innovation**: Fresh knowledge stirs fresh ideas. A developer who takes a course in user experience design might spark an entirely new approach to product development. A marketer who studies data analytics might conceive a new campaign that integrates machine-learning-based targeting.

But fostering continuous learning isn't just about throwing money at fancy workshops or offering LinkedIn Learning subscriptions. You need to cultivate an internal ecosystem that thrives on skill-sharing. Think cross-team hackathons, lunch-and-learns, job-shadowing rotations - so your employees organically grow their repertoire without waiting for top-down commands.

CULTURE OVER COMMANDS

You can't bully people into curiosity. Leadership must model the behavior. If you, as the leader, never admit ignorance or never sign up for new training yourself, your staff will interpret "continuous learning" as empty corporate jargon. The more you humbly show that you're learning too - attending events, reading widely, collaborating with juniors - the more your employees realize it's not just lip service.

To embed continuous learning, tie it into performance reviews or OKRs (Objectives and Key Results). Reward employees who show evidence of newly acquired skills or who took initiative to train others. Shift from praising "static expertise" (the know-it-all mentality) to praising "learning-in-progress" (the perpetual student mentality).

SECTION 2: RESILIENCE AND ADAPTABILITY - BUILDING STRENGTH TO NAVIGATE UNCERTAINTIES

Hand-in-hand with continuous learning is resilience. Why? Because the moment you push into new territory, you're bound to slip up or even face external shocks you can't control. The difference between typical "fixed mindset" leaders and a growth-mindset catalyst is how they deal with adversity.

One concept that's gained traction is **Antifragility**, popularized by Nassim Nicholas Taleb. Being "antifragile" goes beyond mere resilience. A resilient system resists shocks and stays the same; an antifragile system **gets stronger** when jolted by stressors. Think about your muscular system: it rebuilds stronger when you stress it through weight training. In business, if you structure your team and processes to learn from disruptions - maybe through rapid postmortems, real-time course corrections, or quick iterative cycles - each challenge hones your edge rather than dulls it.

EMBRACING ANTIFRAGILITY IN LEADERSHIP

1. **Planned Stress Tests**: Catalyst leaders intentionally stress their systems to reveal weaknesses before crises hit. That might mean simulating a spike in website traffic to see how your servers handle it or rotating key managers to different departments to test cross-functional agility.

2. **Psychological Safety**: You can't absorb stress and emerge stronger if your culture punishes missteps with blame or shame. People will hide problems, limiting your chance to learn. That's why psychologically safe environments - where employees can voice concerns, report failures, and suggest radical ideas without fear - are essential to antifragility.

3. **Iterative Mindset**: Instead of grand, infrequent rollouts, antifragile organizations prefer shorter sprints, quick feedback loops, and phased launches. This approach reveals issues sooner, letting you adapt before a minor flaw becomes a massive crisis.

WHY RESILIENCE AND ADAPTABILITY MATTER MORE THAN EVER

Economies can tilt overnight, supply chains can snap, cultural sentiments can shift unpredictably, and entire technologies can come out of nowhere to overshadow your flagship product. If your leadership style revolves around carefully guarded routines, you'll panic when the environment changes. But if you foster resilience - backed by an antifragile approach - each external jolt becomes a chance to refine, refocus, and recalibrate in ways your stiffer rivals can't match.

ACTION ITEMS

1. Knowledge-Share Hackathons

- Twice a year, host "Knowledge-Share Hackathons." Everyone in the company - developers, marketers, even accounting folks - can propose a quick project or skill they want to develop. Pair up or form small squads. Over one or two days, they tackle real challenges, build mini-prototypes, or even just explore a new domain.

- Conclude with short demos. Encourage every team to articulate what they learned, not just what they built. This fosters continuous learning and a sense that risk-taking is validated.

2. Resilience Fire Drills

- Run "Resilience Fire Drills" every quarter. Simulation exercises that mimic a major crisis or unexpected disruption - like a key vendor going offline or a sudden pivot in consumer demand. Each department or team must come up with an immediate response plan within a set time (say 48 hours).

- Debrief the entire company on the solutions proposed. Ask, "Where were we slow to respond?" or "Which assumptions nearly sunk us?" By structuring these drills, you actively build the muscle of adaptability rather than passively hoping your system handles future shocks.

FINAL THOUGHTS

You stand on the brink of a new frontier for your business and your personal leadership journey. A growth mindset - anchored in relentless learning, resilience, and antifragility - forces you to do more than survive. You thrive amid chaos, flipping challenges into rocket fuel. That's your mandate: Keep evolving, keep pushing, and never let complacency lull you to sleep. As Ernest Hemingway once declared, "The earth is a fine place and worth fighting for." In your world, that translates to: "Your mission is worth evolving for." Embrace the turbulence, roll up your sleeves, and become unstoppable.

The Catalyst Circle

ENVISION

Clarify your future direction. This is where you dream big, pinpoint emerging trends, and set bold targets.

EVOLVE

Reflect on what worked (and what didn't), then integrate new insights. This sets the stage for your next vision.

EMBRACE

Welcome change as your opportunity for reinvention. Instead of fearing the unknown, you lean into it.

EXPERIMENT

Turn ideas into action. Rapid prototyping, brainstorming, testing - whatever it takes to find solutions that break new ground.

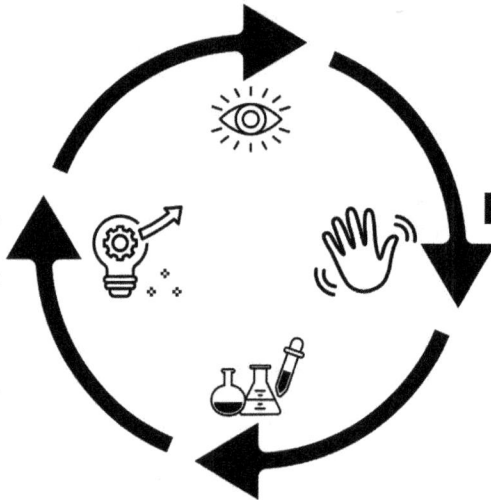

TOOL:
THE CATALYST CIRCLE

Let's get one thing straight: if you're serious about leveling up your leadership, you've gotta ditch the old "play it safe" mentality. Real success doesn't happen by riding the status quo - it's about seeing the opportunities nobody else sees, welcoming change like it's your best friend, and turning problems into possibilities.

The Catalyst Circle does exactly that, giving you a simple, powerful process to sharpen your vision, embrace growth, and stay resilient in an ever-shifting landscape. Ready to rock?

Why It Works To Understand the Catalyst Mindset

Characteristics of Catalyst Leaders

- Visionary Thinking: The Circle starts by challenging you to Envision where you want to go. This first step ensures you're always looking beyond the horizon.

- Embracing Change: The next phase leans hard into Embrace, reframing change from a threat to your greatest ally.

- Innovative Problem-Solving: By design, the Circle encourages you to Experiment, so you don't just dream - you build, tinker, and create solutions nobody else has thought of.

Cultivating a Growth Mindset

- Continuous Learning: The Circle loops, meaning once you cycle through, you start again - always leveling up, always learning.

- Resilience and Adaptability: When you adopt The Catalyst Circle, you practice bouncing back from setbacks, adjusting fast, and keeping the momentum alive.

What Is It?

Think of The Catalyst Circle as four distinct phases that feed into each other:

1. **Envision** - Clarify your future direction. This is where you dream big, pinpoint emerging trends, and set bold targets.

2. **Embrace** - Welcome change as your opportunity for reinvention. Instead of fearing the unknown, you lean into it.

3. **Experiment** - Turn ideas into action. Rapid prototyping, brainstorming, testing - whatever it takes to find solutions that break new ground.

4. **Evolve** - Reflect on what worked (and what didn't), then integrate new insights. This sets the stage for your next vision.

The circle continuously cycles - once you Evolve, you return to Envision with fresh insights, and the process starts again.

Where To Use It

In the Office

- Envision: Kick off Monday meetings by brainstorming one big, forward-thinking goal for the quarter.

- Embrace: Host a monthly "change chat" where teams share new tech, shifting market trends, or even internal processes that need to evolve.

With Your Team

- Experiment: Run quick sprints (one or two weeks) to test new ideas. No endless planning - just do, learn, and iterate.

- Evolve: After each sprint, hold a retrospective where you analyze wins, failures, and next steps.

With Yourself

- Envision: Each month, set one personal growth target - like mastering a new skill or reading a specific leadership book.

- Evolve: Reflect weekly: "How did I handle change? Where can I improve?" Then use that info to refine your vision.

Here's the real talk: being a catalyst leader means never standing still. The Catalyst Circle keeps your leadership game on a constant loop of big thinking, bold action, and non-stop improvement.

Embrace these phases, and you won't just adapt to whatever's next - you'll shape it. Now get out there and prove that you're ready to lead at the highest level!

"Bernstein didn't just conduct music - he orchestrated belief in a larger creative mission."

1ST QUARTER BONUS:
BE A CONDUCTOR, NOT A PLAYER

THE POWER OF CONNECTION:
HOW BERNSTEIN TURNED SOLOISTS INTO A SYMPHONY

When Leonard Bernstein first took the conductor's podium at the New York Philharmonic in the late 1950s, he stepped into an environment stuffed with some of the world's most accomplished and occasionally arrogant musicians.

Many had been playing their instruments for decades - prima donnas who believed they already knew how each passage should sound. Tradition and ego intertwined, stifling risk-taking. The new conductor faced skepticism: Who was this flamboyant, American-born talent to demand they alter their cherished interpretations?

He refused to tiptoe around the veterans. Instead, he made his rehearsal style more than just counting off beats. He'd sing parts himself, vigorously wave his baton, and interject with stories about how certain melodies "should feel." Some seasoned musicians bristled at first, dismissing his passionate flair as showmanship.

But his undeniable musical insight, combined with a relentless positivity, started to win them over. He'd make eye contact with each section, ensuring they felt personally seen. He'd take the time after hours to discuss a clarinetist's phrasing or a violinist's emotional expression, never cutting them short. This combination of intense focus and genuine warmth gradually transformed the ensemble's attitude.

Under Bernstein's guidance, the musicians' performances soared. Audiences could sense the electric synergy. The woodwinds sparkled with renewed confidence, the brass section began to take well-timed risks, and the string players delivered emotional nuance that critics had rarely observed before.

Even the most infamous soloists, known for their defiance of conductors, found themselves swayed by Bernstein's unwavering vision. They realized that while he didn't hold an instrument, he played the entire orchestra through his baton, body language, and dynamic leadership. This transformation is a testament to the potential impact of effective leadership.

Over time, Bernstein's approach set new benchmarks in orchestral performance. His vibrant concerts made classical music more approachable for broader audiences, and musicians discovered that behind each bold direction was a deep respect for their artistry.

By bridging authority with empathy, he turned a group of individual virtuosos into a cohesive, world-class force. Bernstein didn't just conduct music - he orchestrated belief in a larger creative mission. He showed them how to blend individual brilliance with collective harmony, proving that an influential leader doesn't ask permission to innovate. Instead, they paint a vision so compelling that even the most prideful players line up behind it.

THE CONDUCTOR VS. THE SOLO PLAYER

How often do we assume that leadership is about diving in headfirst, micromanaging tasks, or being the loudest voice in the room? In a typical corporate environment, the "leader" often tries to do everything - both the big strategic calls and the nitty-gritty grunt work, overshadowing the team's potential. That's the "solo player" approach: maybe you're the best at performing a certain role, but you limit how others participate.

Bernstein's story is a powerful example of the 'conductor' approach to leadership. As a leader, you don't need to do all the playing. Instead, you orchestrate the synergy and alignment of multiple experts, each bringing their specialized brilliance. You set a grand vision, like a symphony, and empower your 'orchestra' (the team) to interpret and refine that vision. This empowerment is a key aspect of effective leadership, and it can inspire your team to reach new heights.

THE CONDUCTOR'S MINDSET IN CATALYST LEADERSHIP

Catalyst Leadership is about igniting transformation, fueling creativity, and ensuring that every single person in the room feels part of a shared mission. The conductor's baton is more symbolic than literal: it's the tool that orchestrates direction, timing, and emotional texture. In business, it manifests as:

- **Vision:** Everyone in the organization knows the overarching piece you're trying to perform. No hidden agendas; you wave that baton for all to see.

- **Empowerment:** Musicians (employees) each have unique gifts, so the conductor doesn't overshadow them but shapes how their contributions fit into the grand design.

- **Communication:** Effective communication is a cornerstone of leadership. As a leader, your body language, eye contact, and emotional cues matter as much as the content of your words. If you can't convey your direction clearly, the audience (market) hears dissonance. This is why it's crucial to hone your leadership communication skills, ensuring that your team understands and aligns with your vision.

- **Adaptability:** No performance is set in stone. Suppose the environment changes mid-symphony (like consumer preferences shifting). In that case, the conductor must quickly pivot, maybe adjusting tempo or emphasis without losing the melody.

WHY YOU NEED TO SHIFT FROM "PLAYER" TO "CONDUCTOR"

1. **Scaling Beyond Yourself** - You might be a rock star salesperson or an incredible data analyst. But if everything depends on your personal output, you're capping the organization's potential. The conductor harnesses dozens of virtuosos - exponentially expanding impact.

2. **Encouraging Initiative** - A micromanaging "solo player" stifles Initiative because team members feel overshadowed. But under a conductor, everyone becomes accountable for their "solo lines." They adapt on the fly, trusting that the conductor sees the bigger picture.

3. **Maintaining Energy and Creativity** - When employees see that you're not hogging the spotlight but orchestrating synergy, they're more invested. They realize their piece genuinely matters. This fosters relentless creativity - like each musician feeling free to add interpretive flourishes without messing up the ensemble.

4. **Conflict as Harmony** - An orchestra's tension between sections can produce a richer sound if properly directed. The conductor ensures that each voice is heard but balanced, turning potential conflict into layered complexity. Likewise, a Catalyst Leader can let cross-functional tension spawn innovative solutions, provided it's well-guided.

BEING MORE ASSERTIVE: DIRECTING WITHOUT OVERSTEPPING

Bernstein wasn't timid. He stepped onto the podium with conviction, made eye contact, gave clear baton cues, and soared above the noise. Similarly, Catalyst Leaders need a dash of boldness:

- **Confident Vision:** Articulate your direction so forcefully that your team rallies behind you - just like a conductor's downbeat signals the entire orchestra to begin in sync.

- **Respectful Assertion:** You can push your team to excel without belittling them. Directness is not rudeness. Sometimes, a misunderstood "nice approach" leads to muddy directions. When you sense your group slipping, snap them back on tempo.

BEING MORE FOCUSED: KNOW THE SCORE, KEEP THE TEMPO

Bernstein would never have guided an orchestra if he'd only scanned the music minutes before. He studied every note, every rest. For a Catalyst Leader:

- **Master the Essentials:** You don't need to be an expert in every department's micro-tasks, but you must thoroughly grasp your business's "score." Understand the interplay of sales, operations, marketing, and finance.

- **Maintain Momentum:** A conductor can't let the orchestra drift once the performance starts. They must keep them on pace. In a business context, focus is your tempo - don't allow random side projects or internal politics to derail your core mission.

BECOMING AN EVANGELIST FOR YOUR "RELIGION"

Bernstein famously persuaded even stubborn star musicians to buy into his interpretation. He didn't do it by force alone. He exuded passion for the piece, explaining why each phrasing or dynamic shift mattered. Be an evangelist for your "Catalyst Religion" - your organization's overarching cause or goal.

- **Storytelling:** People connect with narratives. Talk about where you started, overcame obstacles, and the future you're orchestrating. Build an emotional resonance so strong that "difficult employees" or "tough clients" can't help but be intrigued.

- **Consistency:** If you're on fire about your vision one day but lukewarm the next, your message loses gravity. Show unwavering commitment. You're the consistent force that reminds everyOne: "This is why we do what we do."

THE CONTRAST: PLAYER VS. CONDUCTOR

Players focus on their own performance, ensuring they execute flawlessly within a narrow scope. Conductors see the entire tapestry, guiding multiple specialized players to produce collective brilliance. That difference is enormous in the business realm. To remain a do-it-all hero, be a top "player." But if you want to orchestrate a movement that outlasts you, become a "conductor."

You might miss the rush of personally "doing it all." But as a catalyst, your role is bigger than personal gratification. You're shaping an ecosystem that thrives on synergy, fosters unstoppable momentum, and compels each member to deliver their best for the group's shared triumph.

TAKE ACTION

1. **Podium Sprints**

- Once a quarter, gather cross-functional teams for what we'll call "Podium Sprints." Each sprint lasts a week or two, focusing on a core challenge - maybe revamping a product feature or launching a new marketing approach.

- As the "conductor," your job is to define the overall objective, set the tempo, and encourage synergy. Resist the urge to micromanage. Encourage each "section" (department) to interpret the challenge in their own creative way.

- Conclude with a "performance review" - not the HR kind, but a public, celebratory rundown of results. People show off what they achieved and how they collaborated. This builds a sense of shared artistry.

2. Conductor's Coaching Sessions

- Host one-on-one or small-group "coaching sessions" with team leads. The point is to teach them how to "conduct" their mini-orchestras: define a clear vision, coordinate across skill sets, and let each specialist shine.

- Provide direct feedback on their communication style - how effectively they align people, how they handle squeaky wheels or strong personalities, etc. This ensures the entire leadership chain can replicate your approach, scaling your "conductor effect."

FINAL THOUGHTS

Stop trying to be the hero who does everything. Step onto the podium, baton in hand, and conduct a masterpiece. Let your team's diverse talents crescendo and converge into something far beyond what any single "star performer" could deliver. That's Catalyst Leadership - a fearless blend of assertiveness, unwavering focus, and evangelism for your mission.

As Beethoven said, "To play a wrong note is insignificant; to play without passion is inexcusable." Dare to set the passion in motion. Leave the self-limiting mindset behind, lead with unstoppable conviction, and orchestrate the show your industry never saw coming.

The "Orchestra Alignment Canvas

This canvas ensures every "player" knows their part, each "solo" is heard, and the final performance (project outcome) resonates like a well-orchestrated symphony.

Score (Objective)

This is your project's "why." It clarifies the big-picture purpose—whether that's launching a product, entering a new market, or staging a major event. Like a symphony's sheet music, the objective anchors everyone to the same endpoint.

Sections (Teams)

Each department—marketing, engineering, sales, finance—becomes its own "section." Note their core functions, resources, and how they fit into the bigger piece. This step prevents duplicate efforts and spotlights potential synergy between sections.

Soloists (Key Players)

Certain individuals hold rare expertise, or they might lead a critical part of the process. Label these "soloists" so everyone recognizes their unique responsibility and respects their moments to shine.

Tempo (Timeline)

Break the project into clear sprints or milestones, defining a "tempo" so each section knows when to come in or hand off. This beats the chaos of a free-for-all with no deadlines or accountability.

Dynamics (Communication Style)

Just as musicians rely on cues for volume and intensity, teams need explicit guidelines for how often they meet or share updates (e.g., weekly stand-ups, Slack channels, short daily huddles). Aligning communication frequencies and formats curtails confusion and fosters cohesion

TOOL:
THE ORCHESTRA ALIGNMENT CANVAS

Picture your business or project as a grand musical performance, with various departments acting as instrument sections, and specific individuals stepping into the solo spotlight when their unique talents are needed.

The Orchestra Alignment Canvas helps you transform that abstract vision into a practical blueprint for action, ensuring every participant understands the collective goal and how they contribute.

Score (Objective) - This is your project's "why." It clarifies the big-picture purpose - whether that's launching a product, entering a new market, or staging a major event. Like a symphony's sheet music, the objective anchors everyone to the same endpoint.

Sections (Teams) - Each department - marketing, engineering, sales, finance - becomes its own "section." Note their core functions, resources, and how they fit into the bigger piece. This step prevents duplicate efforts and spotlights potential synergy between sections.

Soloists (Key Players) - Certain individuals hold rare expertise, or they might lead a critical part of the process. Label these "soloists" so everyone recognizes their unique responsibility and respects their moments to shine.

Tempo (Timeline) - Break the project into clear sprints or milestones, defining a "tempo" so each section knows when to come in or hand off. This beats the chaos of a free-for-all with no deadlines or accountability.

Dynamics (Communication Style) - Just as musicians rely on cues for volume and intensity, teams need explicit guidelines for how often they meet or share updates (e.g., weekly stand-ups, Slack channels, short daily huddles). Aligning communication frequencies and formats curtails confusion and fosters cohesion.

By visually mapping these components, the Orchestra Alignment Canvas harmonizes cross-functional coordination and pinpoints who's in the limelight when. It's your master score for orchestrating success - keeping everyone tuned in, on cue, and ready to perform at peak creativity.

VISIONARY LEADERSHIP & INNOVATION

4

"DO YOU WANT TO BE A
VISIONARY LEADER WHO
DRIVES CHANGE, INSPIRES
YOUR TEAM, AND CREATES
A LASTING IMPACT?"

DEVELOPING VISIONARY LEADERSHIP

Part One:
Crafting a Compelling Vision

Part Two:
Strategic Foresight

Part Three:
Leading with Purpose

"Construct a fierce vision that rouses every corner of your organization to see a future that begs to be created."

PART ONE:
CRAFTING A COMPELLING VISION

HOW INDRA NOOYI BET AGAINST PEPSI'S CASH COWS— AND STILL CRUSHED IT

When Indra Nooyi stepped in as CEO of PepsiCo in 2006, the food and beverage giant was riding high on traditional consumer favorites like soda and salty snacks. However, changes in consumer attitudes toward health and wellness were already simmering. People wanted less sugar, fewer empty calories, and products that aligned with a healthier lifestyle. Internally, some executives hesitated to mess with the cash cows - who wants to tamper with America's favorite soda? Financial analysts wondered if pivoting toward healthier products might slash revenue. The question loomed: Could PepsiCo boldly reshape its portfolio without alienating loyal consumers and risking short-term profitability?

Nooyi didn't flinch. She envisioned a more sustainable, health-conscious future where PepsiCo would embrace better-for-you products alongside its iconic brands. She introduced the "Performance with Purpose" philosophy, aiming to tie corporate profits to societal and environmental benefits. She championed significant R&D investments into low-sugar beverages, nutritious snacks, and sustainable agricultural practices. Internally, her leadership style called for cross-departmental collaboration to revamp product recipes, marketing strategies, and global distribution models. She challenged business units to become ambassadors of this new vision instead of mere gatekeepers of old successes.

The payoff was unmistakable. Over the next decade, PepsiCo's revenue streams diversified, with "good-for-you" and "better-for-you" segments outpacing traditional offerings in growth. Investors, initially skeptical, saw that embracing health trends didn't mean abandoning profits. The company's market valuation soared. Nooyi's unwavering focus on aligning the company's long-term vision with broader health and environmental goals resonated with consumers and revitalized the corporate culture. PepsiCo emerged more decisive, forward-thinking, and relevant in a world increasingly demanding responsible products. Nooyi's story showcases how crafting a bold, purpose-driven vision - and relentlessly communicating it - can transform a sprawling multinational and keep it on the leading edge of consumer expectations.

KEY TAKEAWAYS

Visionary Leadership: Nooyi's vision of aligning business goals with societal and environmental concerns was a key driver of PepsiCo's transformation.

Long-Term Strategic Thinking: Her focus on long-term sustainability and growth, even at the potential cost of short-term profits, was a crucial element of her success.

Adapting to Changing Consumer Preferences: Nooyi's leadership demonstrated the importance of adapting to evolving consumer preferences and market trends.

DEFINING THE POWER OF A COMPELLING VISION

Visionary leadership is more than a poster on the wall or a catchy tagline in your annual report. It's about forging a unifying narrative that ties your daily operations to a broader purpose, pulling everyone - employees, partners, and even skeptical stakeholders - toward a future that your competitors can't see. Without a clear vision, you're just shuffling tasks and chasing quarterly targets. With one, you can rally an entire organization to punch above its weight, persist through adversity, and innovate far beyond what short-term metrics suggest.

SECTION 1: ALIGNING WITH ORGANIZATIONAL GOALS

You can't spin up a random vision that sounds good but ignores the company's fundamentals. The best visions build upon your organization's core competencies and strategic aims. Think about Indra Nooyi: she didn't burn PepsiCo to the ground; she leveraged its global distribution and brand clout to pivot toward healthier offerings. Your vision must resonate with your company's identity and talent base - otherwise, it's a fantasy that never takes root.

Why Alignment Matters

- **Coherent Execution**: People see a logical flow from daily tasks to a higher purpose when the top-level vision syncs with operational goals - like cost targets, product launches, or market expansions.

- **Resource Prioritization**: Big visions often need significant investments. If those investments don't align with your organizational strengths, you risk a messy sprawl of initiatives going nowhere.

- **Employee Buy-In**: Employees want to feel their work matters. If your grand plan overlooks fundamental business objectives, they'll label it fluff and ignore it.

So, how do you ensure alignment? First, articulate your company's core mission or strategic pillars. Then, ask, "How does my vision help accelerate or enhance these pillars?" If you can't answer that succinctly, refine the vision. Don't treat alignment like a constraint; treat it like the structural foundation that lets you stack bigger ambitions on top.

SECTION 2: ENSURING YOUR VISION SUPPORTS BROADER OBJECTIVES

A compelling vision doesn't just align internally - it also resonates with the bigger ecosystem. That might include societal trends (health, sustainability, diversity), regulatory landscapes, or next-gen consumer expectations. If your vision matches cultural momentum, you'll struggle to gain traction or risk future backlash.

Think External:

- **Market Shifts**: Are you anticipating evolving consumer demands or ignoring them? PepsiCo's pivot to healthier options was about riding the wave of wellness. In your case, maybe it's digital transformation, AI integration, or supply-chain resilience.

- **Partnerships and Alliances**: A vision that extends beyond your walls can attract strategic partners. If your aim is to revolutionize renewable packaging, for example, you might team up with raw materials innovators or nonprofits championing the environment.

- **Community and Social Impact**: Today's employees and customers increasingly care about brand ethics. Ensure your vision ties back to something bigger than profit. That's how you win hearts, not just wallets.

By supporting broader objectives - like global sustainability goals or inclusive hiring practices - you create a magnet for talent and goodwill. People see you as a force for positive change, not just another company chasing dollars.

SECTION 3: COMMUNICATING VISION EFFECTIVELY

You can craft the most brilliant vision statement in the world, but if you can't communicate it in a way that ignites hearts and minds, it's wasted potential. A rallying cry that resonates must be clear, concise, and relatable.

Key Principles

1. **Simplicity**: Strip away jargon. People need to grasp it in one sentence.

2. **Authenticity**: Don't parrot cliches. Show genuine commitment. If you're pivoting to "green" initiatives, prove it with real actions and allocated budgets.

3. **Repetition**: Communication isn't a one-and-done. Like a drumbeat, your vision should be woven into town halls, newsletters, project kick-offs, and performance reviews.

4. **Storytelling**: Use anecdotes, case studies, or real employee examples to illustrate why this vision matters. Story hits the emotional chord logic can't always reach.

And please, avoid the corporate-speak that numbs souls. People rally behind visions when they sense passion and conviction, not stiff formalities. Let your voice crack with excitement if you have to. The more human, the better.

SECTION 4: INSPIRING OTHERS TO SHARE YOUR FORESIGHT

This final piece is crucial. You can't implement a grand vision single-handedly; you need an army of believers. That means forging emotional connections. Why does your future scenario matter to an entry-level engineer or a mid-career accountant? Show them how they fit into the puzzle.

Inspiration Tactics

- **Highlight Individual Roles**: In your communications, spell out how each department or role contributes to this larger mission. Emphasize the synergy that emerges when everyone rows in the same direction.

- **Empower Champions**: Identify influencers within the organization - formal or informal leaders - who can evangelize. Let them host discussions, champion pilot programs, and gather feedback.

- **Celebrate Early Wins**: Quick wins validate your vision. Share small success stories - like a product iteration that boosts user engagement or a new partnership that broadens your brand's footprint. These stories reaffirm that the vision isn't some distant ideal; it's happening in real time.

Ultimately, you want your people not just to comply but to champion the vision. Their enthusiasm ripples outward - customers notice, partners see a spark, and you cultivate an ecosystem of unstoppable momentum.

ACTION ITEMS

Vision Alignment Workshop

- Host a half-day workshop with key managers, frontline employees, and even some external stakeholders if relevant. Start by clearly stating your draft vision. Then, facilitate open dialogue on how it plugs into current organizational goals. Where do folks see misalignments or gaps? Where do they see synergy?

- Collect their input, refine the vision, and produce a succinct "Vision & Alignment" document. Distribute it widely, ensuring everyone grasps the direct link to operational goals.

Future Impact Showcase

- Schedule a monthly "Future Impact Showcase" - short presentations (10-15 minutes each) where teams or individuals show how they're contributing to the vision. They might discuss a pilot project, a new technology being tested, or a marketing campaign that ties back to the broader mission.

- Keep it public and celebratory. Applaud even the small steps. This fosters transparency and reminds everyone, in a tangible way, how their daily work moves the vision forward.

FINAL THOUGHTS

Don't stand in the shallows, timidly waiting for change to wash over you. Construct a fierce vision that rouses every corner of your organization to see a future that begs to be created. Speak its purpose loudly, remind people of their role in its unfolding, and paint pictures of the triumph that awaits when everyone unites behind it.

As Walt Whitman said, "Do I contradict myself? Very well then, I contradict myself." Visions worth having often defy neat logic - so defy it. Let your vision be the spark that lights a wildfire of commitment, invention, and unstoppable growth.

"You can't control the future, but you sure can lay a killer foundation to dominate it."

PART TWO:
STRATEGIC FORESIGHT

HOW NOKIA WENT FROM KING TO CAUTIONARY TALE—
BECAUSE THEY PLAYED IT TOO SAFE

At the turn of the 21st century, **Nokia** was the undisputed king of the mobile phone industry. Its simple but reliable devices dominated markets from Europe to Africa to Asia, and the brand name was practically synonymous with "cell phone." Yet behind the shiny success reports, a quiet storm brewed. Consumer tastes leaned toward internet connectivity, color displays, and more sophisticated software experiences. Meanwhile, a handful of tech players - once considered inconsequential - were experimenting with new ecosystems, touchscreens, and advanced operating systems.

Nokia's leadership was aware of these developments but largely discounted their urgency. They doubled down on hardware design - sleeker forms, robust build quality - believing that their reputation for reliability and brand trust would carry them forward indefinitely. Some internal voices recommended pivoting to a stronger software ecosystem, perhaps adopting a more open platform or forging deeper alliances with emerging mobile OS developers. However, the inertia of success and an unwillingness to cannibalize current profit lines dampened any swift shift in strategy.

When Apple's iPhone and Google's Android stormed onto the scene, **Nokia** was caught in a reactive loop. They tried to patch Symbian, introduced half-hearted touchscreen models, and even launched a partnership with Microsoft. None of it could match the user experience revolution that iOS and Android were serving up. Within just a few years, Nokia's global dominance shrank alarmingly. Leadership scrambled but never fully recovered when facing plummeting market share and intensifying pressure. Eventually, Nokia's mobile division was sold off, a bittersweet footnote for a brand that had once seemed unassailable.

What can we learn from this? The story underscores the devastating cost of ignoring future trends and lacking robust scenario planning. Nokia had the resources, the brand, and even early glimpses of the touchscreen future but failed to act aggressively. They had data but lacked the strategic foresight to interpret it as a clarion call rather than background noise. The window for a decisive pivot was gone by the time the threat was undeniable. This cautionary tale sets the stage for why **trend analysis** and **scenario planning** aren't fancy buzzwords - they're the life-or-death skill set of visionary leadership.

KEY TAKEAWAYS

Failure to Adapt to Technological Change: Nokia's failure to adapt to the changing technological landscape, particularly the shift towards software-centric mobile experiences, is the primary reason for their decline.

Underestimating the Competition: Nokia underestimated the threat posed by Apple and Google and failed to recognize the disruptive potential of their new approaches.

Inertia of Success: Nokia's past success created a sense of complacency and made them resistant to change.

Importance of Strategic Foresight and Scenario Planning: The narrative correctly emphasizes the importance of strategic foresight and scenario planning in anticipating future trends and making timely decisions.

INTRODUCTION TO STRATEGIC FORESIGHT

Being a visionary leader isn't just about having a dream that excites people - it's about making that dream bulletproof by anticipating how markets, technologies, and consumer behaviors will shift. And that's precisely what **strategic foresight** brings to the table. It's the discipline of scanning the future - predicting potential disruptions, identifying hidden opportunities, and planning for multiple outcomes so your organization never gets blindsided.

SECTION 1: TREND ANALYSIS – USING DATA TO PREDICT INDUSTRY SHIFTS

Trend analysis is your early warning system. It's how you transform raw data - market reports, consumer surveys, global events - into actionable insights about where the puck will be in six months, one year, or five years. The key isn't just gathering info but interpreting it with nuance, spotting patterns your competitors dismiss as noise.

WHY TREND ANALYSIS MATTERS

- **Preventing Complacency**: If your sales are up 10% this quarter, that's great - until a competitor launches a brand-new product that makes your current offering look prehistoric. Trends can foreshadow that competitor's next move or an industry pivot, giving you the jump on reinvention.

- **Resource Allocation**: Your R&D budget, hiring strategy, and marketing campaigns are all shaped by what you think the future holds. If you spot a consumer trend trending toward subscription models or eco-friendly materials, you can direct resources there ahead of the rush.

- **Informed Decision-Making**: Data is neutral, but how you interpret it determines whether you create or miss opportunities. For example, a spike in online searches for "homegrown produce" could signal a broader shift in consumer values that your brand can tap into with new product lines or marketing angles.

GATHERING DATA VS. GENERATING INSIGHT

It's easy to drown in data. The real mastery lies in bridging data to insight. Maybe you track e-commerce stats, social media chatter, or macroeconomic indicators. Great - but do you have a dedicated team or process that synthesizes these into a coherent picture of emerging consumer desires, potential tech leaps, or next-wave competitors?

- **Qualitative + Quantitative**: Hard numbers on revenue or user analytics are crucial, but so are intangible cues - like influencer chatter, niche community enthusiasm, or signals from edge-case markets. Sometimes, the future is hidden in fringe behavior.

- **Cross-Functional Collaboration**: Trend analysis shouldn't be siloed in a single department. Marketing sees shifting consumer tastes, R&D sees new tech possibilities, and finance sees funding flows. Bring them together to form a holistic view.

SECTION 2: SCENARIO PLANNING -
PREPARING FOR MULTIPLE FUTURE POSSIBILITIES

Even with robust trend analysis, the future remains unpredictable. That's where scenario planning enters the fray. Instead of betting everything on one forecast, you outline multiple plausible futures - best case, worst case, and everything in between - so you're never caught flatfooted.

How Scenario Planning Works

1. **Identify Key Variables**: Maybe it's the adoption rate of a new technology, a potential global recession, or a sudden shift in consumer ethics toward sustainability.

2. **Construct Scenarios**: For each variable, hypothesize how it might evolve - slow or fast, positive or negative. Combine these variables into several narratives, e.g., "Accelerated Tech Utopia," "Sluggish Global Economy," and "Eco-Revolution Consumer Mindset."

3. **Assess Organizational Impact**: How does your business model hold up in each scenario? Which product lines thrive or die? Where could supply chain disruptions cripple you?

4. **Strategize**: Outline contingency plans - like alternate suppliers, new product R&D, or shifts in marketing. If one scenario starts manifesting, you can pivot without panic.

THE POWER OF BEING READY

Scenario planning is not about predicting the future flawlessly - it's about being flexible enough to adapt no matter which future unfolds. It's your competitive advantage in a world where disruption often feels random. When something left-field hits (like a pandemic, a tech revolution, or a significant regulatory change), you're not reacting blindly; you've already gamed out the possibilities.

Suppose Nokia had run multiple scenarios where touchscreen phones suddenly captured massive market share. In that case, they might have pre-emptively allocated resources to software R & D or deeper alliances with forward-thinking partners. Instead, they clung to the scenario that their design and brand loyalty would remain bulletproof - an assumption that scenario planning could have challenged.

ACTION ITEMS

Institutionalize a "Trend Review Board"

- Form a cross-departmental group that meets monthly to review fresh data - consumer research, tech breakthroughs, competitor announcements. They craft a short "Emerging Trends Memo" that circulates across leadership, summarizing any early signals or shifts.

- Encourage them to highlight "wild card" possibilities, no matter how strange. The point is to keep the conversation about future shifts alive, not buried in day-to-day tasks.

Scenario Planning Workshops

- Twice a year, hold scenario planning workshops. Divide your leadership and a few key innovators into teams. Each team crafts 2-3 plausible future scenarios - ranging from bullish to catastrophic - and drafts how the organization could respond.

- Post-workshop, compile a short scenario playbook. Don't let it gather dust. Revisit it whenever new data suggests one scenario is starting to look more likely. This ensures your strategy remains agile and your team psychologically prepared for different futures.

FINAL THOUGHTS

You can't control the future, but you sure can lay a killer foundation to dominate it. Trend analysis keeps your radar sharp, scenario planning keeps you nimble, and both ensure you're not Nokia - scrambling too late to a market that's sprinted miles ahead. The question is, will you be the leader who sees the storm coming and seizes the advantage or dismisses the early gusts until it's a full-blown hurricane?

Winston Churchill once remarked, "The empires of the future are the empires of the mind." Arm your mind with foresight, and you'll build an empire that thrives - no matter what tomorrow brings.

"Purpose-driven leadership isn't just moral high ground - it's the future of market dominance. People don't merely want to buy; they want to belong."

PART THREE: LEADING WITH PURPOSE

HOW A CLIMBER BUILT PATAGONIA BY FLIPPING OFF FAST FASHION AND PLAYING THE LONG GAME

In the 1960s, **Yvon Chouinard** was a restless rock climber, making his climbing gear to support his passion for scaling mountainsides. At the time, the outdoor equipment industry was small, with minimal environmental awareness. Most climbers used iron pitons that damaged the rock, and few companies bothered with eco-friendly materials. Yvon noticed his fellow climbers' impact on natural habitats and grew uneasy. Selling homemade climbing gear from the back of his car, he realized that the "easy money" approach - using cheap but polluting materials - conflicted with his deep respect for the natural world.

He refused to accept that businesses should prioritize profit above all else. Instead, he poured time and resources into designing more sustainable equipment, especially aluminum chocks that could be removed from rock faces without scarring them. The path wasn't smooth. He had to retool production processes, invest in R&D, and educate climbers used to hammering pitons into every crack. Even his small but loyal customer base questioned whether such gear could match the reliability of tradition. But Yvon was relentless about aligning his fledgling business with his values.

That same spirit led him to found **Patagonia**, an outdoor apparel brand that challenged the entire fashion and sporting goods industry to reckon with the footprint they left behind. Rather than scale up quickly with cheap labor, Patagonia sourced eco-friendly materials, introduced organic cotton, and gave employees flexibility for surf breaks or family commitments. Revenues didn't explode overnight, but trust did. Customers who shared Yvon's environmental concerns latched onto Patagonia, seeing it as a brand that walked its talk.

Fast-forward to today: Patagonia is a global powerhouse in outdoor wear, widely lauded for pioneering sustainable business practices. They actively encourage consumers to repair garments rather than buy new ones, donate a chunk of profits to environmental causes, and champion activism for preserving wild places. Instead of doping the market with endless product lines, Patagonia invests in long-lasting items with minimal environmental cost. Yvon Chouinard's ethic - valuing nature over quick gains - transformed the brand into an icon of values-driven leadership. By focusing on purpose before profit, he built an empire that redefined what it meant to run a responsible and influential global enterprise.

KEY TAKEAWAYS

Alignment of Values and Business: The story highlights the importance of aligning personal values with business practices, a central theme in Patagonia's success.

Long-Term Vision and Sustainability: Patagonia's focus on long-term sustainability and environmental responsibility has been a key differentiator and a source of competitive advantage.

Purpose Before Profit: The idea of prioritizing purpose over profit is a core principle that has guided Patagonia's decisions and shaped its brand identity.

INTRODUCING PURPOSE-DRIVEN LEADERSHIP

Leading with purpose isn't some new-age buzzword or marketing gimmick. It's a laser-focused approach to leadership where every decision, every product, and every relationship aligns with a core set of values that transcend short-term profits. Leaders who operate this way create not just companies but movements. They don't merely chase revenue; they build tribes of loyal customers and employees who stand behind something more significant than mere transactions.

SECTION 1: VALUES-DRIVEN LEADERSHIP – ALIGNING ACTIONS WITH CORE PRINCIPLES

Values-driven leadership starts with knowing what the hell you stand for. Not the superficial statements you plaster on a corporate website but the honest, deep-down convictions that shape every choice - even if it costs you in the short run. Think of Yvon Chouinard forging climbing gear that respected nature or refusing to scale up Patagonia at the planet's expense. The point isn't to adopt a cause to look good; it's about integrating that cause - or that set of values - so seamlessly into your operations that you can't separate them from your brand identity.

WHY VALUES MATTER

1. **Guidance in Uncertainty**

   When the economy wobbles, or competitor moves threaten your market share, your values become an internal compass. Instead of panic-selling or pivoting to something that betrays your ethos, you hold tight to the principles that define your brand. This consistent adherence builds trust - internally and externally.

2. **Employee Engagement**

   People don't want to punch a clock for a paycheck; they want to believe in something. A leadership approach anchored in authentic, well-communicated values resonates with employees, fueling loyalty and innovation. Because if employees feel they're part of a meaningful mission, they bring more energy, creativity, and resilience to the table.

3. **Customer Loyalty**

   Consumers are increasingly savvy. They smell corporate hypocrisy a mile away. If your marketing screams, "We care about sustainability!" while your supply chain pollutes rivers, you'll get skewered on social media. But if you walk the talk - using ethical sourcing, supporting fair labor, or championing social causes - customers reward that consistency. They become evangelists for your brand, not just one-time buyers.

EMBEDDING VALUES IN DAILY OPERATIONS

Values can't live in a silo. They must infiltrate your hiring processes, performance metrics, product designs, vendor relationships - everything. For instance, if you claim to prioritize environmental sustainability, then you vet suppliers for eco-friendly standards, design products that last longer, and even accept the cost of recycling or refurbishing. In short, you let those values shape your entire business model.

It also means policing yourself. Are your executives on board, or do they quietly sidestep these ideals when it's convenient? Do your managers regard values-based decisions as optional or champion them? If your leadership isn't modeling these values, your employees won't either.

SECTION 2: CREATING MEANINGFUL IMPACT – FOCUSING ON CONTRIBUTIONS THAT MATTER

Leading with purpose isn't just about brand image or mission statements. It's about tangible impact. If your values revolve around sustainability, your measurable impact might involve drastically reducing your carbon footprint or supporting environmental activism. If you focus on empowering underprivileged communities, your metrics might involve philanthropic investments, job creation, or educational programs.

DEFINING "MEANINGFUL IMPACT"

1. **Social and Environmental Footprint**

   This could be resource consumption, fair wages across your supply chain, or the carbon emissions tied to your logistics. Leading with purpose means actively measuring and reducing negative or amplifying positive impacts.

2. **Innovation That Serves Humanity**

   Instead of asking, "How can we exploit this tech for a quick buck?" you ask, "How can we harness this technology to solve a real problem or elevate people's lives?" That shift in mindset can spawn products or services that do more than fill your corporate coffers - they shift the industry forward.

3. **Community Engagement**

   Real impact often means stepping outside your corporate walls. Partnerships with nonprofits, local communities, or educational institutions can amplify your ability to drive lasting change. For instance, if your goal is bridging the digital divide, you could sponsor coding camps in underrepresented areas or bring broadband to rural schools.

BALANCING PROFIT AND PURPOSE

Skeptics might say, "Sure, meaning is nice, but we have bills to pay and shareholders to satisfy." The good news is that purpose and profit needn't be at war. Numerous studies show that businesses with strong ethical underpinnings often outperform ethically neutral peers in the long run. Why? Because customers trust them, employees love working there, and they're more resilient in the face of scandals or crises. The intangible asset of goodwill can carry you through tough times better than ephemeral marketing campaigns.

That said, leading with purpose might cost you in the short term. Sourcing eco-friendly materials can be pricier, or paying fair wages might squeeze margins. But in a marketplace where brand loyalty and transparency matter more each day, these moves can generate loyalty that's nearly unbreakable. You're playing a marathon, not a sprint.

THE RIPPLE EFFECT

Your influence extends beyond immediate beneficiaries when you lead purposefully and focus on meaningful impact. Partners might adopt similar practices. Competitors might adapt to keep up. Entire supply chains can shift when big companies demand higher standards. It's a chain reaction that can reshape entire industries over time. That's the real power of purpose-driven leadership: it sets new norms for what's acceptable and possible.

ACTION ITEMS

1. **Values Audit**

- Gather your executive team (or top managers) for a half-day retreat. Revisit your core values. Are they clearly defined, actionable, and integrated into everyday decisions? If they're just words on a poster, refine them until they reflect your brand's DNA.

- Next, examine your operations. Does your hiring align with these values? Does your product design process, supply chain management, and marketing embody them? Identify three areas where your actions diverge from your stated values, and craft a 90-day plan to close those gaps.

2. **Impact Blueprint**

- Decide on one central area where you want to create tangible impact - environmental, social, or something else that resonates with your brand's ethos. Host a cross-functional brainstorming session to define measurable goals (e.g., reduce carbon emissions by 30% in two years or fund 100 scholarships for underprivileged youth).

- Form a small "Impact Task Force" to drive these initiatives. Give them authority and resources, and require monthly progress updates. Celebrate small wins publicly - employee recognition, social media blasts - so the organization sees that purposeful action isn't lip service.

FINAL THOUGHTS

Don't settle for running a faceless organization that pushes product. Be the leader who ignites purpose, sets new benchmarks for ethics, and weaves impact into your brand's core. Purpose-driven leadership isn't just a path to moral high ground - it's the future of market dominance. People don't merely want to buy; they want to belong. Give them a cause worth rallying around.

As Victor Hugo said, "There is nothing more powerful than an idea whose time has come." Let your purpose be that idea, blazing a trail so others follow - not because they must, but because they believe.

The Vision ARC

3. COMMIT
Clarify Roles and Expectations
Establish Milestones and Metrics
Share and Inspire

2. FRAME
Synthesize Findings
Create Your Strategic
Vision
Ensure Organizational
Alignment

4. RADIATE
Scale Up and Showcase Wins
Iterate and Refine
Broadcast Beyond Your Walls

1. EXPLORE
Scan the Horizon
Collect Diverse Perspectives
Reflect on Personal Values

TOOL:
THE VISION ARC

Listen, if you want to be more than just a manager punching the clock, you've got to think bigger - and I mean really big. Visionary leadership isn't just about having a cool slogan. It's about painting a future so compelling that everyone around you leans in and says, "I want to be part of that."

The Vision Arc will help you sharpen that crystal-clear focus, scan the horizon for fresh opportunities, and lead with a purpose that goes way beyond quarterly targets. Ready to elevate your game?

Why It Works in Developing Visionary Leadership

Crafting a Compelling Vision

- Aligning with Organizational Goals: The first part of The Vision Arc ensures your big ideas actually support the broader mission - not just your personal wish list.

- Communicating Vision Effectively: Once the Arc is in place, it becomes a blueprint you can share with your entire organization, inspiring them to buy into your foresight.

Strategic Foresight

- Trend Analysis: The Vision Arc includes a step for taking a good, hard look at industry data and future possibilities so you're not making blind bets.

- Scenario Planning: As you progress through the Arc, you naturally spin off multiple scenarios, preparing you for whatever twist or turn the market throws your way.

Leading with Purpose

- Values-Driven Leadership: The Arc helps you anchor your grand vision in core principles, so you don't just chase profits - you make a real impact.

- Creating Meaningful Impact: By refining and clarifying your vision, you focus on the contributions that truly matter - to your people, your customers, and the world at large.

What Is It?

The Vision Arc is a four-stage, iterative process designed to help you develop and maintain a compelling, future-focused leadership vision. Each stage feeds into the next, creating a continuous cycle of discovery, refinement, commitment, and outreach. Here's how it breaks down in more detail:

1. **Explore**

- Scan the Horizon: Begin by gathering insights from market data, technology trends, and conversations with customers or stakeholders. Look for patterns - emerging demands, new tools, or cultural shifts - that might shape your future landscape.

- Collect Diverse Perspectives: Don't limit your exploration to just your immediate team. Talk to people in different departments, different industries, or even different cultural contexts. Their perspectives can spark new ideas and challenge your assumptions.

- Reflect on Personal Values: As you gather information, notice how it resonates with your own leadership philosophy. Ask yourself: "Which of these trends or ideas truly align with what we stand for, both as an organization and as individuals?"

2. **Frame**

- Synthesize Findings: Once you have a pile of raw insights, condense them into clear statements or opportunity areas. Which trends are most relevant to your goals? Which potential directions are most aligned with your core principles?

- Create Your Strategic Vision: Draft a concise vision statement that captures where you see the organization headed. Think of it as a north star - something to guide you and your team through complex decisions.

- Ensure Organizational Alignment: Cross-check this vision with your existing mission and objectives. If there's a conflict, revise until everything flows together. The point is to craft a vision that feels both ambitious and authentic.

3. Commit

- Clarify Roles and Expectations: Identify what each team member - or department - needs to do to bring the vision to life. If people don't know their part, even the best ideas will stall.

- Establish Milestones and Metrics: Commit to concrete targets - both short-term goals and long-term aspirations. Make them visible so everyone knows where you're headed and how progress will be measured.

- Share and Inspire: This stage is all about rallying the troops. Hold kickoffs, workshops, or town halls where you communicate the vision in a way that excites and motivates people.

4. Radiate

- Scale Up and Showcase Wins: Begin rolling out pilot projects or new initiatives tied to your vision. Highlight early successes, no matter how small, so people see that the vision isn't just talk - it's becoming reality.

- Iterate and Refine: Keep an eye on the metrics you set in the Commit phase. If something isn't working, adjust. Stay flexible - every piece of feedback is an opportunity to refine your approach.

- Broadcast Beyond Your Walls: Once you start seeing meaningful progress, share your story externally with customers, partners, or even industry peers. By radiating your vision outward, you attract talent, open doors for strategic partnerships, and further cement your leadership role in shaping the future.

Through these four stages, The Vision Arc transforms the abstract concept of "visionary leadership" into a practical, repeatable process. And because it loops back - after Radiate, you return to Explore - you're never stuck on yesterday's version of success. You keep evolving, staying relevant, and pushing the boundaries of what your organization can achieve..

Each stage flows seamlessly into the next, forming a continuous loop that keeps your vision dynamic and relevant.

How to Use It

In the Office

- Explore: Start by hosting a "Futures Lab" session - invite cross-functional teams to share emerging trends.

- Frame: Convert those raw ideas into a real plan. Whiteboard the overlaps between new opportunities and your existing objectives.

With Your Team

- Commit: Hold a kickoff meeting or workshop where you walk everyone through your refined vision. Let people ask questions and voice concerns early.

- Radiate: Launch smaller pilot projects or initiatives tied to your vision, and track their performance. Share successes quickly - recognition builds momentum.

With Yourself

- Explore: Spend time each week reading about industry shifts or technological advancements. Keep a personal notebook of fresh insights.

- Frame: Reflect on whether these new insights align with your own values and the company's mission. Adjust your personal growth goals accordingly.

Here's the truth: You don't accidentally become a visionary leader. You become one by systematically exploring possibilities, framing them into a compelling path, committing your team, and then broadcasting that vision to the world.

The Vision Arc is your practical roadmap for doing precisely that. Embrace it, and you'll do more than meet your goals - you'll redefine what's possible for your entire organization. Let's make it happen!

5

"DO YOU WANT TO EMPOWER YOUR TEAM TO INNOVATE WITHOUT FEAR AND DRIVE YOUR ORGANIZATION TO NEW HEIGHTS?"

FOSTERING INNOVATION AND CREATIVITY

Part One:
Building an Innovative Culture

Part Two:
Leveraging Technology and AI

Part Three:
Overcoming Barriers to Innovation

"Innovation isn't a checkbox you tick - it's a living pulse that drives your team forward."

PART ONE:
BUILDING AN INNOVATIVE CULTURE

HOW 3M BECAME AN INNOVATION MACHINE - BY LETTING EMPLOYEES TINKER AROUND ON THE CLOCK

In the 1920s, 3M was a scrappy Minnesota-based mining and manufacturing outfit struggling to gain traction in abrasive materials. They had a few success stories, like sandpaper. Still, the company was far from the global powerhouse it would later become. Internally, teams were cautious, avoiding big risks for fear of wasting limited resources. Then William McKnight, originally hired as an assistant bookkeeper, rose through the ranks and shook the status quo. He noticed that top-down control stifled creativity. Employees with unique ideas or side projects often found themselves stonewalled by bureaucracy or dismissed by conservative managers who only cared about immediate returns.

McKnight spearheaded a cultural shift that encouraged employees to pursue hunches and tinker with side projects - even if those projects seemed unrelated to immediate product lines. His mantra was simple: let people experiment, give them the freedom to fail, and support them with time and resources. Some leadership fretted about wasted budgets or misallocating staff hours, but McKnight insisted that true breakthroughs wouldn't emerge from rigid procedures alone.

The results of McKnight's cultural shift were nothing short of transformative. Out of these 'free-time' experiments came products like masking tape and the iconic Post-it Notes - blockbuster innovations that not only turned healthy profits but also expanded 3 M's brand identity far beyond abrasives. Over time, 3M baked McKnight's philosophy into its very DNA, granting employees a portion of their workweek to chase personal R&D projects without immediate oversight. Managers were trained to champion these initiatives rather than squash them. This cultural shift catalyzed a pipeline of discoveries and product lines that fueled 3 M's global expansion, a testament to the power of a culture of experimentation and innovation.

By the mid-20th century, 3M was a beacon of corporate creativity, admired by business leaders worldwide. McKnight's core principle - trust people, give them space to explore, and accept that not all experiments would pay off - proved invaluable. While many corporations were fixated on short-term goals and controlling the daily grind, 3M soared ahead by unleashing a culture where innovation became second nature. That gamble spawned game-changing products and attracted top talent who craved an environment that valued original thinking over rigid compliance. Ultimately, 3M transformed into the multi-billion-dollar conglomerate we know today, all because McKnight believed that experimentation and creative freedom were the lifeblood of true industry leadership.

KEY TAKEAWAYS

Empowering Employees to Innovate: McKnight's key insight was that empowering employees to pursue their own ideas could lead to significant breakthroughs.

Creating a Culture of Experimentation and Risk-Taking: The acceptance of failure and the encouragement of experimentation were crucial elements of the culture he fostered.

McKnight's focus on long-term innovation, rather than just short-term profits, was a key factor in 3 M's long-term success. This emphasis on the long game is a reminder that true innovation often takes time and persistence, and that a culture of experimentation and risk-taking is a marathon, not a sprint.

INTRODUCTION: CULTIVATING AN INNOVATIVE CULTURE

In many corporate boardrooms, "innovation" is a buzzword thrown around to impress investors and employees. But too often, it's tethered to isolated R&D labs or pinned on a sporadic "innovation day" once a year. Real innovation demands a culture that daily fosters creativity, risk-taking, and curiosity. That's the core premise of an "innovative culture": it isn't an event; it's a mindset woven through your entire organization. It liberates talent, fuels problem-solving, and primes you to seize opportunities before your competition even notices them.

SECTION 1: ENCOURAGING EXPERIMENTATION – ALLOWING SPACE FOR TRIAL AND ERROR

Why Experimentation Matters

Experimentation is oxygen for creativity. Without it, ideas suffocate under the weight of "proven methods" or fear of failure. Companies that treat failure as taboo lock themselves into incremental progress and stagnation at worst. Yet breakthroughs - truly disruptive leaps - rarely come from playing it safe. As 3 M's story shows, sometimes the most profitable ideas sprout from side projects with zero immediate ROI. When you empower employees to try out offbeat concepts, you open the door to accidental discoveries, like the creation of Post-it Notes, which started as a glue project gone wrong.

EMBEDDING TRIAL-AND-ERROR IN DAILY OPERATIONS

- **Dedicated Time:** One approach is the "15% rule" 3M popularized, letting employees devote a chunk of their workweek to passion projects or hunches. Google once had a "20% time" concept, producing Gmail and AdSense. The exact percentage may vary, but the principle is constant: free up structured time to tinker.

- **Rapid Prototyping:** Encourage small, quick prototypes. You don't risk blowing up budgets if an idea is cheap and easy to test. If it fails, you fail fast and learn fast.

- **Safe Zones for Failure:** Let's be honest - people aren't going to jump into experiments if they think one misstep will bury their career. So, leadership must cultivate psychological safety. That means praising well-intentioned attempts even if they flop, gleaning lessons, and pivoting quickly.

ROLE OF LEADERSHIP

Leaders must not just endorse but actively model experimental behavior. If you only praise 'sure bets,' your talk about innovation rings hollow. Show you're willing to experiment yourself, whether by championing a new approach to budgeting or trialing an unconventional marketing channel. When employees see leaders diving in, they are more likely to follow suit, reinforcing the importance of leadership in fostering an innovative culture.

COMMON PITFALLS

- **Token Support:** Big announcements about a "new culture of innovation" without structural changes breed cynicism.

- **Over-Policing:** Employees give up on suggesting new ideas if middle managers clamp down with rigid approvals.

- **Ignoring Wins:** No matter how small, early successes from experiments must be celebrated publicly to reinforce the message that creativity is valued.

SECTION 2: RECOGNIZING AND REWARDING CREATIVITY – INCENTIVIZING INNOVATIVE THINKING

Experimentation is one side of the coin, but consistent creative output requires recognition. People need to see that their innovative contributions matter, not just in performance reviews but also in the day-to-day hustle. Otherwise, the zeal for new ideas fizzles out fast.

Why Recognition Fuels Innovation

Humans thrive on validation. If employees see their creative efforts go unnoticed or overshadowed by routine tasks, they'll revert to "doing my job." However, the entire workforce notices when leaders spotlight creative problem-solvers in front of peers, share their stories across the company or provide tangible rewards. Momentum builds. The next employee with a half-baked concept might think, "Why not me?" and pitch it anyway.

BUILDING A RECOGNITION FRAMEWORK

- **Creative Showcases:** Host monthly or quarterly "innovation fairs" where teams present prototypes, ideas, or process improvements. Let the entire company vote for their favorites, awarding small cash prizes or symbolic trophies.

- **Peer Nominations:** Allow employees to nominate colleagues who are creative in solving real problems. This fosters a culture where employees celebrate each other's ingenuity rather than compete for leadership's nod.

- **Career Advancement:** Ensure employees who excel at creative thinking get opportunities to lead new projects, join cross-functional innovation squads, or ascend the leadership ladder. Nothing cements creativity better than associating it with career growth.

ALIGNING REWARDS WITH VALUES

Remember, you get the behavior you incentivize. If your entire bonus structure only rewards short-term revenue, guess what? People chase immediate sales and skip longer-term innovation. So, incorporate creativity or risk-taking achievements into performance metrics. It might be a new product concept tested in a pilot market or an internal hack that slashes overhead. The clearer you tie rewards to innovative outcomes, the stronger the cultural shift.

POTENTIAL DRAWBACKS

- **Overemphasis on Competition:** Beware of turning everything into a contest. Too much competition can hamper collaboration.

- **Rewarding the Loud, Not the Good:** Make sure recognition is based on actual impact or effort, not just who can pitch the loudest. A quiet engineer might have groundbreaking ideas but never push themselves forward if the environment only applauds showmanship.

ACTION ITEMS

1. Innovation Hubs

- Allocate a dedicated physical or virtual space - an "Innovation Hub" - where employees can congregate to brainstorm, prototype, or discuss offbeat solutions. Stock it with basic supplies: whiteboards, prototyping kits, and design thinking tools. Encourage teams to schedule at least one hour weekly in this space.

- Make it official: Leaders should set a target for each department to organize at least two "innovation sessions" per quarter in the hub. Track outcomes, like how many prototypes were tested or pilot programs were launched. This structural support transforms good intentions into real activity.

2. Spotlight Awards

- Institute monthly "Spotlight Awards" that highlight unique creative endeavors - like a developer who coded a time-saving script, a sales rep who discovered a new market angle, or an admin who streamlined the onboarding process.

- Make it a short ceremony - 10 minutes in a company-wide meeting - where leaders publicly honor the winners. This doesn't need to be a huge bonus; a symbolic trophy, front-row parking spot, or a small gift card can suffice. The key is public recognition that says, "We see you, we value you, keep it up."

FINAL THOUGHTS

Innovation isn't a checkbox you tick; it's a living pulse that drives your team forward. Open the floodgates for experimentation, celebrate creativity like it's the lifeblood of your success, and watch as your workforce shifts from "dutiful employees" to audacious problem-solvers. No more treading water in the sea of mediocrity - empower your people to break molds.

As George Bernard Shaw once said, "The reasonable man adapts himself to the world; the unreasonable one persists in trying to adapt the world to himself." Dare to be the latter - unreasonable enough to believe you can shape tomorrow and bold enough to do it.

"Let's cut the crap: If you're not leveraging AI and advanced tech right now, you're flirting with irrelevance in a world that rewards innovation and punishes stagnation."

PART TWO:
LEVERAGING TECHNOLOGY AND AI

HOW NETFLIX WON THE STREAMING WARS -
BY LETTING THE ALGORITHM TAKE THE WHEEL

In the early days of Netflix's transition from a DVD rental service to a streaming platform, the company faced a serious uphill battle. The market was cluttered with competitors, and consumer attention spans were shrinking fast. People were getting frustrated scrolling through endless titles, unsure what to watch. The platform needed a better way to engage users, keep them on the platform longer, and encourage them to explore more content. Despite these challenges, Netflix's successful transition serves as a beacon of inspiration, showing what can be achieved with the right technology and strategy.

Instead of relying on guesswork, Netflix embraced a relatively new frontier at the time - machine learning algorithms. They poured resources into building robust data pipelines, analyzing user viewing habits, search patterns, and even the times people watched certain shows. With enough data, they could train recommendation models to serve personalized suggestions tailored to individual tastes. Engineers iterated these systems rapidly, running experiments and fine-tuning algorithms to boost accuracy and relevance.

The impact was massive. Users started discovering shows and movies they liked without digging through the catalog. Engagement soared, subscriber churn dropped, and Netflix didn't just differentiate itself - it set an industry standard. Competitors scrambled to replicate this data-driven personalization, but Netflix was already miles ahead, refining its models, integrating new analytics tools, and constantly pushing the envelope in AI-driven content recommendations. The company didn't just weather the competitive storm; it defined a new era of streaming driven by technology and data.

Let's cut the crap: If you're not leveraging technology and AI in your organization today, you're flirting with irrelevance. In a world evolving at light speed, clinging to legacy systems and guesswork decision-making is a one-way ticket to the business graveyard. AI and advanced tech tools aren't futuristic luxuries - they're mandatory weapons in your arsenal. They give you speed, precision, and an undeniable edge in a cutthroat market. Embracing these technologies is not just a choice; it's a necessity for any forward-thinking business leader.

INTEGRATING NEW TOOLS

So, what does it mean to integrate new tools effectively? It's not about chasing every shiny object - there are a million "game-changing" apps and platforms popping up daily. It's about identifying which technologies align with your strategic goals and give you the leverage to out-innovate your competition. It's about using these tools to automate the mundane, augment human capability, and unlock insights hidden in oceans of data.

And let's talk about data. Everyone loves to say "data-driven" like it's some magic spell, but most companies are drowning in data they don't know how to use. The difference between leaders and losers is the ability to transform raw numbers into actionable insights. This is where AI steps in. Machine learning models can churn through data at a scale and speed humans can't even dream of. They identify patterns, predict outcomes, and help you make decisions based on empirical evidence rather than gut feelings.

But let's be brutally honest: integrating tech and AI into your workflow isn't a plug-and-play scenario. It demands open-minded leadership ready to invest in training, infrastructure, and continuous iteration. You have to accept that these tools will evolve, and what works today might be outdated tomorrow. This is not a set-it-and-forget-it deal; it's an ongoing commitment to improvement.

There's also the cultural element. If your team sees AI and advanced tools as threats - maybe they fear being replaced or overwhelmed - they'll resist. As a leader, you need to position technology as an enabler, a partner in their work, not their robotic overlord. Show them how these tools free them from drudge work and enhance their creativity by giving them more time to focus on strategy and innovation. Make it clear that the goal is augmentation, not replacement.

And don't limit your view of AI. It's not just recommendation systems or chatbots. It can optimize logistics, forecast market trends, fine-tune pricing strategies, and even help in product design by analyzing customer feedback at scale. The applications are endless, but you need the guts and vision to experiment.

DATA-DRIVEN DECISION MAKING

Let's talk about data-driven decision-making. Gut instincts and experience matter. They give you context and a sense of direction. But relying solely on them is like driving with your headlights off at night. Data illuminates the path. When you merge intuition with empirical evidence, you strike gold. AI just turns that gold into a factory of insights.

At a strategic level, data-driven decisions lead to agility. You spot market shifts earlier, respond faster, and tailor your offerings more precisely. You test new ideas before going all-in, minimizing risk and maximizing upside. In a world where timing is everything, data, and AI help you show up at the right place, at the right time, with the right product.

Some leaders worry that all this reliance on AI will strip away the "human element." That's nonsense. The best leaders know that human creativity, empathy, and vision are irreplaceable. AI gives you a supercharged toolkit to bring those human qualities to fruition more effectively. You still set the vision; AI helps you refine and realize it.

Let's not forget the importance of continuous learning. AI models evolve. The tools you adopt this year might need upgrades next year. Your team's skill set must evolve, too. Invest in learning and development so your people can wield these tools like experts, not amateurs. Celebrate curiosity and reward those who embrace new technologies rather than clinging to outdated methods. By fostering a culture of continuous learning, you empower your team to adapt and thrive in the ever-changing landscape of technology.

The bottom line: If you're not using AI and advanced tech, you're fighting a modern war with medieval weapons. Don't just catch up - leapfrog.

Make the bold moves now, equip your team with the necessary tools, and become the player everyone else is scrambling to emulate. This isn't just about survival; it's about thriving in a world that rewards innovation and punishes stagnation.

ACTION ITEM 1: CONDUCT A 'TECH AND AI AUDIT'

First things first, get your arms around what you have and what you need. Conduct a comprehensive audit of your current technology stack. Identify gaps, overlaps, and opportunities for integration. Don't treat this like a routine IT exercise - bring in cross-functional teams to get fresh perspectives. This audit reveals where AI can provide immediate wins - maybe in predictive analytics for sales, customer segmentation for marketing, or supply chain optimization. Armed with these insights, you can invest in tools that genuinely move the needle.

ACTION ITEM 2: LAUNCH A 'DATA LITERACY BOOTCAMP'

Second, knowledge is power only if people know how to use it. Launch a Data Literacy Bootcamp to up-skill your entire team. Teach them to interpret data, understand basic AI concepts, and ask the right questions. You're not trying to turn everyone into data scientists, but everyone should be comfortable swimming in data's waters. This breaks down the intimidation barrier and makes your workforce more receptive to new technologies.

Consider applying the CRISP-DM (Cross-Industry Standard Process for Data Mining) methodology. It's a proven framework for implementing data-driven projects, from understanding business objectives and preparing data to modeling, evaluation, and deployment. CRISP-DM keeps your AI initiatives aligned with business goals, ensuring that each tech integration drives tangible results rather than becoming a science project that never sees the light of day.

FINAL THOUGHTS

You're at a crossroads right now. You can cling to old-school tactics and hope the world slows down for you - which it won't - or you can seize the tools of the future. This isn't about technology for technology's sake; it's about unlocking your organization's full potential. Embrace AI not as a buzzword but as your secret weapon. Automate the routine, amplify human brilliance, and precisely refine your strategic vision.

As Peter Drucker said, "The best way to predict the future is to create it." So pick up the tools, build your future, and make everyone else chase you.

"Barriers to innovation - fear of failure and siloed thinking - are your real opponents, not the competition outside; tear them down and unleash a creative force that outpaces every rival."

PART THREE:
OVERCOMING BARRIERS TO INNOVATION

HOW SPACEX TURNED EXPLODING ROCKETS INTO BILLION-DOLLAR BREAKTHROUGHS

When SpaceX launched in 2002, its ambition seemed outlandish: make space travel cheaper, accessible, and ultimately a gateway to Mars colonization. Skeptics labeled Elon Musk's vision ludicrous - after all, rocket science was typically the domain of mega-funded government agencies, not a startup. The company's early experiments didn't help quell those doubts. Rockets exploded on the launch pad, test flights failed, and naysayers had a field day mocking Musk's "wasted millions." Internally, morale wavered under the weight of repeated failures, and some engineers questioned whether they could pull off breakthroughs that NASA itself struggled with.

Yet Musk's unwavering leadership transformed the company's approach to failure. He instilled in his team the belief that failure wasn't just an option but a crucial stepping stone to success. Each crash was dissected relentlessly for lessons, data, and improvements. Managers were instructed to avoid finger-pointing and cultivate an environment where people felt safe speaking up about potential flaws. Meanwhile, cross-functional squads of software engineers, propulsion experts, and avionics specialists would literally share the same factory floor, breaking down departmental walls so problems could be tackled holistically. The message was clear: to do what no private company had done - launch reusable rockets into orbit and safely bring them back - SpaceX needed to replace fear and silos with bold risk-taking and genuine teamwork.

Gradually, each rocket iteration improved. Test flights made it further before an inevitable explosion. Then came the groundbreaking moment: Falcon 9 soared into orbit, delivering payloads at a fraction of typical costs.

Even more stunning was the company's success in landing and reusing boosters - an achievement that turned the rocket equation upside down, slashing costs and hinting at future Mars missions. Investors, once cynical, lined up to fund the next stage of development. Young engineers flocked to SpaceX, enticed by its culture of radical experimentation and no-holds-barred collaboration.

Today, SpaceX stands as a pioneering force in commercial spaceflight, boasting a string of landmark achievements. The company's mission to make humankind a multi-planetary species no longer feels like science fiction but a serious objective. Its approach - embracing failure as a data goldmine and demolishing silos for maximum collaboration - reveals precisely how to conquer the biggest barriers to innovation: fear of failure and departmental isolation. If rockets can be landed vertically on drone ships, what stops your organization from tackling its entrenched boundaries?

KEY TAKEAWAYS

Embracing Failure as a Learning Opportunity: Musk's approach to failure is a key lesson from the SpaceX story. He turned failures into valuable data and used them to drive improvement. This approach not only led to the success of SpaceX but also serves as a powerful reminder that failure is not the end, but a new beginning full of potential for growth and innovation.

Importance of Collaboration and Breaking Down Silos: The emphasis on cross-functional collaboration and breaking down departmental barriers was crucial for fostering innovation and solving complex engineering challenges.

Visionary Leadership and Perseverance: Musk's visionary leadership and unwavering perseverance in the face of numerous setbacks were not just essential, but they were the driving force behind SpaceX's success. His ability to see beyond the immediate failures and keep the team focused on the ultimate goal is a testament to the power of leadership in overcoming challenges.

INTRODUCTION: CONFRONTING THE BARRIERS TO INNOVATION

Creativity isn't just a nice-to-have for modern organizations; it's the life-blood that keeps you ahead of market shifts, competitor moves, and the shifting demands of customers who crave novelty. However, as crucial as innovation is, many companies still grapple with internal barriers that choke creative thinking and stall big ideas. Two of the most crippling obstacles are:

1. **Fear of Failure** – A pervasive anxiety that stepping outside the norm or green-lighting an unproven concept will end in embarrassment or job-threatening mistakes. This caution-laden climate paralyzes employees, preventing them from going beyond safe, incremental improvements.

2. **Departmental Silos** – Rigid boundaries between teams that breed turf wars and miscommunication, undermining synergy. Instead of exploring cross-functional solutions, departments stay locked in their corners, focused on their own metrics rather than broader organizational goals.

SECTION 1: ADDRESSING FEAR OF FAILURE – CREATING A SAFE ENVIRONMENT FOR RISKS

Fear of failure is a silent killer of innovative thinking. People don't propose big ideas or experiment with new methods because they're afraid of repercussions - maybe a scolding from top brass, a demotion, or even losing their jobs. This dread leads to "play it safe" mindsets: minimal risk, minimal out-of-the-box thinking, minimal breakthroughs.

But if you look at the boldest success stories - from SpaceX's epic rocket landings to Apple's bet on the iPhone - they often started as leaps of faith, steered by a team willing to risk public face-plants for the chance at transformative success. Catalyst leaders see failure as an essential step in the learning process. Each misstep reveals new data, guiding adjustments that can bring an idea to fruition.

Why Fear Stifles Progress

- **Mediocrity Over Mastery:** Employees offer small enhancements rather than radical leaps.

- **Delayed Decisions:** Teams dither, collecting endless data to avoid blame.

- **Cultural Stagnation:** Morale nosedives; creative people bail for more dynamic environments.

BUILDING A SAFE ENVIRONMENT

1. Openness to Imperfection

Leaders need to explicitly say, "We expect some projects to flop, and that's okay," and back up those words with real behavior. If you preach about the virtues of experimentation but penalize a failed pilot program in annual reviews, you're sending mixed messages. Contrarily, if you publicly dissect a failed initiative, highlight its learning points, and pivot to the next iteration, you instill confidence that it's safe to innovate.

2. Fail-Fast Approach

Borrowing from the agile software world, a fail-fast mindset encourages small, quick tests that let you glean insights rapidly. You fail in a controlled environment, not after months of resource burn. This cycles back into your culture: employees see failures as quick detours, not catastrophic sinkholes. Each "mini-failure" is a rung on the ladder of success.

SECTION 2: BREAKING DOWN SILOS – PROMOTING CROSS-FUNCTIONAL COLLABORATION

The second major barrier is organizational silos. One team might be doing cutting-edge R&D, but if they never talk to marketing, the product might never find a winning go-to-market strategy. Meanwhile, finance might hold the purse strings but remain clueless about the engineering breakthroughs that need timely funding. These walls hamper idea flow, breed mistrust, and stifle synergy.

Consequences of Silo Mentality

- **Redundant Efforts:** Multiple teams might inadvertently solve the same problem, wasting time.

- **Communication Lags:** Vital information gets stuck in departmental echo chambers.

- **Incompatible Goals:** Groups chase departmental KPIs over the organization's strategic vision, causing friction and misalignment.

CULTIVATING CROSS-FUNCTIONAL HARMONY

1. Physical or Virtual Spaces

Sometimes, minor design tweaks can encourage collaboration: open-plan work areas, digital collaboration platforms, or even cross-departmental squads. The idea is to create natural intersections where teams mingle and share insights. Suppose your data analytics group rarely interacts with product designers. In that case, create a weekly jam session or a Slack channel to break the ice.

2. Universal KPIs

Instead of awarding bonuses solely for departmental metrics - like marketing hitting lead targets or R&D hitting patent counts - tie part of the incentive to organization-wide performance. This signals that success is mutual, reducing the "us vs. them" dynamic.

3. Project-Based Integration

Spin up cross-functional teams for critical projects, ensuring that folks from different departments are forced to collaborate daily. Over time, these relationships endure beyond the project's life cycle, weaving an organizational fabric that's more unified and ready to pivot as one entity.

ACTION ITEMS

1. Failure Debrief Sessions

- Establish a monthly "Failure Debrief." Invite teams that attempted ambitious projects or pilot launches but didn't meet targets. They present what went wrong, what was learned, and how they'd do it differently next time.

- Keep the tone constructive. Applaud their boldness. Reward them not with "punishment" but with follow-up resources to tweak the idea. By normalizing this ritual, you convert failure from taboo into actionable intel.

2. Cross-Functional Workshops

- Schedule quarterly workshops where teams from different departments gather to share current challenges and upcoming roadmaps. Marketing meets with engineering, HR meets with the product, and finance meets with IT.

- Each workshop ends with a quick brainstorming session: "Where can we help each other out?" "What synergy might exist across our upcoming plans?" Encourage small, cross-team spin-off tasks. Even something as simple as marketing providing feedback on a product prototype can spark a major improvement.

These two action items - Failure Debrief Sessions and Cross-Functional Workshops - reinforce a culture that tolerates risk and embraces it while simultaneously bridging departmental divides.

FINAL THOUGHTS

Barriers to innovation - fear of failure and siloed thinking - are your real opponents, not the competition outside. Tear them down, and you unleash a creative force that outpaces any rival. Embrace risk like SpaceX, transforming crashes into stepping stones. Break silos like your market share depends on it (because it does). Rally your entire organization around a common cause: explore new frontiers without flinching, cross departmental boundaries without friction, and chase audacious goals without apology.

As Oscar Wilde said, "An idea that is not dangerous is unworthy of being called an idea at all." So go ahead - court danger and watch innovation ignite.

Build An INNOVATION Space

4. LAUNCH

Roll out the best ideas on a larger scale, rallying your team and stakeholders behind the concept.

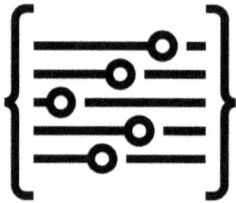

3. TWEAK

Refine, pivot, or scrap what doesn't work. Learn from failures, then adjust the approach.

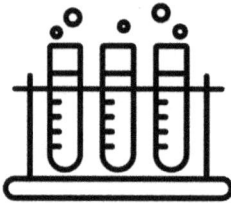

2. TEST

Run small, controlled experiments to see what sticks. Gather data, gather feedback, and stay curious.

1. THINK

Generate bold ideas. Brainstorm without limits; nothing is too "out there" at this stage.

TOOL:
BUILD AN INNOVATION SPACE

Alright, you hungry leaders - innovation doesn't happen by accident. It's a result of giving people the freedom to play and experiment, but sometimes they fail in the process. You want next-level ideas?

You need an environment where your team can roll up their sleeves and get their hands dirty. That's precisely what The INNOVATION Space is about. There is no fluff or red tape - just real, practical steps to kickstart creativity and push your organization forward.

Why It Works With This Chapter

5.1 Building an Innovative Culture

- Encouraging Experimentation: The INNOVATION Space approach allows for trial, error, and reworking ideas.

- Recognizing and Rewarding Creativity: It frames creativity as an ongoing process rather than a one-off event, so team members feel motivated to keep pushing boundaries.

5.2 Leveraging Technology and AI

- Integrating New Tools: By "playing" in the Space, teams test new technology or AI solutions in a low-risk environment.

- Data-Driven Decision Making: The iterative nature of the INNOVATION encourages using actual data to refine and improve ideas.

5.3 Overcoming Barriers to Innovation

- Addressing Fear of Failure: The Space explicitly permits to fail fast and learn, reducing the stigma around mistakes.

- Breaking Down Silos: Collaboration is built into the framework - everyone contributes their unique expertise to shape and strengthen the idea.

By adopting an INNOVATION Space, you'll create a culture where imaginative thinking meets practical execution, all while fostering team unity and excitement for the next big thing.

Let's break it down:

Think – Generate bold ideas. Brainstorm without limits; nothing is too "out there" at this stage.

Test – Run small, controlled experiments to see what sticks. Gather data, gather feedback, and stay curious.

Tweak – Refine, pivot, or scrap what doesn't work. Learn from failures, then adjust the approach.

Launch – Roll out the best ideas on a larger scale, rallying your team and stakeholders behind the concept.

Think of it as an unlimited area of space: a safe place to build, knock down, and rebuild until you have something truly remarkable.

From Think to Test to Tweak to Launch - each step feeds into the next, turning fresh ideas into actionable solutions.

How to Use It

In the Office - Dedicate an "INNOVATION Session" each week where anyone can pitch a quick idea. The team chooses one to test in a mini-experiment, then circles back to share results and refine.

With Your Team - Encourage cross-functional "playdates" where different departments collaborate on an idea. Marketing, engineering, finance - everyone brings a unique viewpoint to the Space.

With Yourself - Keep a "INNOVATION Journal." Whenever you spot a potential improvement or new tech, jot it down. Every month, pick one idea to test, tweak, and either launch or toss. No regrets, just lessons learned.

When you treat innovation like drawing on an infinite whiteboard - testing, tweaking, and sometimes knocking them down to start over - you remove the fear factor and spark real creativity. The INNOVATION Space offers a practical path to turn big dreams into everyday breakthroughs. Jump in, get messy, and watch your team rise to the occasion.

SECTION 03

EMPOWERING TEAMS

6

"DO YOU WANT TO BUILD A HIGH-PERFORMING TEAM THAT THRIVES ON TRUST, COLLABORATION, AND OWNERSHIP?"

EMPOWERING AND ENGAGING YOUR TEAM

Part One:
Developing Team Members

Part Two:
Enhancing Collaboration

Part Three:
Delegating with Purpose

"If you think your job as a leader is to bark orders and watch the numbers roll in, you're delusional. The real currency of leadership is unlocking human potential."

PART ONE:
DEVELOPING TEAM MEMBERS

WHILE CEOS WERE SLASHING BUDGETS, SCHULTZ WAS TRAINING BARISTAS—AND THAT'S WHY HE WON

When Howard Schultz returned to Starbucks as CEO in 2008, the company was on shaky ground. The global economy had taken a nosedive, and Starbucks - once the darling of the coffee world - had lost its edge. Store closures, declining sales, and morale at an all-time low painted a bleak picture. Many leaders in his position would have responded by slashing training budgets and doubling down on cost-cutting measures, hoping to ride out the storm. But Schultz knew better. He understood that the company's soul lay in its people - the baristas who created that "third place" experience for customers. If they lost their passion, Starbucks would be just another commodity coffee shop.

So he took a different approach. Instead of tightening belts to the point of strangulation, he invested in his team. He reopened the coffee training school, brought baristas and store managers together for intensive skill development sessions, and launched new mentorship initiatives. Starbucks didn't just teach employees how to pull the perfect espresso; they taught them the company's values, its mission, and why their role mattered. Experienced managers mentored newcomers, seasoned baristas coached green recruits, and everyone got a refresher on what made Starbucks unique.

As the economy clawed back, Starbucks emerged stronger. Armed with renewed skills and a deeper understanding of their purpose, employees delivered a better customer experience. The relationship between team members and leadership was more authentic and built on trust and mutual respect. Profits followed suit. Starbucks bounced back from near-disaster to become stronger than ever - partly because Schultz understood that developing his team was not a luxury but a necessity. The people behind the counter became brand ambassadors, not just order takers. They were proud to wear the apron, engaged in their work, and dedicated to the company's success.

If you think your job as a leader is to bark orders and watch the numbers roll in, you're delusional. Wake up. The real currency of leadership is unlocking human potential. Your team isn't a bunch of cogs in a machine; they're dynamic, creative, hungry individuals waiting for the right environment to unleash their talent. The question is, will you create that environment or kill their spirit?

KEY TAKEAWAYS

- **Investing in People as a Key to Success:** Schultz's experience at Starbucks demonstrates the importance of investing in employees as a driver of business success.

- **Leadership as Unlocking Human Potential:** The case study correctly emphasizes that effective leadership is about unlocking human potential and creating an environment where employees can thrive.

- **The Importance of Company Culture and Values:** Reconnecting employees with the company's culture and values was a crucial part of the turnaround.

PERSONAL GROWTH OPPORTUNITIES

Developing team members isn't optional - it's the lifeblood of sustainable success. You can't expect growth, innovation, or adaptability if your people stagnate. Let's get one thing straight: Personal growth opportunities and mentorship aren't "nice-to-have" perks. They are strategic necessities. The market evolves, competitors get more innovative, and technology never stops advancing. If your people aren't growing, they're dying professionally. And when your team withers, so does your company.

Personal growth opportunities come in many forms: training sessions, workshops, online courses, conferences, cross-functional projects, and even side gigs within the organization where employees can test new skills. This isn't just about padding resumes or satisfying HR checkboxes - it's about fueling a culture of constant improvement. When you invest in training and development, you send a loud message: "I believe in your potential. I want you to get better, not just for me, but for yourself."

And guess what? That belief is contagious. When employees know you've got their back and are willing to invest in their future, they show up with more energy, loyalty, and creativity. They'll go the extra mile because they feel valued, not just compensated.

But let's not talk about growth opportunities without mentioning mentorship and coaching. Talent doesn't flourish in a vacuum. It needs guidance, feedback, and a model to follow. Mentorship is the secret sauce that transforms raw potential into refined skill. Think about it: even the greatest athletes have coaches, and the top CEOs have mentors. Without that guidance, all that raw talent can go in circles, never realizing its full potential.

A mentor is more than a teacher; they're a guide who helps navigate the complexity of a career path. They share wisdom, but more importantly, they challenge assumptions. They say, "You can do better," and show you how. They hold a mirror up to your performance and help you see what you can't see on your own. Good mentors push you out of your comfort zone and help you grow into a version of yourself you didn't know was possible.

Coaching, on the other hand, is about unlocking performance at a granular level. Coaches aren't there to give you all the answers; they're there to ask the right questions. "Why did you approach the project this way?" "How could you handle that client differently?" Coaching is the tool that transforms good employees into great ones by focusing on mindset, approach, and technique. Where mentorship might be broader and longer-term, coaching can be tactical and immediate, addressing specific performance issues or growth areas.

Leaders who invest in personal growth opportunities and mentorship play the long game. They're not interested in quick wins that come at the expense of their team's development. They understand that building a high-performing team means nurturing each member's evolution. When you do this right, your team becomes a pipeline of leaders who can rise through the ranks, carry the torch, and keep the innovation engine humming.

But don't fool yourself into thinking this is just about them. As you help your team grow, you become a more accomplished leader. Your legacy isn't the projects you personally completed; it's the people you've empowered. The ripple effect is enormous: a well-developed team means less micromanagement, fewer fires to put out, and more strategic thinking from everyone involved.

Now, I know what some of you are thinking: "I don't have time for this." That's a cop-out. If you don't have time to develop your people, you don't have time to be a leader. This is not a task you can outsource or put on the back burner. It's integral to your role. And here's the kicker: developing your team members saves you time in the long run. The more competent and autonomous they become, the less you have to spoon-feed them or double-check their work. You're not just saving time; you're multiplying your impact.

Another excuse I hear: "What if I invest in their development and they leave?" Newsflash: people who feel stagnated are more likely to leave anyway. At least if you invest in them, you'll get top-tier performance while they're with you. And if they go, you'll have a reputation as a leader who builds talent, which attracts even more capable people to replace them. It's a virtuous cycle, not a zero-sum game.

Let's get concrete. Offering personal growth opportunities could mean paying for relevant courses, bringing in trainers for hands-on workshops, or partnering with educational platforms that allow employees to develop new skill sets. It means creating an environment where continuous learning is baked into the company culture. You're not just training employees; you're making learning part of their job description.

MENTORSHIP AND COACHING

Formalize mentorship and coaching. Don't rely on ad-hoc, backchannel relationships. Create mentorship pairings, set goals, and measure progress. Encourage mentors to be transparent about their failures and lessons learned. Don't let mentorship become a stale checkbox activity. Make it vibrant, challenging, and growth-oriented.

For coaching, equip managers with the skills and frameworks they need for meaningful conversations. Provide them with tools, question guides, and role-playing scenarios to help them become effective coaches.

The bottom line is that developing team members is a strategic imperative, not a fluffy add-on. When done right, it strengthens your team's backbone, sparks innovation, and elevates the entire organization's trajectory.

ACTION ITEM 1: LAUNCH A "PERSONAL GROWTH BUDGET" PROGRAM

Set aside a dedicated budget for each team member to spend annually on their professional growth. This could cover online courses, conference tickets, or specialized training. Make it simple and transparent - no convoluted approval processes that kill motivation. The message should be loud and clear: "We trust you to invest in yourself." When employees have control over their learning, they become proactive about seeking new skills and experiences. They don't wait to be told what to learn; they drive their own growth.

ACTION ITEM 2: ESTABLISH A FORMAL MENTORSHIP NETWORK

Don't leave mentorship to chance. Identify experienced team members or leaders who can serve as mentors and pair them with mentees eager to learn. Set clear expectations: How often will they meet? What goals will they set? Track progress and celebrate milestones. By making mentorship an institutionalized practice, you create a culture where knowledge transfer and personal development are standard operating procedures, not sporadic nice-to-haves.

FINAL THOUGHTS

Picture a team that isn't just meeting targets but surpassing them, composed of people who are constantly evolving, hungry for new challenges, and driven by more than just a paycheck. Imagine a workplace where mentorship isn't a formality but a flame that lights the path forward. That's the kind of energy that fuels market disruption, brand loyalty, and unprecedented growth.

As you double down on personal growth and mentorship, you're investing in a future where your team members don't just follow your lead - they become leaders in their own right. This isn't just how you build a high-performance culture; this is how you build a legacy that outlives your tenure. And as Warren Buffett said, "Someone's sitting in the shade today because someone planted a tree a long time ago." Be that someone. Plant the seeds of growth, watch your team flourish, and bask in the shade of their collective brilliance.

"When trust and professional diversity converge, human beings can do the unimaginable."

PART TWO:
ENHANCING COLLABORATION

NO EGO, ALL HUSTLE:
NASA'S EPIC COLLAB THAT LANDED A MAN ON THE MOON

When NASA set its sights on landing a man on the moon in the 1960s, the organization faced a staggering array of obstacles. It wasn't just the physics and engineering challenges - those alone were daunting. It was also the mess of human complexity beneath the polished veneer of America's premier space agency. Thousands of engineers, scientists, military test pilots, and administrators came from different backgrounds and different regions of the country and often held stubbornly different viewpoints about how to solve the next big problem. Technical specialists guarded their domains fiercely, communication didn't flow as freely as it should, and trust sometimes faltered. After all, who would take personal responsibility for a catastrophic failure that could cost American lives and prestige on the global stage?

NASA's leadership knew the only way forward was to unite these fragmented teams into a cohesive force. They forced cross-departmental collaboration, demanding that scientists talk directly to engineers, that test pilots share real-world feedback with designers, and that contractors break out of their silos and listen to one another. They enforced processes to ensure open communication, scheduled frequent joint briefings and encouraged personal accountability. If a component wasn't functioning properly, they'd bring the relevant teams into the same room - often literally locking them in until they figured out a solution. The agency recruited talent from a wide range of backgrounds, including women and minorities, who, despite the era's prejudices, contributed innovative ideas and offered unique perspectives that helped solve intricate technical puzzles.

The payoff wasn't just the iconic moment of Neil Armstrong stepping onto lunar soil; it was the creation of a collaborative machine so finely tuned that it pioneered the frontier of human space exploration. By the time Apollo 11 blasted off, NASA had transformed into a deeply interconnected network of experts who trusted each other's abilities and respected each other's differences. Communication channels were wide open, responsibilities were clear, and mutual respect was ingrained. The result: a historic achievement that captured the world's imagination and proved that when trust and diversity converge, human beings can do the unimaginable.

KEY TAKEAWAYS

Importance of Collaboration in Complex Projects: The Apollo program demonstrates the critical role of collaboration and communication in achieving complex goals.

Overcoming Organizational Barriers: NASA's efforts to break down silos and promote cross-functional collaboration were essential to their success.

The Value of Diverse Perspectives: The contributions of women and minorities, despite their limited numbers, highlight the value of diverse perspectives in problem-solving and innovation.

INTRODUCTION: ENHANCING COLLABORATION

You can talk about collaboration all day long, but if you're not building trust and leveraging diversity, you're just making noise. Let's get something straight: collaboration isn't a warm, fuzzy concept for corporate retreats. It's a hard strategic necessity. If your team isn't working together seamlessly - if they're not communicating openly, if they don't trust each other, if they all think the same way and bring the same narrow set of experiences to the table - you're dead in the water. Your competition will eat you for lunch, and you'll be left wondering what the hell went wrong.

Here's the truth: no single genius is going to save your company. The era of the lone wolf hero is over. Real breakthroughs - those that define markets, reshape industries, and kick the competition to the curb - happen when a diverse group of talented people come together, share their insights, challenge each other's assumptions, and support one another through the turmoil of trial and error. That only happens in a culture where trust is not negotiable and diversity is not a checkbox but a core value.

BUILDING TRUST: FOSTERING OPEN COMMUNICATION AND RELIABILITY

Trust is the lubricant that keeps the machinery of collaboration running smoothly. Without trust, your team operates like a car running on an empty tank - stalled, sputtering, and going nowhere. Trust isn't built by slogans on the wall or by empty speeches from the corner office. It's earned through consistent action. It's when your words and deeds line up every single day. It's when team members know that if they raise a concern, they won't be punished. It's when someone makes a mistake, and instead of a witch hunt, there's a conversation about how to learn and improve.

You want trust? Start by showing your team you've got their back. Keep them informed. Don't hoard information like some twisted form of currency. If your people don't know what's going on, they'll fill in the blanks with fear and suspicion. Commit to transparency: share the good, the bad, and the ugly. When people know the truth, even if it's tough, they respect you more. Reliability is also key. If you promise something, deliver. And if you can't deliver, explain why. Reliability creates predictability, and predictability fosters trust.

But trust isn't just leader-to-employee. It's peer-to-peer. Encourage your team members to become reliable partners to one another. If your marketing lead promises a report to product development by Tuesday, it better land in their inbox by Tuesday. If it doesn't, own it, apologize, and make it right. Over time, this culture of personal accountability and follow-through turns your team into a unit that not only respects each other's commitments but also trusts that everyone is pulling their weight.

DIVERSITY AND INCLUSION:
LEVERAGING DIVERSE PERSPECTIVES FOR INNOVATION

Now let's talk about diversity and inclusion. And let's get real: This isn't about meeting some corporate quota or putting on a PR show. It's about strengthening your team's creative arsenal. Different backgrounds, experiences, cultures, genders, ages, and skills mean different ways of seeing problems. Homogenous teams are prone to groupthink and blind spots. They overlook opportunities and mistakes because everyone's perspective is the same.

You want innovation? You need friction - the positive kind. You need people who come at problems from angles you never considered. When a team includes different voices, there's a higher chance someone will point out the flaw in the plan, propose a radical alternative, or build on someone else's idea to create something extraordinary. Diversity is your secret weapon in a marketplace that rewards agility, creativity, and boldness.

But diversity is meaningless without inclusion. If you bring different people in but don't give them a seat at the table or genuinely value their input, you're just window-dressing. Inclusion means everyone feels safe to speak up. Everyone knows their perspective matters. It means you're not just asking for opinions - you're listening to them and acting on them.

Let's not romanticize this. Embracing diversity and fostering inclusion is hard work. It means confronting our own biases and preferences for comfort. It's easier to be around people who think like we do, who won't challenge us. But comfort is the enemy of greatness. If you want to break boundaries, you need to break out of your safe bubble and invite people in who'll test your assumptions.

Bringing trust and diversity together creates a cultural powerhouse. When your team trusts each other, they're not afraid to disagree. When they're diverse, disagreement becomes productive tension, not destructive conflict. Ideas are judged on merit, not on who proposed them. The best ideas rise to the top, the weak ones fall away, and the team grows stronger, smarter, and more resilient.

Don't expect this to happen overnight. Building trust takes time, demonstrating reliability takes consistent effort, and nurturing diversity and inclusion takes deliberate action. But the payoff is massive. You get a team that's not just functional but highly adaptive, creative, and downright unstoppable. You'll see it in their energy, their willingness to tackle tough challenges, and their ability to thrive under pressure.

ACTION ITEM 1: CREATE "TRUST FORUMS"

Enough with the top-down memos. If you want to build trust, let your people talk to each other openly. Schedule regular "Trust Forums" - no formal agenda, PowerPoints, or scripted speeches. Give your team space to discuss issues, fears, successes, and opportunities. Maybe it's a monthly lunch where everyone can share what's on their mind. The only rule? Listen. Don't argue, don't interrupt - just listen. Over time, these forums become a place where honesty and transparency are the norm, not the exception.

ACTION ITEM 2: HOST A "DIVERSITY IDEA JAM"

If you want to leverage diversity for real innovation, create a structured event that brings various team members together to brainstorm solutions to a current business challenge. Mix departments, seniorities, backgrounds, and personalities. The more eclectic, the better. Give them a problem - maybe improving a product feature, enhancing customer experience, or streamlining a process - and let them go wild. Recognize and reward the best ideas but also the most surprising insights. This signals that you value fresh perspectives and that different voices shape your company's future.

FINAL THOUGHTS

Picture a team that doesn't flinch at tough conversations, embraces differences without hesitation, and treats each setback as a lesson learned together. Imagine a work environment where everyone's got each other's back, where every voice adds a new dimension of insight, and where the combined creativity of your team forms a fortress no competitor can breach.

This isn't some utopian fantasy - it's your next move. Trust doesn't cost a dime, but it pays out like a jackpot. Diversity won't always make life comfortable, but it will make your organization formidable.

As Henry Ford said, "Coming together is a beginning; keeping together is progress; working together is success." Are you ready to cross the finish line with a team that's locked in, fired up, and ready to rewrite the rules of your industry? It's time to make collaboration your secret weapon. Embrace it, invest in it, and watch your team roar.

"If you want to ignite real innovation, inspire ownership, and free yourself from endless micromanaging, you must delegate purposefully."

PART THREE: DELEGATING WITH PURPOSE

FROM DINOSAUR TO DOMINATOR: HOW JACK WELCH UNLEASHED GE'S INNER HUSTLER

When Jack Welch took over as CEO of General Electric in 1981, the company was a massive conglomerate with layers upon layers of bureaucracy. People waited for orders from on high, no one wanted to take risks, and decisions trickled painfully down a long chain of command. This sluggishness starkly contrasted with an evolving marketplace that demanded speed and agility. Welch saw that if GE continued to operate like a lumbering dinosaur, it would be devoured by nimbler competitors. He knew the clock was ticking. The company needed to break free from its old habits and give power back to the people working on the ground.

Instead of micromanaging from the top, Welch began stripping away layers of hierarchy. He encouraged managers to push decision-making authority down to the front lines. He demanded that department heads stop treating their teams like cogs and start treating them like empowered professionals. He made it crystal clear: no more waiting for permission on every little thing. If you have the knowledge and the skill, you have the mandate to act. Alongside this new autonomy, Welch implemented rigorous accountability measures - if you took on a decision, you owned the outcome. No scapegoats, no excuses.

The effect was electric. Freed from bureaucratic chains, employees started seizing opportunities and experimenting with new approaches. They stopped passing the buck and began making decisions that drove actual results. Over time, GE transformed into a leaner, more responsive powerhouse that consistently outperformed its competition for decades. Welch's approach to delegation - empowering decision-making and holding people accountable - became a benchmark for effective leadership, proving that when you trust your team and give them freedom and responsibility, they deliver beyond expectations.

KEY TAKEAWAYS

Empowerment and Accountability as Key Drivers: Welch's focus on empowering employees while simultaneously holding them accountable was a key driver of GE's improved performance.

Breaking Down Bureaucracy: His efforts to reduce bureaucracy and streamline decision-making were crucial for increasing the company's agility.

"Rank and Yank" (or "Vitality Curve"): While the provided case study focuses on the positive aspects of Welch's leadership, it's important to acknowledge the controversial "rank and yank" performance management system he implemented. This system, also known as the "vitality curve" or "forced ranking," involved annually ranking employees and dismissing the bottom 10%, which generated both praise and criticism. While it aimed to drive performance and eliminate underperformers, it also created a highly competitive and sometimes cutthroat work environment. This is often part of the discussion of Welch's legacy and is a notable omission from the provided story.

Focus on Shareholder Value: Welch's focus was strongly on increasing shareholder value, and many of his decisions were driven by this objective.

INTRODUCTION: DELEGATING WITH PURPOSE

Let's face it: Most leaders suck at delegation. Yeah, I said it. They talk a big game about "empowering the team" but still cling to every decision like a toddler clutching a security blanket. Stop. You're choking the life out of your team's potential. If you want to ignite real innovation, inspire ownership, and free yourself from endless micromanaging, you must delegate purposefully.

Delegation isn't just dumping work off your plate onto someone else's desk. It's a strategic decision to trust your people with autonomy and provide them with the structure they need to succeed. When you delegate effectively, you're not just transferring tasks - you're transferring authority, accountability, and, most importantly, the belief that your team can make the right calls.

EMPOWERING DECISION-MAKING: ALLOWING AUTONOMY TO ENCOURAGE OWNERSHIP

First, let's tackle autonomy. Autonomy means giving people the freedom to choose their own path to the goal. It's about setting a target and letting them figure out how to hit it. This is the exact opposite of micromanagement. Micromanagement is where you dictate every step, suffocating creativity and discouraging independent thought. Autonomy signals trust. It says, "I believe you have the skills, judgment, and initiative to handle this."

Why does this matter? Because people who feel trusted step up. They become more resourceful when they know you're not breathing down their necks. They think critically, own their work, and go the extra mile to produce results. Instead of waiting passively for instructions, they become active problem-solvers. This shift in mindset from "just doing what I'm told" to "I'm making decisions that matter" is rocket fuel for performance.

Of course, empowering decision-making isn't about letting anarchy reign. You need boundaries. Autonomy works when paired with clarity. Ensure your team knows the objectives, the constraints (like budget, deadlines, or compliance issues), and what success looks like. Give them the context they need to make smart decisions. Do this, and you'll watch them amaze you with their ingenuity.

ACCOUNTABILITY STRUCTURES: SETTING CLEAR EXPECTATIONS AND FOLLOW-UPS

Now, let's talk about accountability. Autonomy without accountability is a recipe for chaos. If no one's on the hook for the results, tasks drift, deadlines slip, and standards erode. Accountability provides the backbone that supports autonomy. It tells people: "You have the power to make decisions, but you also bear the responsibility for what happens next."

Accountability isn't about threats or blame games. It's about fairness and ownership. When everyone knows who's responsible for what - and how they'll be evaluated - they can focus on delivering the best possible outcome. They're not looking for someone else to take the fall or waiting for more instructions. They're engaged, committed, and solution-oriented.

To implement accountability structures, be explicit about your expectations. Assign responsibilities clearly - no vague "someone should handle this" nonsense. Put names next to tasks and deadlines. Check in periodically, not to micromanage, but to support and provide feedback. Set measurable goals and track progress. When something goes wrong, address it directly: What happened? What did we learn? How can we prevent this next time? This approach turns mistakes into growth opportunities rather than sources of fear.

When autonomy and accountability dance together, you get a high-performance culture. Instead of dragging your team along, you become a conductor, guiding skilled musicians who know their parts and play them brilliantly. Instead of shouldering every decision, you're empowering a network of capable leaders who handle challenges as they arise. Your role evolves from puppeteer to coach, mentor, and strategist.

Imagine a team where people take pride in their decisions, where they don't hide behind their bosses but step forward to say, "I've got this." A team where leaders have the mental space to think strategically because they're not bogged down in every detail. A team where risk-taking is balanced by accountability, and creativity thrives within the guardrails of clear expectations. That's what purposeful delegation creates.

But let's get real: delegating with purpose isn't always comfortable. It requires you to let go of control. It demands that you trust people, even when you're not 100% sure they'll handle it perfectly. Guess what? Sometimes they won't. They'll drop the ball or make bad calls. That's okay. That's how they learn. Without the freedom to fail, no one grows. Without accountability, no one learns from their mistakes.

Your job as a leader is to make peace with that. Instead of seeing delegation as a gamble, see it as an investment. Every time you delegate, you invest in your team's development. You're building a bench of future leaders who can scale the business, innovate, and adapt. Over time, the return on this investment is huge. You get a more capable, more engaged workforce, and you free yourself to focus on what really matters - steering the ship, not rowing it alone.

So why do so many leaders resist delegating with purpose? Fear. Fear that someone else won't do it as well as they can. Fear that it'll take longer to explain than just doing it themselves. Fear that if the team member fails, it'll reflect poorly on them. But these fears are short-sighted. Ultimately, if you refuse to delegate, you'll become the bottleneck. Your team will stagnate, you'll burn out, and your company will miss growth opportunities.

Get over yourself. Your team is capable if you've hired right and cultivated a strong culture. Give them the keys, show them the road, and let them drive. Monitor the journey, but don't backseat-drive. Correct course when needed, and always circle back for lessons learned. This is how you build a team that can handle whatever the market throws at them - because they have the autonomy to respond and the accountability to deliver.

ACTION ITEM 1: DELEGATE A HIGH-PROFILE PROJECT TO A RISING STAR

Pick a project that you'd normally handle yourself and assign it to a promising team member. Set clear goals, boundaries, and timelines, but let them decide the approach. Check in only at scheduled intervals - no hovering. When the project concludes, hold a debrief. Discuss what went well, what didn't, and what they learned. Over time, repeat this with other team members. You'll create a culture where people crave responsibility because it's genuinely empowering, not just extra workload.

ACTION ITEM 2: CREATE A "DECISION JOURNAL"

Encourage each team member to maintain a personal Decision Journal. Whenever they make a significant decision - especially one delegated to them - they jot down the context, their reasoning, and their expected outcome. Later, when results are in, they review their entries. This simple practice builds accountability by making decision-making processes transparent and reflective. People begin to see patterns in their thinking, understand where they excel, and pinpoint where they need to improve.

FINAL THOUGHTS

Picture a team that thrives under pressure because everyone understands their role and revels in the freedom to execute it their way. Imagine no more bottlenecks, no more frantic firefighting, no more leaders exhausted by trivial decisions. Instead, you have a lean, mean, decision-making machine, fueled by trust and anchored in accountability.

That's what happens when you delegate with purpose. It's not just about offloading tasks; it's about unleashing potential. As Andrew Carnegie said, "No man will make a great leader who wants to do it all himself or get all the credit for doing it." So hand over the reins, embrace the journey, and watch your team rise to the challenge. That's leadership. That's how you multiply your impact and turn your vision into reality.

The Empowerment Flow

Provide Growth Tools

Offer training, personal development programs, and resources so team members can sharpen their skill sets.

Spark Membership

Pair seasoned pros with rising talents. This ensures knowledge transfer and continuous coaching are front and center.

Foster Collaboration

Encourage cross-functional projects, trust-building activities, and open communication channels to break down silos.

Delegate with Purpose

Assign responsibilities that challenge your team while aligning with their strengths, giving them real autonomy to innovate.

Maintain Accountability

Set clear goals and follow-up processes. Everyone knows what's expected and how to measure success, keeping momentum high.

TOOL: THE EMPOWERMENT FLOW

Look, if you think you can scale your business and build an all-star team by hogging the spotlight, you're missing the point. Real success comes when you empower your people to grow, collaborate, and take on real responsibility. The Empowerment Flow is all about cutting through the noise and giving your team the freedom (and framework) to crush it at every level. Ready to light a fire under your leadership approach? Let's go!

Why It Works With This Chapter

Developing Team Members

- Personal Growth Opportunities: The first stage of The Empowerment Flow pushes leaders to invest in each individual's development, turning potential into performance.

- Mentorship and Coaching: By building mentorship into the flow, you set up a natural, ongoing system for passing along skills and insights - no stale "once-a-year" training.

Enhancing Collaboration

- Building Trust: Collaboration doesn't thrive in a vacuum. The Empowerment Flow guides you in creating transparency and open communication so that trust can grow.

- Diversity and Inclusion: You need varied perspectives to spark innovation. Incorporating different voices in The Empowerment Flow ensures you're leveraging every talent on the team.

Delegating with Purpose

- Empowering Decision-Making: Delegation isn't just about handing off tasks; it's about giving your people the latitude to make real choices - something The Empowerment Flow bakes right in.

- Accountability Structures: When expectations are clear, ownership skyrockets. The final step of the Flow locks in accountability and keeps everyone on track.

How It Works:

Think of The Empowerment Flow as a series of five key actions that create a cycle of growth, engagement, and responsibility:

1. **Provide Growth Tools** - Offer training, personal development programs, and resources so team members can sharpen their skill sets.

2. **Spark Mentorship** - Pair seasoned pros with rising talents. This ensures knowledge transfer and continuous coaching are front and center.

3. **Foster Collaboration** - Encourage cross-functional projects, trust-building activities, and open communication channels to break down silos.

4. **Delegate with Purpose** - Assign responsibilities that challenge your team while aligning with their strengths, giving them real autonomy to innovate.

5. **Maintain Accountability** - Set clear goals and follow-up processes. Everyone knows what's expected and how to measure success, keeping momentum high.

Each step feeds into the next, forming a continuous loop of empowerment and engagement.

How to Use It

In the Office

- Kick off a monthly meeting by reviewing what growth tools or training opportunities are available. Then, identify who will mentor whom for the next quarter.

- Encourage collaboration by mixing departments for projects - marketing meets operations, finance meets R&D - so fresh ideas spark.

With Your Team

- Assign tasks that push team members out of their comfort zone but align with their career goals. This builds confidence and competence at the same time.

- Use weekly check-ins to confirm everyone is meeting their goals and upholding accountability. If something's off, adjust quickly.

With Yourself

- Reflect on your own growth. Sign up for that leadership course or conference you've been eyeing. Show your team that learning never stops.

- Identify areas where you can delegate more effectively. If you're still micromanaging, it's time to free yourself - and empower someone else.

Empowerment isn't just a buzzword - it's the fuel that drives team engagement and skyrockets performance. The Empowerment Flow offers a straightforward path to develop your people, foster collaboration, and delegate like a pro. Put this framework into action, and you'll be amazed at how quickly your team levels up. This is how you build a culture of trust, ownership, and unstoppable momentum.

"Don't tiptoe around your vision or let your calendar bury your ambitions. Step up, streamline, and connect like your legacy depends on it - because it does."

HALF-TIME BONUS:
BEING MORE ASSERTIVE, MORE FOCUSED,
AND BECOMING A NETWORKING EXPERT

This chapter isn't about turning every leader into a chatty extrovert - far from it. It's about equipping you with assertiveness tools and networking strategies that work on your own terms. You don't have to be the life of the party or the one who 'works the room.' That's okay. You can still build powerful connections, guide your team with clarity, and stand tall in your leadership.

This chapter shows you how to tap into your strengths - empathy, deep observation, thoughtfulness - while leveling up skills like focused communication and targeted networking. No forced small talk, no personality overhaul. Just solid tactics to help you own your influence, connect authentically, and drive your organization forward, one genuine relationship at a time.

TOM CRUISE: TOTAL POSITIVITY, DARING VISION, AND GAME-CHANGING MOVES

Tom Cruise was once just a scrappy kid with a dream of making it big in Hollywood. Early on, he faced the skepticism that every rising actor confronts: Would audiences take him seriously? Could he step beyond the teen heartthrob niche? But he had an unrelenting fire - he didn't wait for anyone's validation. He seized roles that demanded more than a handsome face; he sought out mentors, studied the craft, and built relationships behind the scenes. Agents told him, "Play it safe. Don't rock the boat." He refused, determined to carve a unique path.

He turned the entertainment model upside down by pouring total positivity into every interaction. Directors, co-stars, crew - Cruise showered them with unwavering attention, remembering small details about their lives, exuding genuine warmth. It wasn't a gimmick. People recognized his authenticity and gravitated to him. Instead of waiting for studios to offer him "safe" blockbuster deals, he collaborated with top producers to develop high-stakes projects - sometimes even co-financing them. Then he doubled down, launching world tours to promote each film like it was a personal mission, forging direct bonds with fans worldwide.

Over time, Cruise's approach shifted Hollywood norms. He pioneered the concept of the globally coordinated movie release tour, turning each premiere into an event that captured global media attention. Audiences connected with him not just as an actor but as a brand that delivered top-tier action and heartfelt performances. He took massive risks, including performing his own stunts. The result? Record-breaking box-office returns, unwavering fan loyalty, and a filmography that redefined how stars interact with their audience. Cruise became the ultimate example of fearless, people-centric leadership.

WHY ASSERTIVENESS, FOCUS, AND NETWORKING EXPERTISE MATTER

In the story of Tom Cruise - both on-screen and behind the scenes - we see a relentless drive that merges unwavering assertiveness, pinpoint focus, and a level of networking mastery rarely matched in Hollywood. Think about it: this is a guy who meets fans with an energy that feels personal, not staged. He invests wholeheartedly in relationships - be they with directors or stunt coordinators - and he's not shy about pushing boundaries for the sake of delivering next-level experiences.

Now, let's translate that to your world. We might not all-star in billion-dollar action franchises, but the principles that catapulted Cruise to the A-list can supercharge your leadership game. Being more assertive means not waiting for permission to innovate or lead. Being more focused means channeling your energy where it counts and resisting distraction. And being a networking expert? That's your secret weapon to unite teams, partners, and stakeholders around your vision.

SECTION 1: BEING MORE ASSERTIVE - NO APOLOGIES, NO PERMISSION

Assertiveness is often misunderstood. People equate it with aggression, but they're worlds apart. Aggression bulldozes people's feelings and ideas. Assertiveness, on the other hand, states your vision or boundary firmly yet respectfully. It's about stepping up and saying, "Here's what I see, here's what I propose, and I'm inviting you to join me." This is not about being aggressive; it's about being confident and in control.

WHAT ASSERTIVENESS LOOKS LIKE IN LEADERSHIP

1. **Clear Vision, Clearly Stated** - You don't sugarcoat your objectives. If you want your team to pivot in six months, you say so outright, with confidence. You invite pushback but make it clear you're not dabbling in half-measures. For instance, if you're leading a project and you believe a certain approach is the best, you assertively communicate this to your team, inviting their feedback but making it clear that you're not open to compromising on the quality of the work.

2. **Decisive Action** - Indecision drains momentum. An assertive leader pounces on opportunities, even if the path isn't 100% guaranteed. Picture Tom Cruise performing his own stunts - he's weighed the risks and consulted experts but ultimately steps forward without wavering.

3. **Respectful Boundary-Setting** - Assertiveness means you don't yield to scope creep or never-ending demands that drain resources. You learn to say "No" when something doesn't align with your core mission or your capacity. That "No" preserves energy for the big yes's that truly matter. It's about taking charge of your time and resources, and not letting them be dictated by others.

AVOIDING THE AGGRESSION TRAP

Being assertive doesn't mean dominating every conversation. You still need to listen. If your team sees you bulldozing, they'll eventually clam up or push back with resentment. The sweet spot is projecting authority while respecting input. You harness the best ideas by inviting them, not by stifling them.

SECTION 2: BEING MORE FOCUSED –
BLOCKING OUT NOISE, DOUBLING DOWN ON ESSENTIALS

Focus, in the context of leadership, is your ability to zero in on what truly matters and block out the rest. Tom Cruise invests in massive projects but ensures each one gets the deep attention it deserves. Whether it's training for a stunt or personally connecting with fans, he doesn't half-commit. So, how do you replicate that focus in your own leadership context? It's about identifying the key priorities in your role, such as strategic planning or team development, and dedicating your time and energy to these areas while delegating or minimizing tasks that are less important or can be handled by others.

Why Focus?

1. **Complexity Overload** - We live in an age where Slack notifications, endless emails, and back-to-back meetings can nibble away at your mind space. Without a solid system to protect your focus, you become reactive - a slave to urgent tasks that might not be truly important.

2. **Impact Amplification** - Focus is a force multiplier. Knock out one big objective - like launching a new product or forging a strategic alliance - and watch how it cascades into breakthroughs. Scatter your attention across 50 small tasks, and your net impact fizzles.

3. **Consistency Builds Trust** - People trust a leader who stays consistent and on message. If you're pivoting every other week, your team's faith in your direction wavers. By focusing on a few core priorities, you project reliability and seriousness.

How to Stay Laser-Focused

- **Prioritize Ruthlessly**: Identify your top 1-3 tasks that align with your biggest strategic goals each morning. Everything else is secondary.

- **Time Blocking**: Schedule uninterrupted blocks for crucial work - no email, phone calls, or "quick question" pop-ins. This is your dedicated creation zone.

- **Delegate and Empower**: The more you do personally, the less you can remain focused on overarching leadership. Hand off tasks that others can handle competently, freeing you to do what only you can do.

SECTION 3: BECOMING A NETWORKING EXPERT – BUILDING THE TIES THAT BIND

You can't lead in a vacuum. Great leaders like Tom Cruise forging relationships with directors, co-stars, and fans know that forging strong professional and personal connections is non-negotiable. In business, the right network can open doors to partnerships, new markets, or top-tier talent. And it's not about superficial schmoozing - it's about genuine, reciprocal relationships.

Why Networking Rocks

4. **Collaboration** - A robust network means you can assemble "dream teams" quickly. If your next project requires specialized skills, you know exactly who to call or who can introduce you to a prime candidate.

5. **Idea Flow** - In a network of trusted peers, knowledge flows freely. People share best practices, cautionary tales, and cutting-edge insights. That intel can be a competitive edge if you integrate it fast.

6. **Brand Amplification** - Word of mouth is still powerful. If you consistently show up as a helpful, authentic presence, your name travels further than any LinkedIn ad campaign.

REAL NETWORKING VS. FAKE NETWORKING

Shaking hands and exchanging business cards at a conference is not enough. That's transactional. Real networking means delivering value. You remember small details about someone's personal life or project needs and follow up with relevant solutions or intros. It's a long game fueled by sincerity, curiosity, and a willingness to help before you're helped.

ACTION ITEMS

1. **Assertive Goal-Setting Sessions**

•   Schedule a monthly "Assertive Goal-Setting" meeting with your team or key leaders. For each top priority, clarify the "why," define success metrics, and assign ownership. Don't wait for consensus to be perfect - drive the conversation toward a decisive plan.

- Encourage each participant to articulate at least one bold action they'll take before the next session. This trains everyone to be more assertive about commitments.

2. **Networking Sprint**

- Commit to a short "Networking Sprint" every quarter. Identify 3-5 people - industry peers, potential mentors, or even lateral connections - who might offer fresh perspectives or collaboration opportunities.

- Over a two-week period, schedule coffee chats or Zoom calls with these individuals. Come prepared with ways to help them (resources, intros, or actionable insights). Then, follow up with a concise summary of your conversation and a sincere "thank you."

- By the end, measure your success not by how many leads you got but by how many authentic connections you genuinely advanced.

FINAL THOUGHTS

Assertiveness, focus, and an unshakable network are the trifecta that can catapult you from a decent leader to a game-changer. Don't tiptoe around your vision or let your calendar bury your ambitions. Step up, streamline, and connect like your legacy depends on it - because it does. People gravitate toward those who project clarity and confidence, cut through the noise, and bring genuine value to every relationship.

Bruce Lee once said, "I'm not in this world to live up to your expectations, and you're not in this world to live up to mine." Channel that vibe: lead fiercely, stay sharp, and build connections to amplify your mission beyond your wildest dreams.

The Assertiveness Barometer

Jerk
Obnoxious & Uncaring

Everyone is afraid if they speak up, they will be branded a 'Jerk'. Rarely do we act like a jerk, but we all work with one.

Assertive
Hey, this needs fixing

Sometimes you have to push yourself into this level to get what you want. But you're not being a 'Jerk'.

Professional
Direct & Pleasant

This is where normal people hang out. You're amenable to most decisions, but are critical to the wacky ones.

Laid Back
Give your team some space

Sometimes you should relax and watch the fireworks happen. Jump in when it's safe. But don't be a pushover.

Pushover
Easy To Manipulate & Careless

This is where we think we are - and sometimes we're right. I want you to stay in the professional, assertive, and laid back levels only.

TOOL:
THE ASSERTIVENESS BAROMETER

COPY FOR HALFTIME CHAPTER MASTERING THE ASSERTIVENESS BAROMETER STAYING PRO, GOING ASSERTIVE, NEVER A JERK

Let's get real: People will test you. An employee pushes back on your authority, a client drags out their payment or a peer tries to burn you in front of your boss. You've got two choices - roll over and let them walk all over you or step up and show them you mean business. That's where Catalyst Leadership kicks in: you've got to champion your ideas and your team without turning into a raging jerk or a powerless pushover.

Too many people fear being labeled "the jerk," so they slip into "pushover" mode. Meanwhile, others stay so wary of being a pushover that they default to an overbearing approach. Neither extreme serves your cause. Look, being a doormat is not leadership and being a tyrant sure as hell won't win hearts. But there's a broad space in between, and you can use it to assert your ideas, keep your respect, and maintain healthy relationships.

Here's the deal: **Professional** sits in the middle, right where we want to be most of the time - clear, direct, respectful, fair. That's your day-to-day sweet spot. But stuff happens. Maybe your associate oversteps or a client tries to dodge an invoice yet again. Go ahead and lean into **Assertive**. That's not being a **Jerk**. It's stepping up and stating, "Hey, this needs fixing. Here's what's going to happen." It's short and sharp, and it draws a boundary. People respect that. They may grumble, but they know where you stand, and they see that you're defending your cause.

On the other side, you've got **Laid Back** - perfect for those moments when you can give your team space to experiment or let a situation resolve on its own. But if you drift too far, you risk sliding into total **"Pushover"** territory. Don't be that person who never takes a stance or shrugs at real issues. On the flip side, going all-out "**Jerk**" means barking orders and stomping on feelings - and guess what? Jerks don't give a second thought to how they sound, so if you're worried, you're not one.

You probably work with a **Jerk**. And you probably are surrounded by **Pushovers**. You CANNOT play in either domain.

Ultimately, Catalyst Leaders keep their center in "**Professional**," occasionally pivoting to "**Assertive**" or "**Laid Back**" as the situation demands. This is how you maintain respect without muzzle-loading your people with fear, and how you protect your boundaries without stifling collaboration. You're here to make moves, not tiptoe around conflict. Embrace your role with a balanced approach. Don't hide behind politeness or aggression - pick the right spot on the leadership range and own your decisions. That's how you get your ideas heard, drive your team forward, and stay relentlessly effective.

NAVIGATING TECHNOLOGICAL & CULTURAL SHIFTS

7

"ARE YOU READY TO LEAD YOUR ORGANIZATION THROUGH THE AI REVOLUTION WHILE STAYING TRUE TO YOUR VALUES?"

NAVIGATING TECHNOLOGICAL TRANSFORMATIONS

Part One:
Understanding AI's Impact

Part Two:
Preparing Your Team for Change

Part Three:
Ethical Considerations

"If you're still sitting on the sidelines when it comes to AI, you're signing your own death warrant in business terms."

PART ONE:
UNDERSTANDING AI'S IMPACT

GAS GUZZLERS TO AI AVENGERS:
HOW TESLA OBLITERATED THE OLD-SCHOOL CAR GAME

When Tesla entered the automotive scene, it didn't just introduce electric vehicles - it aimed to redefine the entire concept of driving. The established players, from Detroit to Germany, were comfortable iterating on old blueprints: internal combustion engines, routine maintenance schedules, and cars that got you from point A to point B without much intelligence. For decades, the industry had followed a predictable pattern, confident that incremental improvements and brand loyalty would carry it forward.

But Tesla saw a different future. With technology evolving at breakneck speed, Tesla recognized that cars could become rolling computers, learning machines that adapt to drivers and environments in real-time. Traditional carmakers were slow to embrace this shift. While they focused on horsepower and sleek aesthetics, Tesla poured energy into leveraging AI - machine learning and computer vision - to transform its vehicles into something far more dynamic.

So they got to work. Instead of outsourcing the "brain" of the car, Tesla took a DIY approach. They developed sophisticated neural networks fed by data from thousands - eventually millions - of miles driven by their customers. Every swerve, stop sign, and highway lane change contributed to a massive database of driving scenarios. Over-the-air updates allowed Tesla to improve its self-driving features continuously without making customers buy new models. As more data poured in, these systems learned at an astonishing pace, handling increasingly complex situations. They didn't just react to the immediate surroundings; they predicted and adapted based on patterns gleaned from a global fleet.

As a result, Tesla set a new standard for what a car could be. Traditional players were caught off-guard, forced to scramble to incorporate their own

AI solutions. Tesla's vehicles weren't just modes of transportation - they were learning platforms. The industry realized the old rulebook was obsolete. Intelligence, adaptability, and data-driven insights replaced outdated assumptions. By the time competitors woke up, Tesla had redefined customer expectations, and there was no going back. This is what AI can do: uproot entrenched business models, challenge conventional roles, and create a new normal where continuous improvement and adaptation outshine stagnation and complacency.

Let's be brutally honest here: If you're still sitting on the sidelines when it comes to AI, you're signing your own death warrant in business terms. AI isn't a gadget you bolt onto your existing operations and call it a day; it's a force that transforms industries from the ground up. It demands that you reassess your structures, your people, and your entire value proposition. Tesla showed the automotive world that intelligence - algorithmic, data-driven intelligence - would shape the future of mobility. Now it's your turn to recognize how AI will shape your sector.

KEY TAKEAWAYS

Software and AI as Key Differentiators: Tesla's focus on software and AI has been a major factor in its success and has disrupted the traditional automotive industry.

Data-Driven Development: The use of real-world data to train and improve AI systems is a crucial aspect of Tesla's approach.

Over-the-Air Updates as a Game Changer: Over-the-air updates allow Tesla to continuously improve its vehicles and add new features without requiring customers to bring their cars to a service center. This is a significant advantage.

Disruption of Traditional Business Models: Tesla's approach has disrupted the traditional automotive business model, which was based on incremental improvements and annual model updates.

DISRUPTION OF TRADITIONAL ROLES –
IDENTIFYING AREAS OF CHANGE WITHIN YOUR INDUSTRY

Think of your industry's landscape. Chances are, you've got traditional roles that have remained stable for years - maybe decades. Whether it's a bank relying on human tellers and credit analysts, a manufacturing plant counting on manual quality inspectors, or a logistics firm depending on schedulers hunched over spreadsheets, these roles used to make perfect sense. They were the backbone of your operations.

But AI changes the game. Tasks that once required meticulous human attention can now be automated and optimized by algorithms that never get tired, never need a break, and never make a decision based on emotion or bias. It's not about hiring robots to replace humans; it's about recognizing that the grunt work, the repetitive and error-prone activities, can be offloaded to machines. This frees human talent to tackle higher-order challenges: strategy, creative problem-solving, relationship-building, and innovation. If you're clinging to the old ways, guess what? Your competitors will embrace AI first, streamline their operations, and leave you in the dust.

Look closely at your processes. Which parts are repetitive and rules-based? Which parts produce a ton of data that could reveal insights if only you had the tools to interpret it? Which aspects of your product or service delivery feel slow, cumbersome, or prone to human error? Those are the pressure points where AI can deliver a knockout punch. Identify these areas before the market identifies them for you.

The disruption of traditional roles also means retraining and repositioning your workforce. The skill sets that propelled your company last decade may not cut it now. You're going to need data analysts, machine learning experts, and people who can interpret algorithmic outputs to make strategic decisions. Don't wait until you're in crisis mode. Start grooming your team for the future. Show them that learning and adapting are not optional extras; they're the price of admission to the next era of business.

Some will resist this change - "We've always done it this way," they'll say. That mindset is a death sentence. Tradition alone can't shield you from technological disruption. The best leaders understand that some roles will shrink, some will vanish, and entirely new ones will emerge. Instead of viewing this as a threat, see it as an opportunity to elevate your team's capabilities. Challenge them to develop new skills, explore different areas of the business, and become the kind of workforce that thrives in an AI-driven world.

OPPORTUNITIES PRESENTED BY AI – ENHANCING EFFICIENCY AND CREATING NEW SERVICES

Now, let's flip the narrative - enough about fear and disruption. AI isn't just a wrecking ball; it's also a master builder, ready to help you construct something better. If you approach AI with the right mindset, you'll find a wealth of opportunities to enhance efficiency and create entirely new streams of revenue.

Efficiency is the low-hanging fruit. AI can spot inefficiencies in your supply chain, predict inventory needs before you run out of stock, and optimize pricing strategies based on real-time market data. It can handle customer inquiries through smart chatbots, freeing human support staff to handle more complex problems. It can forecast maintenance requirements for your machinery, reducing downtime and extending equipment life. Every corner of your business has a data-driven insight waiting to be unlocked.

But let's dream bigger than just efficiency. AI enables you to play in arenas you never considered before. It can reveal consumer behaviors and preferences hidden behind oceans of data. It can identify niche markets, tailor product recommendations to individual tastes, and accelerate your R&D by simulating countless scenarios before you commit to costly prototypes. With AI, you're not just improving what you already do; you're discovering what you could do if you harness the power of predictive analytics, pattern recognition, and continuous learning.

Let's say you're in healthcare. Traditionally, you diagnose diseases by relying on a doctor's expertise and a handful of tests. AI can analyze patient histories, genetic information, and current symptoms against a global database of cases to identify risk factors and recommend treatments. That's not just efficiency - it's a quantum leap in care quality.

If you're in retail, you can move beyond batch marketing campaigns and blast emails. You can create personalized shopping experiences that anticipate what a customer wants before they even know it. That's not just efficiency - it's rewriting the rules of customer engagement.

This is the promise of AI. It unleashes a level of insight and adaptability that can turn you into a market leader rather than a follower. You don't have to know all the answers upfront. Start experimenting. The market is changing so fast that a willingness to try new things - supported by AI insights - will keep you ahead of the curve.

Of course, taking advantage of these opportunities requires guts. You need to be willing to invest in the right tools, talent, and training. You need to accept that AI projects might fail, that you'll need to pivot, and that learning is an ongoing journey. But the alternative - clinging to outdated methods and hoping the storm passes - is far riskier. The storm is here to stay, and only those who navigate it will survive.

ACTION ITEM 1: THE "AI OPPORTUNITY AUDIT"

Don't wait for inspiration to strike. Conduct an "AI Opportunity Audit" right now. Get your executive team, data analysts, and frontline managers together in a room. Ask them: Where are we wasting time? Where do mistakes frequently occur? What data are we collecting but not using? What would we love to know about our customers, supply chain, and product performance that we currently don't?

List these opportunities out and prioritize them. Start with a couple of high-impact areas and commit to implementing an AI-driven solution within a set timeframe. Don't debate forever - act.

ACTION ITEM 2: UPSKILL YOUR WORKFORCE

Your employees need new weapons for this new battlefield. Invest in training sessions, online courses, workshops, and certifications that help them understand AI fundamentals. They don't all need to become data scientists, but they should know what's possible, what's not, and how to interpret AI-driven insights.

Encourage cross-functional learning: your sales team should understand what's happening in R&D, and your logistics team should know how marketing could leverage predictive analytics. Knowledge silos will kill you in a data-driven era, so break them down before it's too late.

FINAL THOUGHTS

Imagine a future where you don't cower at the mention of AI but embrace it as your competitive edge. A future where your team isn't grumbling about lost jobs but celebrating newfound autonomy and creativity. Where customers rave about personalized experiences that feel tailored just for them - and they were, by algorithms that understand them better than any human ever could.

This is the moment where you decide whether you'll ride the wave of technological transformation or get smashed into the rocks. AI can be your accelerant, your secret weapon, pushing you to out-innovate, out-think, and out-perform everyone else. Don't wait until you're forced to adapt - by then, it might be too late.

As Charles Darwin said, "It is not the strongest of the species that survive, nor the most intelligent, but the one most responsive to change." Will you be responsive, or will you be extinct? The choice is yours.

"You're delusional if you think your team will magically handle disruptive shifts without proper preparation - upskilling and change management aren't optional."

PART TWO:
PREPARING YOUR TEAM FOR CHANGE

FROM BOXED TO BOMBSHELL: ADOBE'S SAVAGE SUBSCRIPTION PIVOT THAT BLEW UP OLD-SCHOOL SOFTWARE

When Adobe decided to shift from selling boxed software to a cloud-based subscription model, not everyone was on board. For years, engineers, product managers, and sales teams had worked under a straightforward paradigm: develop a static product, box it up, ship it, and collect revenue from annual updates or entirely new versions. However, the industry was evolving, and Adobe saw that customers wanted constant improvements, immediate updates, and flexible pricing. To meet these demands, the company bet its future on the Creative Cloud platform - an always-on, subscription-based model delivering continuous enhancements. The old guard balked: sales teams weren't used to long-term subscription upsells, and developers had to consider iterative releases, not massive yearly product launches.

Rather than forcing people to adapt blindly, Adobe invested heavily in up-skilling its workforce. Engineers learned new development practices suited for agile release cycles. Sales reps received training to master recurring revenue models and value-based selling. The company brought in experts, scheduled internal workshops, and encouraged peer mentoring so traditional "boxed software" veterans could learn new digital-first strategies. Initially, it was rocky. Old habits die hard, and some employees resisted, clinging to methods they'd mastered over decades. However, leadership was relentless in its support: new training materials appeared, Q&A sessions were held, and managers highlighted early wins from teams who embraced the new approach.

The payoff was enormous. Adobe's transition to Creative Cloud didn't just boost recurring revenue; it transformed the entire culture. The workforce became more flexible and inventive, adapting smoothly to rolling releases instead of rigid schedules. Customer satisfaction soared as users got fresh features automatically. The team that once dreaded massive shifts learned to welcome them, confident in their ability to pivot, acquire new skills, and thrive in uncharted territory. By committing to preparing its people for monumental change, Adobe didn't just survive the transition - it redefined its place in the industry. They emerged as a powerhouse in the era of constant software evolution.

You're delusional if you think your team will magically handle disruptive shifts without proper preparation. Skilled employees don't spontaneously morph into wizards of new technology just because the market demands it. They need guidance, training, and a roadmap. That's where upskilling, reskilling, and change management come into play. When the ground beneath your industry trembles, ensuring your team's foundation is rock solid is the only way to keep your balance.

Today, Adobe's subscription-first strategy has become so entrenched that most users don't even remember when Creative Cloud came in a cardboard box on a store shelf. A decade ago, plenty of naysayers grumbled about monthly fees; today, many creatives see constant updates and integrated services as the norm. With an expanded app ecosystem - from design and video to UX prototyping and AI-powered features - Adobe's subscription model is less a controversy than a convenience. Emerging competition still bristles at Adobe's market dominance, but industry voices praise how Creative Cloud's iterative releases drive collective innovation. In short, Adobe's once-radical shift has settled into a broadly accepted - and arguably indispensable - method of delivering creative tools worldwide.

KEY TAKEAWAYS

Proactive Adaptation to Market Changes: Adobe's transition demonstrates the importance of proactively adapting to changing market conditions and customer demands.

Importance of Upskilling and Reskilling: The success of the transition was heavily reliant on Adobe's investment in upskilling and reskilling its workforce.

Effective Change Management: The company's focus on effective change management, including communication, training, and support, was crucial for overcoming internal resistance and ensuring a smooth transition.

UPSKILLING AND RESKILLING –
PROVIDING EDUCATION ON NEW TECHNOLOGIES

Let's get one thing straight: yesterday's hot skill set is today's ancient artifact. Markets evolve, customers grow more demanding, and technology sprints ahead - if you're not investing in your team's skills, you're already behind. Upskilling and reskilling aren't optional exercises for "nice-to-have" scenarios. They're critical, strategic moves that separate the winners from the has-beens.

Upskilling is about elevating existing competencies. Maybe your data analysts need to learn machine learning techniques, or your customer service reps need to master AI-driven chat tools. Reskilling involves teaching entirely new skills - like transitioning a desktop software developer into a cloud-native architect. Both strategies are about future-proofing your workforce. Without them, you'll face resistance every time a new technology emerges, and guess what? It's not going to slow down for you.

Stop thinking of training as a line item on your budget that you grudgingly approve. It's an investment in agility, plain and simple. When your employees see you're willing to invest in their growth, they become more engaged, more loyal, and more creative. Instead of dreading the next big shift, they'll ask, "What can we learn next?" That's the kind of culture that puts you ahead of the competition - where continuous learning is the norm, not the exception.

Don't half-ass this. Sending your team to a random webinar once a year isn't upskilling. A serious approach means crafting a learning roadmap. It means identifying the skill gaps by analyzing industry trends, emerging technologies, and future customer demands. Then, match training programs, workshops, online courses, or even mentorship arrangements to address those gaps. Don't rely solely on external experts; internal champions who've mastered new tools can become mentors, spreading expertise organically throughout your organization.

Will your team love it at first? Not necessarily. Some will fear they can't learn fast enough. Others might resent being pulled out of their comfort zones. Tough. The reality is that stagnation is a slow death in business. Your job as a leader is to set the tOne: embrace growth or get left behind.

CHANGE MANAGEMENT STRATEGIES – GUIDING YOUR TEAM THROUGH TRANSITIONS

Now, let's address the elephant in the room: fear. Change is scary. People worry about losing relevance, status, or even their jobs. You're fueling a powder keg of resentment and pushback if you try to force new technologies or processes without acknowledging these fears. Change management is the antidote - your blueprint for moving from old ways to new paradigms while keeping the team intact and committed.

Change management isn't just a set of HR buzzwords. It's a disciplined approach to guiding people through transitions. It starts with communication - real, honest, no-BS conversations about why this shift is happening. Spell out the stakes. Don't sugarcoat it. Acknowledge that this won't be easy, but highlight what's in it for them: career growth, staying relevant, and being part of a market-leading organization. Transparency builds trust, and trust makes change palatable.

Next, involve your people in the process. Please don't treat them like passive passengers on a runaway train. Give them a voice. Let them provide input on how new technologies are integrated. Ask them what training methods work best. The more they own the process, the less they'll resist it. Recognize that not everyone learns at the same pace. Some will adapt quickly, while others need more support. Tailor your change initiatives to accommodate different learning styles, skill levels, and temperaments.

Also, celebrate small wins. Did a team member master a new tool that boosted productivity by 15%? Shout it from the rooftops. Did a department successfully integrate an AI-driven workflow? Hold a mini-celebration. These milestones prove that change isn't just pain - it's progress.

You must also accept that some people won't make the journey. If someone consistently refuses to adapt, no matter how much training or support you provide, it may be time to part ways. Harsh? Maybe. Necessary? Absolutely. The success of your organization hinges on a collective willingness to evolve. Dead weight drags everyone down.

Change management is about painting a vision of the future that's so compelling and achievable that people choose to embrace it rather than fight it.

Instead of threats and decrees, you offer clarity, guidance, and the promise of a brighter horizon. That's how you transform fear into fuel for growth.

ACTION ITEM 1: HOST A "FUTURE-SKILLS BOOTCAMP"

No more excuses. Pick a week and transform your office into a learning arena. Bring in industry experts to run workshops on emerging technologies relevant to your business. Set up internal sessions where team members who've mastered certain tools teach their peers. Make it hands-on, interactive, and results-oriented.

By the end of the bootcamp, everyone should have at least one new skill to show off. You're not just handing out knowledge; you're setting a precedent: this company invests in its people's growth.

ACTION ITEM 2: CREATE A "CHANGE NAVIGATOR" GROUP

Identify a handful of employees - across different departments and seniority levels - who show enthusiasm and adaptability. Make them your "Change Navigators." Their job: serve as liaisons between leadership and the broader team. They gather feedback, share insights, and help troubleshoot problems as people adapt to new tools.

These Navigators become your on-the-ground ambassadors, building trust and smoothing the path through rough transitions. When people see peers embracing change, it feels less threatening and more attainable.

FINAL THOUGHTS

Picture this: a workforce that doesn't flinch at new technology, that runs towards skill-building opportunities instead of away from them. Imagine a team so comfortable evolving that they eagerly anticipate what's next. That's what happens when you take upskilling seriously and master change management. You don't just survive market upheavals; you thrive amid them, turning every shift into a launchpad for more tremendous success.

As Bruce Lee said, "Be water, my friend." Adapt, flow, and reshape yourself to fit new containers. Don't fear the future - mold it to your advantage by preparing your team to rise, learn, and dominate whatever challenges come their way.

"When you build trust, you lock in loyalty; when you wield AI responsibly, you become a leader - instead of a cautionary tale."

PART THREE:
ETHICAL CONSIDERATIONS

FROM DATA GRAB TO DATA GLORY:
GOOGLE'S PRIVACY 180° THAT EARNED GLOBAL TRUST

When Google found itself at the center of increasing scrutiny around data usage, it wasn't business as usual anymore. Over time, the company built powerful AI tools and amassed vast amounts of user information - search histories, location data, and browsing patterns. These assets supercharged their advertising engine and product development, but regulators and the public demanded more transparency. Europe's introduction of GDPR raised the stakes; suddenly, data handling practices that had slipped under the radar were now unacceptable. The conversation had shifted from "Can we do this?" to "Should we do this?" Failure to adapt risked reputational damage, loss of user trust, and crippling fines.

Determined not to be seen as a villain in the digital age, Google revamped its privacy policies, simplified user controls, and integrated robust safeguards into its AI systems. Privacy dashboards gave users granular control over what the company collected and stored. Engineers overhauled product features to incorporate differential privacy and anonymization techniques. Ethicists and compliance experts were brought into the product design process early on, not as an afterthought. Teams underwent training to ensure they understood not just how to build innovative tools but how to do it responsibly, respecting the rights and dignity of users.

The outcome was more than regulatory compliance - it was a cultural shift. Despite initial pushback from some executives who feared restrictions might stifle innovation, the company discovered that respecting users 'data and demonstrating responsible AI use strengthened customer loyalty. Trust soared as people recognized that their information wasn't just being harvested blindly but managed carefully and responsibly. Far from halting progress, these ethical frameworks freed Google to innovate with a clear conscience, laying the groundwork for products and services that benefited users and respected their autonomy and privacy.

KEY TAKEAWAYS

Shift from "Can We Do This?" to "Should We Do This?": This key point captures the changing ethical landscape around data usage.

The Importance of Transparency and User Control: It is crucial to build trust that users have transparency and control over their data.

Privacy by Design: Integrating privacy considerations into the product design process is a best practice.

Ethical Considerations in AI Development: The moral implications of AI and the importance of responsible AI development are increasingly important.

RESPONSIBLE AI USE – ENSURING TECHNOLOGY SERVES ETHICAL PURPOSES

You're dead wrong if you think ethics is just a PR stunt. Ethical considerations are the new competitive edge in a world where artificial intelligence can predict behavior, recommend actions, and even manipulate opinions. AI isn't just another tool - it's a powerful force that can shape societies, influence decisions, and change economies. You can't afford to view it solely through the lens of profit.

Responsible AI means designing systems that respect human rights, avoid bias, and serve the greater good - not just your bottom line. It's about building transparency into the algorithms so users understand how outcomes are generated. It's about accountability, ensuring that if your AI screws up - makes a discriminatory decision, for instance - someone steps up to fix it rather than hiding behind a black box of inscrutable code. The days when you could shrug and say, "That's just the algorithm," are gone. Own your technology's impact.

This isn't just about avoiding scandals. It's about unlocking long-term value. When users and partners know your AI systems are trustworthy, they're more likely to embrace them. When regulators see you taking proactive measures, they ease up on the hammer. Employees who understand that ethical AI isn't negotiable build better products. Responsibility doesn't slow you down; it keeps you from running into a brick wall at full speed.

Don't wait for a crisis to start caring. Bake ethics into your development process from day one. Evaluate training data for bias - test algorithms with diverse scenarios. Get ethicists, sociologists, and philosophers in the room with engineers, breaking the silo that says only techies can design tech. Decide which metrics define "good" outcomes for your AI. Hint: it's not always about more clicks, profits, or conversions. Sometimes, it's about fairness, safety, and preserving the user's autonomy.

One core principle of responsible AI is that technology exists to serve humans, not vice versa. You've failed if your AI exploits vulnerabilities promotes harmful content, or discriminates against certain groups. In an era of increased user awareness and vocality, failing ethically is business suicide.

DATA PRIVACY AND SECURITY – PROTECTING INFORMATION IN THE DIGITAL AGE

Let's face it: data is the oil fueling the modern economy. Except this oil isn't buried underground - it's personal information about real people with rights and expectations. In the digital age, privacy is currency; if you mismanage it, you're throwing money away. Users don't just want features; they want to know their data isn't being sold to the highest bidder or locked in an unsecured vault waiting for the subsequent breach.

Data privacy isn't a chore; it's a differentiator. If you can promise users that you'll guard their information fiercely and handle it ethically, you'll stand out in a crowded marketplace. It's not just about slapping a cookie banner on your site. It's about actively minimizing what you collect, encrypting it properly, and giving users meaningful choices. It's about complying with laws not because you have to but because it's right.

Data security goes hand-in-hand with privacy. You can't claim to be ethical if your servers are leaky buckets. Invest in top-notch encryption, intrusion detection systems, and rapid response teams that treat breaches like the emergencies they are. Train your staff on cybersecurity best practices. Don't just rely on IT to solve security problems - make it everyone's responsibility. One careless click on a phishing link can compromise an entire database.

The balance is tricky: you need data to train your AI, improve your offerings, and understand your customers. But more data isn't always better. Sometimes, the fewer details you collect, the safer everyone is. Sometimes, anonymizing data or using synthetic datasets can help you achieve your goals without putting user information at risk. Explore these options. Show that you respect your users enough to think twice before grabbing every scrap of their digital footprint.

This isn't paranoia. It's reality. Massive breaches have taken down giants, leaving customer trust in tatters. You're either naive or arrogant if you think it can't happen to you. And arrogance is a bad look when asking people to trust you with their digital lives.

ACTION ITEM 1: ESTABLISH AN ETHICAL REVIEW BOARD

Don't count on ad-hoc moral judgments. Create a dedicated team - a cross-functional Ethical Review Board. This board should include engineers, legal experts, data analysts, ethicists, and external advisors. Their mandate is to review AI projects and data initiatives before they launch. Do the algorithms handle sensitive data responsibly? Are there biases in the training set? Are the privacy safeguards robust enough? Institutionalizing ethics in your decision-making eliminates guesswork and reduces the risk of ugly surprises.

ACTION ITEM 2: IMPLEMENT A "PRIVACY BY DESIGN" FRAMEWORK

Stop bolting privacy protections onto systems as an afterthought. Privacy by Design means building safeguards into your products from the ground up. It starts with minimal data collection, robust encryption, user consent forms written in plain language, and regular audits. Make it a mandatory part of your development pipeline. If a product doesn't meet privacy standards, it doesn't ship. This sends a message that you care about people, not just profit.

FINAL THOUGHTS

Imagine a world where technology doesn't just dazzle with its capabilities but earns your respect through its moral compass. That world is possible if you stop treating ethics as a burden and start seeing it as your secret weapon. When you build trust, you lock in loyalty. When safeguarding privacy, you court new customers who value sincerity over showmanship. When you wield AI with responsibility, you become a leader, not a cautionary tale.

Maya Angelou once said, "Do your best until you know better. Then, when you know better, do better." You know better now. Don't just innovate - innovate ethically. Don't just transform - transform with integrity. It's the only way to shape a future worth living in.

The Tech Triad

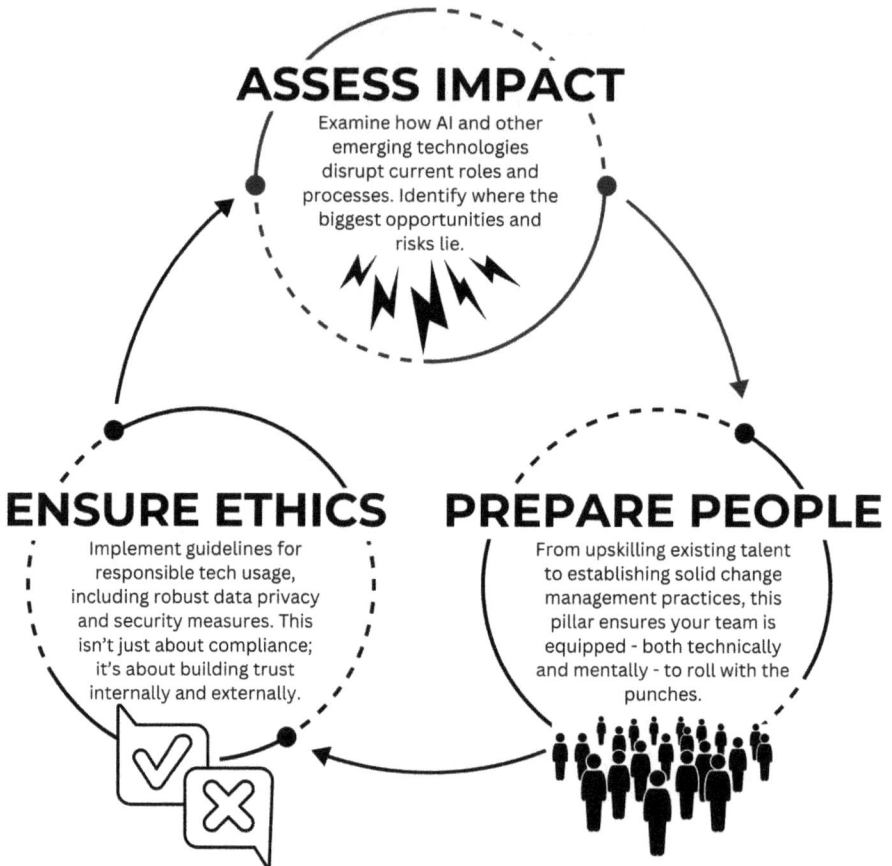

ASSESS IMPACT

Examine how AI and other emerging technologies disrupt current roles and processes. Identify where the biggest opportunities and risks lie.

ENSURE ETHICS

Implement guidelines for responsible tech usage, including robust data privacy and security measures. This isn't just about compliance; it's about building trust internally and externally.

PREPARE PEOPLE

From upskilling existing talent to establishing solid change management practices, this pillar ensures your team is equipped - both technically and mentally - to roll with the punches.

TOOL:
THE TECH TRIAD

Let's get real. Technology is blowing up the old rules of business, and if you're not ready to adapt, you'll get left behind. But here's the upside: AI and other emerging tech can take your leadership game to a whole new level if you know how to harness them responsibly. The Tech Triad is your roadmap for staying ahead of the curve without losing your mind (or ethics). It's about understanding the impact of AI, prepping your team for the inevitable changes, and keeping your moral compass front and center. Ready to level up?

Why It Works in This Chapter

Understanding AI's Impact

- Disruption of Traditional Roles: The Tech Triad helps you spot which roles might shift or shrink so you can adapt proactively.

- Opportunities Presented by AI: Instead of panicking, you'll learn to capitalize on AI's strengths - enhancing efficiency, boosting productivity, and creating new value streams.

Preparing Your Team for Change

- Upskilling and Reskilling: This framework emphasizes continuous learning, so your people won't just survive the changes - they'll thrive in them.

- Change Management Strategies: We're talking real-world, hands-on leadership moves to guide your team from "Oh no, it's AI!" to "We've got this."

Ethical Considerations

- Responsible AI Use: The Triad keeps ethics at the core, so you're not just chasing shiny new tools but ensuring they serve the greater good.

- Data Privacy and Security: Protecting your organization and customers isn't optional - The Tech Triad bakes this right into your approach.

How It Works

The Tech Triad is made up of three interconnected pillars:

1. **Assess the Impact** - Examine how AI and other emerging technologies disrupt current roles and processes. Identify where the biggest opportunities and risks lie.

2. **Prepare Your People** - From upskilling existing talent to establishing solid change management practices, this pillar ensures your team is equipped - both technically and mentally - to roll with the punches.

3. **Ensure Ethics** - Implement guidelines for responsible tech usage, including robust data privacy and security measures. This isn't just about compliance; it's about building trust internally and externally.

Each pillar supports and informs the others, forming a stable structure for navigating tech transformations.

How to Use It

In the Office

- Assess the Impact: Start monthly leadership meetings with a tech "disruption report," highlighting recent AI tools or market shifts that could affect your business.

- Prepare Your People: Schedule mini-training sessions or workshops to keep everyone sharp. Involve your team in brainstorming how to integrate AI ethically and efficiently.

- Ensure Ethics: Appoint an internal "AI Ethics Advocate" to spearhead discussions on responsible usage. Update privacy and security protocols as a team.

With Your Team

- Encourage open dialogue about fears and hopes around AI. When people feel heard, they're more likely to embrace change.

- Recognize employees who upskill or proactively find ethical solutions to tech challenges - it'll inspire others to follow suit.

With Yourself

- Challenge your own biases. Are you overhyping AI, or are you clinging to outdated methods? Make time to learn more - whether reading up on data ethics or taking a quick online course.

- Reflect on how each pillar is playing out in your leadership style. If you're all about the shiny tech but ignoring the ethics piece, it's time to rebalance.

Here's the deal: Technology isn't slowing down for anyone. You can resist it, or you can learn to ride the wave. The Tech Triad offers a balanced approach - understand where AI can drive real value, prep your people to navigate new challenges, and keep your moral compass in check. Embrace this framework, and you'll do more than survive in a tech-driven world - you'll thrive and lead with integrity.

8

"DO YOU WANT TO LEAD
WITH AUTHENTICITY, BUILD
TRUST, AND UNLOCK YOUR
TEAM'S FULL POTENTIAL?"

CULTIVATING EMOTIONAL INTELLIGENCE

"Don't let your leadership potential die on the battlefield of unchecked emotions - channel your self-awareness and self-regulation like a high-voltage battery."

PART ONE:
SELF-AWARENESS AND SELF-REGULATION

FROM SHOES TO BILLION-DOLLAR SMILES:
HOW ZAPPOS TURNED EQ INTO ROI

In the early 2000s, Zappos was an online shoe retailer struggling to differentiate itself from a sea of e-commerce sites that sold identical products at similar price points. They faced a harsh reality: shoes weren't a rocket science product, shipping was shipping, and discounts only got you so far. The question became: how do you stand out in an industry where brand loyalty is rare and competition is brutal?

Zappos 'leadership, led by Tony Hsieh, decided to double down on **culture** as their secret sauce. But it wasn't just about offering free lunches or a quirky office environment. The real pivot came when they realized the root of many operational problems was emotional disconnection - employees felt siloed, customers felt like transactions, and stress built up in the call centers. They needed a shift in leadership style: leaders had to become more emotionally intelligent to foster an environment where staff felt valued, open to new ideas, and genuinely motivated to delight customers.

To tackle this challenge, they instituted new training focused on empathy and self-awareness. Managers were encouraged to do "check-ins" with their teams, not just about metrics but about emotional well-being and personal growth. Customer service reps were given the liberty to handle calls in a personable way - no scripts, no clock-ticking pressure - so they could engage with customers as humans. Far from a soft approach, Zappos quickly discovered that this emotional intelligence emphasis boosted team morale and hammered down turnover rates. More engaged employees turned into brand ambassadors for the company culture, delivering experiences that excited customers.

The result? Zappos saw repeat customers and viral word-of-mouth marketing that drastically cut acquisition costs. Their legendary service stories - like reps spending hours on calls to help a customer - spread across the internet, building an almost cult-like following. Eventually, Amazon acquired Zappos for over a billion dollars. Despite joining the Amazon umbrella, Zappos retained its unique culture and management style. They'd proven that emotional intelligence wasn't just a feel-good concept; it was an operational edge that fueled loyalty, brand equity, and unstoppable growth. By focusing on self-awareness among leaders and emotional connection with customers, Zappos rewrote the rules of e-commerce success.

TAKEAWAYS

Culture as a Competitive Advantage: Zappos's story demonstrates how a strong company culture can be a significant competitive advantage, especially in a commoditized market.

Importance of Emotional Intelligence in Leadership and Customer Service: The emphasis on emotional intelligence in leadership and customer service was a key factor in Zappos's success.

Customer Service as a Marketing Strategy: Zappos effectively used exceptional customer service as a form of marketing, generating positive word-of-mouth and building brand loyalty.

THE ROLE OF EMOTIONAL INTELLIGENCE

Emotional intelligence has been studied, debated, and championed as a critical skill for modern leaders. But let's get real - **it's not** a fluffy HR ideal or just about "being nice." It's about forging genuine connections, building trust, and navigating conflict or crises without losing your cool. Leaders with emotional intelligence handle the chaotic swirl of business with a level head and an open heart. They spot the underlying moods, triggers, and interpersonal dynamics that can make or break an initiative.

Sure, you can be a strong leader with average emotional intelligence, but you risk leaving a trail of bruised egos, sky-high turnover, or a creativity drought. In an era where teams are increasingly diverse, remote, or global, the ability to communicate with empathy and maintain composure is a strategic advantage. And let's be honest: If your management style consistently makes people feel belittled or emotionally drained, you might churn out short-term results, but you'll never sustain momentum or loyalty.

SECTION 1: UNDERSTANDING PERSONAL STRENGTHS AND WEAKNESSES – REFLECTING ON YOUR LEADERSHIP STYLE

Self-awareness is the cornerstone of emotional intelligence. If you don't have a clear sense of who you are - your triggers, blind spots, personality quirks - how can you regulate your emotions or empathize with others? Think of self-awareness as a mirror that reveals both your assets and liabilities. This is no vanity mirror, though; it's a tool for diagnosing where you shine and where you sabotage your own leadership.

WHY SELF-AWARENESS MATTERS

1. **It Prevents Knee-Jerk Reactions** - If you know you get defensive when someone critiques your ideas, you can catch yourself mid-reaction and shift to a more constructive response. Instead of snapping back or shutting down, you ask clarifying questions or take a breather.

2. **It Builds Authenticity** - When you understand your own values, motivations, and insecurities, you communicate more transparently. People can sense authenticity a mile away. Conversely, they can also sniff out pretense or insecurity, which undermines trust.

3. **It Guides You Toward Effective Delegation** - Admitting your weaker areas helps you delegate to those who excel in them. The best leaders aren't generalists doing everything; they're orchestrators who leverage each team member's strengths and fill gaps with complementary skill sets.

Digging Deep

Self-awareness requires introspection. Maybe you're a strong visionary but stink at follow-through. Perhaps you excel at conflict resolution but avoid data analysis. Admitting these truths to yourself sets the stage for growth. Tools like 360-degree feedback or personality assessments (Myers-Briggs, Enneagram, CliftonStrengths) can serve as starting points, but real self-awareness emerges from day-to-day reflection - journaling after heated meetings, debriefing with peers about tough decisions, or even listening to your gut when you sense tension.

SECTION 2: MANAGING EMOTIONS –
RESPONDING RATHER THAN REACTING TO CHALLENGES

If self-awareness is the mirror, self-regulation is the muscle. It's the ability to pivot from raw emotional impulses - anger, fear, frustration - into measured responses that align with your values and objectives. Without self-regulation, your leadership can veer off course in a single heated outburst or meltdown. In a high-pressure environment, that meltdown might cost you credibility or alienate key talent.

EMOTIONAL REGULATION IN PRACTICE

1. **Recognize Emotional Cues** - Watch for physical or emotional signals: tightness in your chest, flushed cheeks, a racing heartbeat. These clues often precede a blow-up or meltdown. The earlier you spot them, the easier it is to intervene mentally.

2. **Pause and Reassess** - Sometimes all it takes is a few seconds of controlled breathing or stepping out of the room. The trick is to disrupt the immediate emotional reaction so your rational brain can catch up. This might look like saying, "Give me a minute to think," instead of blurting out an angry retort.

3. **Channel Emotions Productively** - Anger can fuel righteous action if channeled wisely. Anxiety can prompt thorough planning if you don't let it spiral into paralysis. The key is to let emotions inform you without letting them hijack you. A catalyst leader uses the spark from strong feelings to drive constructive solutions, not personal vendettas.

4. **Create Psychological Safety** - You might handle your own emotions well, but do you inadvertently spark fear in others? If your presence in a meeting makes people clam up, you're not effectively managing the emotional climate. Self-regulated leaders encourage open dialogue by showing calm confidence, not hostility or intimidation.

The Ripple Effect

When you model emotional control under stress, your team picks up on that vibe. If you're flipping out or blaming others, you license them to do the same. Conversely, if you maintain composure and empathy, you shift the entire team's approach to conflict resolution and brainstorming sessions. This culture of level-headedness fosters creativity, because fear of blowback is reduced. People dare to speak their minds, share edgy ideas, and trust that even if they fail, the reaction won't be explosive condemnation.

TAKE ACTION

1. **Personal SWOT Analysis for Emotional Traits**

- Combine personal reflection with peer input. Identify your emotional strengths (e.g., empathy, adaptability) and weaknesses (e.g., impatience, defensiveness). Don't sugarcoat it - this is your chance to lay it all out.

- Pair each weakness with a plan. If you struggle with impulsive anger, commit to a 2-"minute cool-down rule" before replying to tense emails or debates. If you're impatient, practice active listening exercises once a week to slow yourself down.

2. **Develop a "Pressure Check" Protocol**

- Introduce a protocol in meetings: if discussions heat up, anyone can say "Pause for Pressure Check." Everyone takes 30 seconds to regroup, reflect on emotional states, then propose solutions calmly.

- Store these "Pressure Check" references in your meeting logs, so you track how often stress spikes occur and whether the protocol is defusing them. Over time, this normalizes emotional resets, reducing the risk of outbursts that derail progress.

FINAL THOUGHTS

Don't let your leadership potential die on the battlefield of unchecked emotions. Channel your self-awareness and self-regulation like a high-voltage battery - charged, focused, unstoppable. The difference between a mediocre boss and a legend often boils down to emotional intelligence. Think bigger: your calm, your empathy, and your composure in chaos can spark breakthroughs your team never dared dream of.

As the Dalai Lama once said, "A disciplined mind leads to happiness, and an undisciplined mind leads to suffering." So discipline your mind, harness your feelings, and steer your team with unwavering emotional clarity. That's the unstoppable engine of catalyst leadership.

"Empathy isn't a soft extra - it's a hardcore accelerator for trust, loyalty, and fearless innovation."

PART TWO:
EMPATHY IN LEADERSHIP

HOW AIRBNB TURNED COUCH CRASHING INTO A BILLION-DOLLAR EMPIRE—BY ACTUALLY LISTENING

In the late 2000s, Airbnb was a scrappy startup founded by a couple of friends who rented out an air mattress in their apartment to make some extra cash. The idea of letting strangers pay to crash in your living room seemed bizarre, even laughable, to most people. Back then, travelers trusted hotels and official bed-and-breakfasts. The concept of staying in a stranger's home triggered concerns about safety, privacy, and reliability. Investors were hesitant; customers were cautious. Meanwhile, existing online travel platforms mocked the notion that a few guys in an apartment could upend the hospitality industry.

However, the Airbnb team responded differently: they listened - really listened - to what hosts and guests were worried about. Instead of dismissing fears, they empathized. Hosts wanted to feel safe opening up their homes. Guests wanted assurance that they wouldn't show up to a dump or a scam. The founders interviewed early users, solicited every complaint and suggestion, and even visited properties to see what was working and what wasn't. Slowly, they iterated features like verified IDs, photo verifications, secure payment systems, and transparent reviews - each step addressing an emotional concern expressed by the community.

As they addressed these emotional touchpoints, trust grew. More hosts signed up, tempted by extra income and simpler listing processes. More travelers booked, drawn by the personal touches that hotels couldn't match - like local hosts eager to offer city tips or homemade breakfast. Revenue climbed, and venture capital poured in, fueling Airbnb's global expansion. Yet the real tipping point wasn't a marketing hack or a fancy redesign - it was empathy at scale. By deeply understanding the emotional triggers of both hosts and guests, Airbnb created a platform that made intangible connections feel safe, intimate, and worthwhile.

The result? Airbnb is now a global juggernaut valued in the tens of billions, transforming how millions travel. Traditional hotel chains race to emulate the "home sharing" vibe, while Airbnb continues to innovate on community-driven experiences. The key takeaway? Empathy - authentic, unforced, and practical empathy - proved to be more than a soft skill. It was a game-changing catalyst for trust, loyalty, and explosive growth, forging a category that barely existed before.

TAKEAWAY

Empathy as a Key Driver of Success: The narrative correctly emphasizes the role of empathy in Airbnb's success. By understanding and addressing the emotional needs of both hosts and guests, Airbnb built trust and created a booming marketplace.

Building Trust in a New Market: Airbnb's story is a good example of how to build trust in a new market with inherent concerns about safety and reliability.

User Feedback and Iteration: This section also highlights the importance of listening to user feedback and iterating on the product based on that feedback.

EMPATHY AS A LEADERSHIP SUPERPOWER

In an era of fierce competition, disrupted industries, and remote work, empathy isn't just a feel-good virtue - it's a strategic advantage. The transformative power of understanding and sharing in another person's emotional reality can revolutionize your entire approach to leadership. Suppose you truly grasp what your team members, customers, and partners are going through. In that case, you make better decisions, build deeper trust, and spark creative collaboration at a level that numbers alone can't generate. Empathy fosters loyalty, boosts morale, and consistently leads to results that outpace old-school command-and-control models.

But let's bust a myth: Empathy isn't about being a pushover or coddling people. You can remain assertive, set ambitious goals, and hold high standards while practicing radical empathy. It's about listening fully, acknowledging concerns, and then forging a path that addresses them without sacrificing your vision. This is the sweet spot, the synergy between empathy and assertive leadership that reassures your team and instills confidence in your leadership.

SECTION 1: UNDERSTANDING TEAM NEEDS – LISTENING ACTIVELY TO CONCERNS AND IDEAS

Team members bring personal histories, emotional baggage, unspoken fears, and ambitions to work daily. As a leader, actively listening to their concerns and ideas is not just a task but a commitment to understanding and supporting them. If you never take time to listen - listen - you risk missing out on the creative gold and potential synergy locked inside their heads.

ACTIVE LISTENING IN PRACTICE

1. **One-on-One Check-Ins** - Don't let formal reviews be the only time you discuss personal or professional growth with an employee. Schedule frequent, casual check-ins. Ask open-ended questions like "What's the biggest hurdle for you this week?" or "Where do you see a growth opportunity I haven't noticed?" Then, shut up and let them talk.

2. **Reading Between the Lines** - Sometimes, employees won't blurt out their frustrations directly. They might hint at workload stress or dissatisfaction with a new process. Pay attention to body language and changes in tone. If you sense discontent, probe gently: "I get the feeling you're not fully comfortable - what's up?"

3. **Tech-Assisted Listening** - In a remote or hybrid world, you might rely on Slack, Zoom, or project management tools to stay connected. Encourage your team to share "pulse checks" or quick emotional statuses during the day. While not a replacement for face-to-face, these digital signals can help you catch issues early.

THE ROI OF LISTENING

When employees feel heard, they become emotionally invested. They're more open to feedback, willing to collaborate, and less likely to harbor silent resentments that erupt later. Listening also cuts down on misunderstandings that cost time and money to fix. It's a productivity hack disguised as a soft skill. Plus, people become more creative when they sense their voices matter. They'll propose bolder ideas, confident they won't be dismissed out of hand.

SECTION 2: BUILDING STRONG RELATIONSHIPS – CONNECTING ON A PERSONAL LEVEL TO INSPIRE TRUST

Empathy isn't a one-time event; it's a relationship currency you accumulate over time. The deeper you connect with people beyond superficial tasks, the more they trust you. Trust is the backbone of every innovative move. If team members trust you, they'll follow you into uncertain territories. If they don't, even the best strategic plan might flop due to half-hearted execution.

GOING BEYOND PROFESSIONAL TITLES

If you see your employees solely as "assets" or "resources," you'll never unlock their full potential. But if you take the time to know them - understand their personal goals, hobbies, and families - they sense a level of care that fosters loyalty. This doesn't mean prying into private matters. It means being human: remembering who's got a significant family milestone coming up, who's dealing with a personal challenge, or who's itching to learn a new skill.

ENCOURAGING COLLABORATION OVER RIVALRY

Departments often become siloed, each chasing its metrics. Empathy helps you connect individuals across these divides. When marketing empathizes with engineering's workload and constraints, synergy emerges. When product managers empathize with sales' customer-facing challenges, they refine product features that sell. Your job? Model this cross-functional empathy. In meetings, nudge different departments to voice each other's perspectives. Once empathy becomes the default mode of inter-department communication, relationships blossom, forging powerful alliances that accelerate progress.

THE TRUST MULTIPLIER

In practical terms, empathy-laced relationships yield high-trust interactions. People want to do right by colleagues they respect and like. They'll go the extra mile on a team project, share key intel without being asked, and offer help spontaneously. That trust further cements a culture where risk-taking feels safer because you know your colleagues have your back. In short, empathy weaves a safety net that catches stumbles and turns them into learning experiences rather than blame-fests.

ACTION ITEMS

1. **Empathy Rounds**

- Just like medical professionals do "patient rounds," schedule monthly "empathy rounds" where you move from department to department, not to check on tasks but to understand morale and concerns. Ask open-ended questions about workload, personal challenges, or workflow friction. Record these notes systematically, watch for recurring themes, and then share a condensed version of your findings with leadership.

- The point is visibility. Employees see you actively caring, listening, and addressing issues. Over time, empathy rounds have become an anticipated tradition rather than a dreaded managerial oversight.

2. **Peer Mentorship Program**

- Launch a program pairing employees from different levels or departments to meet monthly. It's less about formal mentoring and more about cross-pollinating experiences. In these sessions, they discuss each other's professional or personal hurdles and brainstorm solutions together.

- Provide minimal structure, just enough to keep it from derailing: a monthly topic (e.g., conflict resolution, career planning, stress management) and a recommended 30-minute format. This fosters empathy horizontally, not just top-down. People learn to appreciate each other's roles and challenges, forging relationships that transcend departmental barriers.

FINAL THOUGHTS

Forget the illusion that empathy is "soft." It's a hardcore accelerator for trust, loyalty, and fearless innovation. When your people believe you genuinely care about their hurdles, they'll run through walls for you and do it with creative gusto.

As Maya Angelou once said, "People will forget what you said, people will forget what you did, but people will never forget how you made them feel." So, make them feel respected, heard, and valued. Charge forth with empathy as your competitive edge, forging a workplace and a community where leaders and teams unite around a shared purpose and unstoppable drive.

"Stop tiptoeing around tough conversations - authentic leaders see conflict as a gateway to innovation, not a roadblock."

PART THREE:
SOCIAL SKILLS AND INFLUENCE

SCOOP DREAMS: HOW BEN & JERRY'S MIXED EQ WITH ICE CREAM TO BUILD A BILLION-DOLLAR BRAND

When **Ben Cohen** and **Jerry Greenfield** started their iconic ice cream shop in a renovated gas station in Burlington, Vermont, they had more passion than business acumen. They whipped up quirky flavors, used the best ingredients they could find, and sprinkled in a generous dose of social responsibility.

Customers loved the decadent scoops, but as the company grew, cracks in the internal structure emerged. Communication across different departments - from flavor R&D to distribution - became sporadic. Tensions flared when certain employees or managers felt their voices weren't being heard regarding new flavor releases or philanthropic initiatives. Meanwhile, co-founders Ben and Jerry were forced to juggle a rapidly expanding enterprise and their mission to be more than just another ice cream brand.

To handle these internal issues, the founders put a renewed emphasis on transparent, respectful dialogue. They scheduled informal "town hall" meets where staff at every level could propose ideas or vent frustrations about policies. Each voice was treated with equal respect, from seasonal scoopers to finance leads.

Simultaneously, Ben & Jerry's formalized conflict-resolution approaches, hiring mediators when departmental rifts threatened morale or productivity. They taught managers how to listen actively and articulate disagreements without escalating tensions. The result was an organizational culture where employees felt valued and were more open to speaking up about both creative improvements and social-impact programs.

Over time, the brand soared. Customers adored not only the funky flavor names but the spirit of camaraderie and social activism the company projected. The internal synergy fed the external mission: cohesive teamwork allowed for quick rollouts of new flavors tied to social causes, increasing consumer loyalty.

When Ben & Jerry's eventually merged with a global conglomerate, employees insisted on retaining these open communication norms and conflict-resolution practices. Their brand identity - and the sense of purpose employees felt - remained intact, fueling their ongoing success. This story exemplifies how strengthening social skills and influence - through effective communication and constructive conflict resolution - can safeguard a brand's soul even amid rapid expansion and external pressures.

TAKEAWAYS

Culture as a Core Value: Ben & Jerry's story demonstrates the importance of company culture as a core value and a driver of success.

Open Communication and Collaboration: The emphasis on open communication, dialogue, and collaboration within the company contributed to its positive work environment and its ability to effectively implement its social mission.

Social Responsibility as a Business Strategy: Ben & Jerry's demonstrated that social responsibility can be a successful business strategy, building brand loyalty and attracting customers who share their values.

WHY SOCIAL SKILLS AND INFLUENCE MATTER

Emotional intelligence is more than just self-awareness and self-regulation. If you can't communicate those insights effectively, or if you melt down the second there's friction on the team, your personal breakthroughs do little to propel the organization forward. That's where **social skills** and **influence** kick in. They turn your internal clarity into external impact - leading others, shaping culture, and driving powerful collaborations.

SECTION 1: EFFECTIVE COMMUNICATION – ARTICULATING IDEAS CLEARLY AND PERSUASIVELY

At its core, communication is about two outcomes: clarity and connection. You want your message to be easily understood (clarity) and resonate with your audience's values and feelings (connection). Confusion reigns when a leader fumbles this, projects stall, and team morale dips. Crisp, targeted messaging, on the other hand, can unify teams around a common objective or rally them during adversity.

KEY ELEMENTS OF EFFECTIVE COMMUNICATION

1. **Simplicity** - Strip out the corporate jargon. Nobody wants to wade through buzzwords to find your actual intent. The more straightforward you are, the less likely your words get twisted or watered down.

2. **Empathy** - Great communicators tailor their message to the audience's perspective. If you're talking to front-line staff, address their concerns about workload or daily tasks. If you're pitching to executives, highlight strategic growth or ROI. Empathy ensures that when people hear you speak, they feel seen and understood.

3. **Authenticity** - If you're passionately introducing a new idea, let that passion show. People rally behind genuine emotion. Conversely, if you deliver tough news, don't sugarcoat it - candor builds trust. Authenticity is what stops your message from being perceived as a "corporate spin."

4. **Active Listening** - Communication isn't a monologue. Real leaders listen as fiercely as they speak. This means noticing nonverbal cues, following up on team feedback, and adjusting your stance if you realize you missed a key point.

BENEFITS OF COMMUNICATING WITH IMPACT

-   **Alignment**: Everyone knows the "why" behind a directive or change, so they can execute with fewer misunderstandings.

-   **Agility**: Crisp communication shortens feedback loops. Teams pivot quickly because they don't waste days clarifying instructions.

- **Culture-Building**: People feel valued when leaders talk to them, not at them. This fosters loyalty and a willingness to go above and beyond.

SECTION 2: CONFLICT RESOLUTION – NAVIGATING DISAGREEMENTS CONSTRUCTIVELY

No matter how harmonious you try to make your workplace, conflicts arise. Ideas clash, deadlines loom, personalities grate on each other. Conflict in itself isn't the problem - it's how you handle it. Managed poorly, conflict can tear teams apart, creating a toxic environment. Managed well, conflict can be an engine for innovation, forcing teams to consider multiple perspectives and refine their strategies.

COMMON CONFLICT PITFALLS

- **Avoidance**: Leaders who pretend conflicts don't exist allow tensions to simmer beneath the surface, eventually bursting out in harmful ways.

- **Confrontation Without Structure**: Others might barge in like a bulldozer, squashing dissent and fueling resentment. Sure, you "win" the argument, but you lose your team's respect.

- **Personalization**: Conflict over ideas morphs into personal attacks. Emotions run high, and objective problem-solving goes out the window.

PRINCIPLES OF CONSTRUCTIVE CONFLICT RESOLUTION

5. **Focus on the Issue, Not the Person** - Separate behaviors or ideas from individual identities. You can reject a proposal without rejecting the person proposing it. This keeps the dialogue respectful and idea-centric.

6. **Encourage Contrarian Views** - Great leaders actually solicit opposing viewpoints. If your entire table nods in unison, you might be missing a critical flaw. Conflict, when respectful, unearths hidden risks and leads to more robust outcomes.

7. **Listen First, Then Debate** - Let each side articulate their concerns and rationale. Summarize back what you heard - this ensures everyone feels acknowledged. Only then do you weigh in with counterpoints.

This layered approach prevents conflating "not being heard" with losing the argument.

8. **Seek Common Ground** - Even in heated conflicts, there's often a shared overarching goal - like delivering value to customers or hitting a product launch deadline. Identifying this larger mission can unify parties who otherwise differ in details.

CULTIVATING A CONFLICT-POSITIVE CULTURE

When employees see conflict resolution handled fairly and maturely, they no longer fear voicing dissent or alternative ideas. They realize disagreements can spark breakthroughs rather than sabotage careers. That's rocket fuel for innovation - teams aren't shy to propose new directions or question conventional wisdom. The result: an environment where the best ideas triumph, not just the loudest voice or the highest rank.

ACTION ITEMS

1. **Weekly "Open Forum" Check-Ins**

• Dedicate 15 minutes at the end of each weekly team meeting to an open forum. Anyone can raise a conflict or confusion, from resource constraints to overlapping projects. The aim is to tackle them head-on instead of letting them brew.

• Establish ground rules: speak respectfully, focus on the issue not the individual, and propose at least one potential solution. This consistent format normalizes small doses of conflict and fosters transparent communication.

2. **Two-Minute "Empathy Pause"**

• Before diving into a potentially contentious conversation or debate, institute a "two-minute empathy pause." Each side briefly states the underlying feelings or stakes that matter most to them. For instance, one side might say, "We're worried about brand integrity," the other might say, "We're stressed about budget constraints."

- This pause forces participants to see the human reasons behind each position, resetting the conflict from "my plan vs. yours" to "we share concerns; let's address them together." Over time, employees internalize empathy as a standard procedure for conflict resolution.

FINAL THOUGHTS

Communication and conflict resolution aren't add-ons; they're the grease and gears that roar your leadership machine. Stop tiptoeing around tough conversations or sugarcoating feedback - dive in with clarity and empathy. Authentic leaders use words not just to manage but to spark transformation. They see conflict not as a roadblock but as a gateway to more substantial, innovative teams.

As Ernest Hemingway once quipped, "The world breaks everyone, and afterward, many are strong in the broken places." Let your team be that strong - bonded by open dialogue, fearless challenge, and the unshakeable trust built by nailing social skills and taming conflict.

The Emotional Compass

NORTH
Self-Awareness
Understanding your triggers, strengths, and blind spots. Reflect daily on how you feel and why.

WEST
Social Skills

Influencing, collaborating, and resolving conflicts with integrity. Communicate clearly and build genuine connections.

EAST
Self-Regulation

Guiding your emotional energy in a productive direction. Harness your reactions to serve your goals, not derail them.

N
W — CONNECTION — E
S

SOUTH
Empathy
Stepping into your team's shoes. Listen more than you talk, and validate experiences.

At the center is **Connection** - the magnetic core that ties all four points together, reminding you that emotional intelligence is the foundation of meaningful relationships and effective leadership.

TOOL:
THE EMOTIONAL COMPASS

All right, let's cut to the chase: You can have the best business strategy on the planet, but if you're ignoring emotional intelligence, you're only firing on half your cylinders. Leaders who get EQ right are the ones that build loyalty, drive innovation, and maintain serious momentum - even when the pressure's on. The Emotional Compass is here to help you navigate your own emotions, understand your team on a deeper level, and influence outcomes in a way that elevates everyone. Ready to level up? Let's do it.

Why It Works in Cultivating Emotional Intelligence

Self-Awareness and Self-Regulation

- Understanding Personal Strengths and Weaknesses: The Compass forces you to look at your "True North" of authenticity, so you know exactly where you stand as a leader.

- Managing Emotions: By checking in with your Compass regularly, you'll learn to respond thoughtfully instead of reacting impulsively.

Empathy in Leadership

- Understanding Team Needs: The Compass aligns you with the emotions of others, guiding you to ask better questions and truly listen.

- Building Strong Relationships: When you lead with empathy, you create genuine trust - and trust is the glue that keeps teams together.

Social Skills and Influence

- Effective Communication: A solid EQ foundation improves how you articulate ideas and persuade stakeholders.

- Conflict Resolution: The Compass gives you a clear direction for approaching disagreements with empathy, clarity, and a solutions-oriented mindset.

What Is It?

The Emotional Compass consists of four cardinal points - each representing a key facet of emotional intelligence:

1. **North (N) – Self-Awareness** - Understanding your triggers, strengths, and blind spots. Reflect daily on how you feel and why.

2. **East (E) – Self-Regulation** - Guiding your emotional energy in a productive direction. Harness your reactions to serve your goals, not derail them.

3. **West (W) – Empathy** - Stepping into your team's shoes. Listen more than you talk, and validate experiences.

4. **South (S) – Social Skills** - Influencing, collaborating, and resolving conflicts with integrity. Communicate clearly and build genuine connections.

At the center is Connection - the magnetic core that ties all four points together, reminding you that emotional intelligence is the foundation of meaningful relationships and effective leadership.

How to Use It

In the Office

- Start team meetings with a quick "Compass Check." Ask folks to share something they're working on emotionally - like staying calm under deadlines or actively listening to colleagues.

- Post the diagram in a common area as a reminder that emotional intelligence isn't just fluffy talk - it's a leadership necessity.

With Your Team

- Encourage mentorship pairs to discuss each point of the Compass weekly. For instance, a mentor might guide a mentee to practice empathy (W) by actively listening to a frustrated coworker.

- Organize role-playing scenarios for conflict resolution (S). People can take turns practicing addressing issues using empathy (W) and self-regulation (E).

With Yourself

- Spend five minutes every morning journaling on how you feel, which relates to Self-Awareness (N). Note any triggers that might pop up that day.

- Reflect nightly: Did you keep your emotional response in check (E)? Did you show empathy (W) in challenging moments? Did you communicate effectively (S)?

Here's the bottom line: Emotional intelligence isn't optional - it's the game-changer for anyone serious about effective leadership. The Emotional Compass gives you a clear, straightforward guide to tap into your own EQ and create stronger bonds with your team. When you use this method consistently, you'll see your relationships, communication, and overall leadership style evolve in real time.

Now, go crush it with confidence and a whole lot of heart!

"Stop enabling the 'I'm so busy' script - pull back the curtain, demand clarity, and watch your real innovation engine roar."

3RD QUARTER BONUS:
STOP THE "I'M SO BUSY" EXCUSE AND START LEADING

ALAN MULALLY AT FORD: REINVENTING A CULTURE OF EXCUSES

Early in the 2000s, Alan Mulally stepped into Ford Motor Company as CEO, confronted by an entrenched culture of finger-pointing, territorial attitudes, and endless claims of being "too busy." Department heads frantically protected their own silos, never admitting mistakes. Each group insisted it was swamped with tasks, yet critical vehicle programs stalled, quality suffered, and market share plummeted. Meanwhile, high-level executives were so buried in disclaimers - "We're busy this quarter," "We can't pivot that fast" - that they overlooked the gaping holes in Ford's lineup.

Mulally marched in with an outsider's perspective and zero tolerance for deflections. He demanded straightforward weekly updates (the famous "business plan review" meetings), requiring executives to label project statuses as green, yellow, or red. Early attempts to reveal "red" statuses were met with fear - nobody wanted to admit they were failing. Mulally's approach was to kill that fear with radical transparency and a supportive atmosphere. Rather than punishing someone who said, "We're in trouble," he'd ask the team how to help solve it. This shift forced leaders to move beyond safe excuses like "We're busy" or "That's not my department."

The results were explosive. Once people stopped hiding behind "busy" signals, resource bottlenecks surfaced, cross-functional problems came to light, and solutions got hammered out in real time. Morale began to climb as managers realized that admitting roadblocks or ignorance wasn't a career death sentence. Collaboration soared, Ford launched vehicles that better matched consumer needs, and the brand's financial performance rebounded. By confronting "I'm too busy" mindsets and tackling them head-on, Mulally pulled Ford back from the brink without a government bailout, restoring the company's global credibility. This story reveals a key

Catalyst Leadership principle: Busy is often an excuse for inaction or lack of accountability. Strip away the illusions, and people become free to innovate - and free to get real work done.

THE "I'M SO BUSY" FALLACY

You've heard it a million times: "I can't do that, I'm swamped." "We're too busy to try new ideas right now." or the corporate classic, "I've got a thousand things on my plate." Sure, there are days when real workloads spike, but let's be honest: half the time, "I'm so busy" is a smokescreen, an unconscious shield for avoidance or incompetence. People use it to mask disorganization, an unwillingness to learn, or a refusal to step outside their comfort zone.

Catalyst Leaders see right through it. They don't shrug and say, "Oh well, guess we'll shelve that initiative." Instead, they ask tough questions: Are you truly at capacity with critical tasks, or are you burying yourself in busywork to dodge bigger responsibilities? Are you incompetent at prioritizing, or are you just lazy?

Yes, I said it: incompetent or lazy. Those are the two big "buckets" behind the incessant "too busy" mantra. Let's break down how they manifest and why they matter:

THE "INEPT" TYPE: IT'S NOT MALICE, IT'S SKILL GAPS

Some folks simply lack the skill sets or organizational strategies to handle their responsibilities smoothly. They bounce from email to email, meeting to meeting, never structuring their day or clarifying real deliverables. They're not dumb - they might even be brilliant in specific knowledge areas - but they've never learned to systematically break tasks down. That lack of skill or process yields a constant state of flurry: they're always on the edge of meltdown, claiming zero bandwidth for anything new.

WHY IT'S DANGEROUS

- **Bottlenecks:** Projects stall because an "Inept" associate never gets the fundamentals right, forcing the rest of the team to pick up slack or wait around.

- **Passive Aggression:** They might interpret your request for account-ability as an attack, leading to friction in the group dynamic.

- **Wasted Talent:** Maybe they have potential in a specialized domain, but their chaotic method means they never harness it effectively.

CATALYST LEADER'S APPROACH

Identify whether the issue is purely a skill gap. If so, training or direct coaching can solve a huge chunk of the "busy" problem. By showing them time-management frameworks, how to prioritize critical tasks, or how to break big goals into smaller, daily targets, you convert them from frantic to functional.

THE "LAZY" TYPE: DODGING ACCOUNTABILITY

On the flip side, some people know their job but prefer minimal exertion. "I'm too busy" becomes the perfect smokescreen. It wards off extra projects, hides procrastination, and frames them as a "victim" of an overwhelming schedule. Meanwhile, crucial tasks languish, or they offload responsibilities onto more dedicated teammates.

Why It's Dangerous

- **Suffocates Team Morale:** Others feel used and start questioning why they're busting their butts while this individual skates by with the "busy" excuse.

- **Missed Opportunities:** Potential game-changing tasks get ignored or delayed. The team collectively suffers because one person's inertia holds everyone back.

- **Erodes Trust:** If everyone sees through the charade - except leader-ship - your credibility as a leader takes a hit.

Catalyst Leader's Approach

You can't "train" someone out of laziness; it's an attitude issue. The key is accountability. Show them that tasks have measurable outcomes, timelines, and success criteria. If they fail to meet them consistently with no legitimate reason, reassign them or escalate consequences. A Catalyst Leader doesn't let one anchor sink the entire ship.

WHY THIS MATTERS TO CATALYST LEADERSHIP

Catalyst Leadership is all about driving transformation and momentum. That means tasks, missions, or side projects can't be derailed by fake "I'm busy" deflections. In a fast-moving environment, if you let "busyness" stand unchallenged, your entire innovation engine stalls. You need to ensure that every rung of your organization is optimized for real productivity, not frantic motion.

Moreover, Catalyst Leaders place a huge premium on authenticity. If someone's using "busy" to cover up skill gaps or laziness, you're not dealing with the real issues - like training, motivation, or job fit. And ignoring reality never ends well.

A CULTURE THAT SQUASHES THE "BUSY" SHIELD

Imagine a workplace where no one can wave "I'm so busy" as a get-out-of-jail-free card. Instead, they'd have to say, "I'm stuck," "I don't know how to do this," or "I'm not motivated to take this on." That level of honesty might be awkward initially, but it fosters genuine problem-solving:

- If they're incompetent: Provide quick upskilling or real-time coaching.

- If they're unmotivated: Figure out if it's a job-fit mismatch or a personal slump. Could a new challenge or a different role spark their drive?

BALANCING COMPASSION AND TOUGH LOVE

Catalyst Leadership isn't about steamrolling people. Sometimes the "I'm too busy" lament is a cry for help. Maybe they've taken on too many responsibilities due to poor team delegation. Or maybe they're dealing with personal turmoil outside the office. A dash of empathy goes a long way. Ask clarifying questions, see if you can reduce friction or reassign tasks. But also be firm: no one gets a perpetual free pass.

At the end of the day, removing "I'm so busy" from the corporate dictionary helps unearth real issues and real solutions. People flourish when they can't hide behind illusions - once illusions are gone, they either step up or self-select out. As a Catalyst Leader, you want a team of unstoppable go-getters, not an army of excuse-makers.

And yes, you should reflect on yourself too. Are you projecting an "I'm so busy" aura that discourages your team from approaching you with ideas or concerns? Leadership sets the tone. If you demonstrate that busyness is not a status symbol but a potential sign of disorganization, your people will follow suit, focusing on real productivity and skill-building instead.

TAKE ACTION

1. **Busy-Check Surveys**

- Roll out a quick monthly or quarterly poll asking employees to rank their perceived busyness vs. actual productivity. Let them highlight specific bottlenecks - maybe it's a confusing approval process, outdated software, or poorly defined roles.

- Compile results, share top findings with the team, and commit to addressing at least one major issue each cycle. By bringing "I'm so busy" out into the open, you eliminate default excuses and push for real solutions.

2. **Skill Audit and Accountability Sessions**

- Conduct a "Skill Audit" for each employee, focusing on time management, project execution, and relevant job capabilities. If someone appears incompetent in a critical area, set up targeted training or coaching sessions.

- For the presumably lazy ones, institute weekly accountability check-ins. They present their top priorities and the status of each. If they're slipping, confront it immediately. Reiterate that the team's success depends on honest ownership of tasks.

Between these two steps, you tackle the root issues behind "I'm so busy" - either by upskilling or spotlighting slackers. The net effect is a culture where people stop hiding behind busyness and start owning results.

FINAL THOUGHTS

Stop enabling the "I'm so busy" script. It's time to dethrone busyness as a badge of honor and replace it with actual performance and growth. Whether your associates are genuinely overwhelmed, incompetent, or just lazy, your job as a Catalyst Leader is to yank back the curtain and demand clarity. Tackle skill gaps head-on, call out slackers, and reward real contributions.

As Teddy Roosevelt once said, "In any moment of decision, the best thing you can do is the right thing." So do it: cut the excuses, amplify real impact, and create a culture where hustle means progress, not chaotic stagnation.

The "Priority Ladder"

The Priority Ladder is a simple yet powerful framework that slices through the "I'm too busy" clutter by forcing your team to actively rank everything on their plate.

1. List All Tasks

Each team member writes down every project, from urgent tasks to "someday maybe" items.

2. Rank In True Hierarchy

Forced rank them from top priority to bottom, linking each to a core strategic goal. No ties allowed; you must decide what's literally #1, #2, #3, etc.

3. Allocate Time Blocks

Based on this ladder, employees carve out time blocks. The top third get the prime hours, the middle chunk gets leftover slots, and the bottom rung is optional or delegated away.

4. Review Weekly

Each Monday, a quick review ensures tasks align with real outcomes, not just busywork.

TOOL:
THE "PRIORITY LADDER"

The Priority Ladder is a simple yet powerful framework that slices through the "I'm too busy" clutter by forcing your team to actively rank everything on their plate.

Instead of juggling endless tasks without a clear plan, employees learn to differentiate what truly impacts the organization's goals from what just adds noise.

This practice not only dismantles the illusion of perpetual busyness but also unleashes targeted productivity.

1. **List All Tasks**

- Each team member compiles a comprehensive list of responsibilities - projects, tasks, even wishlist items that might never see the light of day. No filtering at this stage; the idea is to get everything out in the open.

- Encourage absolute honesty. If someone's sneaking in a "quick side project" or random favor from another department, it needs to be on this list. Visibility is power.

2. **Rank in True Hierarchy**

- This is where the magic happens. Force everyone to label each task from #1 down to #N, prohibiting ties. The top slot might be "Launch New Product Beta," while the bottom could be "Reorganize email folders."

- Have them justify each ranking by linking it to a strategic goal or big metric. Why is task #1 so urgent or important? If it doesn't tie directly to a key outcome, does it really belong at the top?

3. **Allocate Time Blocks**

- The top tasks earn prime real estate on the calendar - peak mental hours like early morning or post-lunch sprints, depending on when the person is most alert.

- Middle-ranking tasks go into leftover slots. The bottom rung? Either schedule them in the final open windows of the week, delegate them, or decide they're not worth doing at all. The main point is to stop letting them linger and clog up everyone's "busy" bandwidth.

4. **Review Weekly**

- Every Monday (or Friday, if that's your jam), hold a quick check-in: Did we tackle the top priorities, or did last week get derailed by random junk tasks? If so, let's find out why. Is there a repeated pattern of "urgent-but-not-important" requests from another department? Tweak processes accordingly.

- Adjust the list based on new developments - maybe a new high-impact opportunity appears, or a critical deadline shifts. By staying agile, you maintain momentum instead of letting tasks accumulate and spiral into chaos.

WHY IT WORKS

The Priority Ladder demolishes passive complaints about being slammed. Instead, it imposes structure and demands accountability. By encouraging forced ranking, you can't just throw up your hands and say, "I have too much to do." Instead, you pick what's truly worth doing. Teams learn to let go of low-impact tasks and funnel energy into what genuinely moves the needle. The result? A culture where "busy" transforms into purposeful, and hustle leads to quantifiable outcomes rather than scattered burnout.

9

LEADING THROUGH CHANGE

"Talent alone isn't enough -
true catalyst leaders push
beyond what comes naturally,
embracing change and inspiring
others to do the same."

PART ONE:
THE DYNAMICS OF CHANGE MANAGEMENT

ARE YOU A CATALYST LEADER OR A DINOSAUR? BEZOS KNOWS THE DIFFERENCE

"Never be proud of your gifts."
Jeff Bezos

It's a declaration confronting conventional wisdom and striking at the heart of emotional intelligence and change leadership. Bezos believes your natural talents - starting gifts - are not the pinnacle of success. They're merely the foundation.

For leaders, the real challenge isn't leveraging these gifts but growing beyond them. Success demands emotional awareness, resilience, and the courage to lead through change. This is where catalyst leaders, those who not only lead change but also inspire it, shine.

EMOTIONAL INTELLIGENCE: THE INNER CATALYST

Imagine Bezos in 1994: a promising young Wall Street analyst surrounded by brilliance. He had it all - a six-figure salary, job security, and a clear path to partnership. But something gnawed at him.

Bezos observed his knowledgeable and naturally gifted colleagues settling into roles that came quickly. They were successful but stagnant, avoiding challenges that might stretch their emotional and professional boundaries.

Catalyst leaders, however, know that comfort is the enemy of growth. Bezos recognized the emotional toll of staying safe and avoiding risk. It takes self-awareness to see this trap and self-regulation to resist it. His decision to leave a stable career wasn't impulsive - it was deliberate, grounded in the clarity of his values and vision.

SELF-AWARENESS AND SELF-REGULATION:

Bezos demonstrates the first principles of emotional intelligence: understanding your inner drivers and managing your emotional responses. Walking away from security to pursue an unproven idea - selling books online - wasn't easy. It required courage and a deep belief in his ability to adapt to uncertainty.

This is a critical lesson for leaders: Emotional intelligence isn't just about managing relationships. It's about controlling yourself - your fears, ambitions, and courage to overcome discomfort. It's about being brave enough to face the unknown and lead your team through it, inspiring them with your bravery.

LEADING THROUGH CHANGE: FROM COMFORT TO CALLING

Bezos's journey is also a masterclass in change leadership. When he pitched his online bookstore idea to his boss, the response was cautious: "That's a great idea... for someone who doesn't already have a good job."

This advice represents the traditional leadership mindset: stay safe, protect what you have, and avoid unnecessary risks. But Bezos had a broader perspective. He believed leadership wasn't about maintaining the status quo but transforming it.

Catalyst leaders embrace change not as a threat but as an opportunity. They understand authentic leadership is about helping others navigate uncertainty, adapt to new realities, and grow.

TAKEAWAYS

1. **The Emotional Journey of Change** - Bezos experienced the discomfort of stepping away from a stable career. But he also recognized the emotional cost of staying. Change, while unsettling, is a necessary catalyst for growth.

2. **Communicating Change** - When Bezos began pitching Amazon to investors, he faced skepticism. Online shopping was untested, and many dismissed his idea as impractical. Yet he communicated his vision with clarity and conviction, focusing not on what was easy but on what was possible.

3. **Building Momentum** - Bezos's journey wasn't without setbacks, but he understood the power of incremental progress. His mantra, "Slow is smooth, and smooth is fast," reflects the importance of deliberate, consistent effort in driving change and instilling patience and persistence in leaders.

THE TALENT PARADOX: FROM FIXED TO ADAPTIVE LEADERSHIP

Many leaders fall into the trap of relying on their natural talents. These gifts can secure initial success but often become barriers to growth. Bezos's insight flips this script: "You can't be proud of your gifts because they were given to you. Be grateful for them, but be proud of the choices you make."

For catalyst leaders, this is a call to action. Talent alone isn't enough. Emotional intelligence - self-awareness, empathy, adaptability - matters more. It allows leaders to stretch beyond their gifts and embrace change challenges.

Key Questions for Leaders Facing Change:

- Will you rely on what comes easily or push into the unknown?

- Will you protect your comfort zone or grow through discomfort?

- Will you resist change, or will you lead others through it?

These questions define the difference between traditional and adaptive leadership. Adaptive leadership is about making growth the default, about pushing into the unknown, about embracing discomfort, and about leading others through change. It's about being the catalyst for transformation, not just in your organization, but in yourself and your team.

LEADING WITH EMOTIONAL INTELLIGENCE IN A CHANGING WORLD

Bezos's story is a powerful reminder that leadership is as much about mindset as strategy. It's about cultivating the emotional intelligence to face uncertainty and the adaptive leadership to turn change into opportunity.

As we navigate increasingly complex business landscapes - disrupted by globalization, AI, and shifting cultural norms - leaders must embrace the traits that Bezos embodied:

1. **Empathy for Team Needs** - Leading through change requires understanding the fears and concerns of those you lead. Bezos didn't just focus on his vision - he built Amazon's culture around experimentation, growth, and resilience, ensuring his team could navigate the risks of innovation, showing care and consideration for his team's needs.

2. **Resilience and Adaptability** - Change isn't linear. It's messy, unpredictable, and full of setbacks. Bezos's journey from an online bookstore to the world's most valuable company is a testament to the power of staying the course, adapting strategies, and learning from failure.

3. **Visionary Communication** - Great leaders don't just see the future - they inspire others to pursue it. Bezos didn't sell books; he sold a vision of what online commerce could be.

THE CATALYST'S CHALLENGE

At its core, Bezos's philosophy challenges every leader: Will you rely on your gifts, or will you make the bold choices that define a life of impact?

Catalyst leaders don't settle for what comes easily. They cultivate emotional intelligence, embrace change, and lead with purpose. They make deliberate choices that stretch beyond their natural talents, ensuring their legacy isn't written by their gifts but by their growth.

When you look back at your journey, what will you see? A life of comfort? Or a legacy of transformation?

ACTION ITEMS

Being a catalyst leader isn't about coasting on your title or waiting for change to happen. It's about creating momentum, smashing through barriers, and inspiring your team to reach levels they didn't even know they had in them. Here's how to *do the work*:

1. Make Growth the Default

Stop letting your team play it safe. The real enemy is comfort. Push your people to tackle projects that make them sweat a little. Comfort zones don't lead to greatness - discomfort zones do.

Take Action:

- Assign stretch goals to every team member - tasks that force them to learn, adapt, and expand their skill set.

- Hold weekly "growth huddles" to celebrate risks, even if they failed. Show your team that failure is fuel.

2. Kill the Fear of Change

People cling to what's working because they fear what might not. Your job is to crush that fear and turn it into excitement. Get your team to see change as an *opportunity*, not a threat.

Take Action:

- Share a story of a terrifying past change that paid off big. Make it personal. People connect with authenticity.

- Run a "Change Challenge" in which the team identifies one thing they can do differently next quarter and then actually does it.

3. Speak Vision, Not Tasks

Most leaders manage tasks; catalyst leaders sell *why* the work matters. People don't get fired up for spreadsheets - they want to know how their work changes the game.

Take Action:

- Kick off every major project with a rallying cry: What's the big goal? Why does it matter? Get your team emotionally hooked.

- When someone gets stuck in the weeds, remind them of the bigger picture. Every email and task ties to something epic.

4. Build Relentless Feedback Loops

Great leaders don't assume they're getting it right - they ask, listen, and pivot. A feedback loop isn't just a nice-to-have; it's the rocket fuel for leadership growth.

Take Action:

- Schedule monthly one-on-ones where you ask your team, "What's one thing I could do better as your leader?" and then act on it.

- Foster peer feedback - run team reviews where people constructively call out strengths and blind spots in a safe environment.

5. Light the Fire and Step Back

Catalyst leaders don't micromanage - they empower. Once you've set the vision and given clear direction, step back and let your team crush it. But stay close enough to course-correct if they veer off.

Take Action:

- • Give ownership of a key project to someone ready to level up, even if they're not 100% confident. Be their safety net, not their crutch.

- • During meetings, talk 20% of the time. Listen 80%. Empower your team to drive the conversation and the solutions.

6. Recognize Effort, Not Just Wins

If you only celebrate the endgame, you're missing the point. Success is built in the daily grind. Call out effort, risks, and the baby steps that lead to big leaps.

Take Action:

- Start a weekly "Wins & Risks" moment in team meetings. Shout out to someone who took a chance, whether or not it paid off.

- Write one handwritten thank-you note a week to a team member who's been grinding hard. Authenticity builds loyalty.

7. Be a Growth Junkie Yourself

You can't lead a team to growth if you're standing still. Show them what it looks like to evolve every damn day.

Take Action:

- Share one book, podcast, or insight you're consuming weekly with your team. Let them see you learning and leveling up.

- Attend a workshop or training yourself and share what you learned with the team. Show them that no one - even the boss - is done growing.

FINAL THOUGHTS

Catalyst leadership isn't just about *managing* people; it's about *unlocking* them. Keep your team up and moving forward, and watch as they turn small wins into massive momentum. You don't just lead - you transform. Let's go.

"They pivoted out of a flop by acknowledging - and transforming - resistance into renewed momentum."

PART TWO:
OVERCOMING RESISTANCE

FROM GAME OVER TO GAME CHANGER:
HOW SLACK TURNED A FLOP INTO A FORTUNE 500 COMPANY

Slack had a drastically different focus when it was still a fledgling startup. The company began as Tiny Speck, a small team building an online game called "Glitch." The original vision was bold: a whimsical, collaborative gaming universe for players worldwide.

Yet despite an enthusiastic core user base, the game struggled to gain traction in a saturated market. It drained resources, demanded constant updates, and left the company at a crossroads. Some employees passionately believed in the original vision. In contrast, others quietly admitted the game might never achieve the success needed to sustain the business.

The founders noticed something unexpected - an internal communication tool they'd developed for the team was proving far more valuable than the game itself. Engineers, designers, and community managers had grown accustomed to using this tool all day, every day, to streamline collaboration. This homegrown messaging platform was the real catalyst for productivity. Suddenly, the leadership team realized they might be on to something bigger than "Glitch."

But pivoting away from the game wasn't easy. Some employees felt betrayed at the idea of shelving their cherished creative project. Others were worried about job security. Investors questioned the viability of jumping into the already crowded software space. Resistance simmered beneath the surface, threatening morale and risking a mass exodus if not handled delicately.

The founders, however, decided to lean into this new direction with a deep commitment to their team's well-being. They recognized the root of their team's anxiety: fear of wasted effort, fear of the unknown, and fear of losing their identity as game developers.

Instead of bulldozing concerns, they set up open forums where every team member could voice doubts and propose ideas. They demonstrated how the pivot could leverage existing strengths - creativity, collaboration, user-centric design - while addressing real-world problems in workplace communication.

Gradually, employees began to see that shifting focus to the messaging platform wasn't a betrayal of creativity but a reinvention. The pivot happened. Slack was born. The business scaled rapidly, evolving into a staple of modern workplace communication.

That success was only possible because leadership acknowledged and addressed resistance rather than ignored it. By understanding those fears and methodically easing concerns, they transformed a potential mutiny into a unified march toward a bold new goal.

TAKEAWAYS

Recognizing Opportunity in an Unexpected Place: The Slack story is a great example of a company recognizing an opportunity in an unexpected place - their internal tool - and having the foresight to capitalize on it.

Importance of Addressing Internal Resistance to Change: How the founders handled the internal resistance to the pivot was crucial to its success. By acknowledging and addressing employee concerns, they were able to bring the team on board.

From Failure to Success: The story highlights how a perceived "failure" (Glitch's lack of commercial success) can lead to tremendous success if the company adapts and pivots.

Identifying and Addressing Resistance

You might think, "If my idea is good, why would my team resist it?" Newsflash: humans don't operate solely on logic. They're driven by emotions, biases, personal stakes, and the dreaded "what-if" scenarios. No matter how brilliant a strategy or how lucrative a market pivot might be, resistance is almost inevitable. Sometimes, it's overt, with team members voicing concerns or outright defiance. Other times, it's subtle - people nod politely but drag their feet when it's time to execute.

This chapter digs into the nitty-gritty of overcoming resistance in two major parts:

1. Identifying Sources of Resistance – Understanding where those fears and objections come from.

2. Strategies to Address Concerns – Providing concrete support, reassurance, and a sense of partnership so your people actually want to follow you.

SECTION 1: IDENTIFYING SOURCES OF RESISTANCE – UNDERSTANDING FEARS AND OBJECTIONS

Let's get brutally honest: you can't fix it if you don't know why people are pushing back. Identifying the root cause is the crucial first step. Sometimes resistance stems from job security fears - no one wants to feel replaceable. Sometimes, it's a worry about increased workload or new skills they're not confident they can master. Sometimes, it's a philosophical disagreement; maybe your team believes the new direction betrays the company's core values. Or perhaps they suspect leadership is just chasing trends without a solid plan.

Fear of the Unknown

One of the strongest drivers of resistance is plain old uncertainty. When you announce a major shift - be it a pivot in product strategy, a new organizational structure, or a technology overhaul - some people imagine the worst. They ask themselves: Will I still matter in this new scenario? Will I have to learn something I can't handle? Is this going to disrupt my work-life balance? These internal monologues often go unspoken, leading to rumor mills and half-truths filling the vacuum.

Ego and Status Quo

Another critical factor is ego. People get attached to their current roles, methodologies, or even office politics that keep them comfortable. A change might force them out of that comfort zone. They'd rather cling to what they know than risk being "newbies" again or losing internal influence. Some might feel they've "paid their dues" to the old system and resent having to adapt.

Past Failures

Your team has a memory. If they've lived through a disastrous reorganization before or seen half-baked initiatives come and go, skepticism is bound to run deep. They'll think, "Why should this time be any different?" Suppose you don't acknowledge that history and show how things will differ. In that case, they'll remain stuck, expecting yet another doomed exercise that wastes time and morale.

Gaps in Communication

Last but not least, a big cause of resistance is poor communication. If you're springing changes on people at the last minute, you're basically sending a signal: "I don't value your input." That's like pouring gasoline on a small campfire of skepticism, turning it into a forest fire of resentment. Without transparent dialogue, assumptions fill the void, and you end up with a swirling storm of misinformation, fear, and confusion. Open and honest communication is key to addressing these concerns and fostering a sense of inclusion and understanding.

SECTION 2: STRATEGIES TO ADDRESS CONCERNS – PROVIDING SUPPORT AND REASSURANCE

Once you know what's fueling the resistance - fear of obsolescence, uncertainty, or old baggage - it's time to tackle it head-on. This isn't about coddling your team or letting them call all the shots. It's about persuading them through empathy, clarity, and shared vision so that they opt-in rather than drag their heels or quietly sabotage progress.

Transparent Communication

First off, over-communicate. Explain the "why" behind your decision. Show the data, talk about market signals, and paint a compelling picture of the risks of staying put. Then, articulate the benefits of making the leap.

Don't sugarcoat the downsides or challenges; your team isn't stupid. By being transparent, you demonstrate respect. You also give them the cognitive tools to rationalize the change instead of feeling blindsided.

Co-Creation and Inclusion

No matter how brilliant you think your plan is, if your people feel zero ownership, they'll resent it. Look for opportunities to involve them in refining the strategy. Solicit feedback. Incorporate relevant suggestions. The more your team sees their fingerprints on the final approach, the more they'll champion it. This co-creation also helps you spot hidden pitfalls that you, from your vantage point, might be missing.

Skill Development and Support

If your plan requires new competencies - be it learning a new software platform or adopting agile methodologies - offer concrete training and resources. Fear often arises from a lack of confidence. People think, "I can't do that. I'll look incompetent." Show them you're invested in their growth. Provide workshops, mentorships, or even a buddy system. They'll be far less resistant if they see a clear path to becoming proficient in the new paradigm.

Small Wins and Pilot Projects

Grand transformations can feel overwhelming. Break it down. Launch a pilot project where a small team tests the new process, technology, or strategy. Celebrate any early success - no matter how modest. Those small wins serve as tangible proof that the change can work, deflating skeptics' doom-and-gloom narratives. Momentum builds. People start thinking, "Hey, maybe this isn't so scary after all." Over time, that pilot becomes the blueprint for broader implementation.

Empathy and Active Listening

Look, not everyone is going to jump on board the moment you say "go." Some might have personal circumstances or deep-seated concerns you never considered. Take the time to talk individually. Ask them, "What worries you most?" Then shut up and listen. Validate their feelings. That doesn't mean you agree with their every objection, but you acknowledge it. Often, just feeling heard eases half the tension.

Accountability and Consistency

If you promise resources or training, deliver them. Do it if you say you'll reevaluate the strategy in three months. If you claim your door is always open, then respond when someone knocks. Every unfulfilled promise fuels cynicism. Every consistent action fosters trust. Overcoming resistance is part logic, part emotional currency. If people trust you to keep your word, they'll ride the bumps in the road with far less friction.

TAKE ACTION

1. Conduct a "Resistance Mapping" Workshop

Gather your key leaders and stakeholders in a room. Dedicate at least an hour to systematically map out potential areas of resistance for your upcoming initiative. Start by listing every department or role that will be impacted. Next to each, brainstorm possible fears, questions, or objections. For example, if you're implementing new software, the finance department might worry about cost overruns, while HR might fear employees lacking training time. Then, propose a countermeasure for each concern - like additional budget clarity, training sessions, or open Q&A forums.

This exercise does two things:

- It pre-empts silent sabotage by acknowledging it before it festers.

- It helps you tailor your messaging and support specifically to each group's anxieties.

Have someone take detailed notes and then distribute these "Resistance Maps" to all involved. This fosters transparency and accountability. Everyone knows which concerns exist and who's responsible for addressing them.

2. Launch a "Concerns Hotline"

This might be as simple as a dedicated Slack channel or an online form. The key is that it provides a safe, easy way for employees to voice objections, worries, or even anonymous feedback about the change. Assign a trusted person or small team to monitor it. Don't just collect feedback - address it publicly or privately, as appropriate. People need to see that you take their concerns seriously and are not just paying lip service. Over time, this "hotline" can serve as an early-warning system for emerging issues and a valuable source of improvement ideas. If used well, it becomes a real-time pulse check on organizational sentiment.

FINAL THOUGHTS

Resistance isn't the enemy; it's the heat that forges your plan into something stronger. If you dodge objections, you'll end up with a brittle blueprint that shatters under pressure. Embrace the friction, tackle fears head-on, and watch your team transform from wary bystanders into passionate co-creators. Remember, no great revolution ever happened because everyone was polite and timid.

As Nelson Mandela once said, "It always seems impossible until it's done." So lock arms with your critics, rally your believers, and march forward. Your boldest moves deserve a team that's fully lit with conviction - ignite that spark by shattering resistance at its core.

"Momentum is the lifeblood of audacious goals - once you lose sight of those tangible wins, your revolution fizzles before it ever truly begins."

PART THREE:
SUSTAINING MOMENTUM

KICKSTARTER: THEY DIDN'T JUST BUILD A PLATFORM, THEY BUILT A REVOLUTION.

When Kickstarter was still a scrappy, up-and-coming crowdfunding platform, it found itself at a critical juncture as projects flooded in from around the globe.

The team had nailed the concept - connecting creators with backers to bring innovative ideas to life - but they struggled to maintain the energy that had fueled their early success. Requests for new features piled up, skeptics questioned the long-term viability of the business model, and internally, people started losing steam as daily tasks devolved into a repetitive grind. Leadership realized that if the company lost its fervor, it wouldn't just stall - the entire ecosystem of creators and backers could lose faith, taking Kickstarter's credibility down with it.

Instead of ignoring the issue, the founders took decisive actions to reignite the team's passion and sustain the platform's momentum. They implemented a transparent tracking system highlighting the most promising creative projects reaching their fundraising goals. Each milestone, such as a creator surpassing 100 backers or achieving 50% of their funding target, was showcased on a live dashboard in the office.

The excitement over each small victory was infectious. Simultaneously, the leadership promoted continuous beta testing for new site features, encouraging employees to gather feedback directly from users. This dynamic feedback loop enabled them to swiftly adjust - scrapping or refining features that didn't resonate and enhancing those that did.

Over time, both internal and external stakeholders rallied behind Kickstarter's mission with renewed vigor. The pace remained robust and accelerated, propelling the platform to global prominence in launching creative projects.

TAKEAWAYS

The Kickstarter narrative underscores the significance of actively managing growth and sustaining momentum, particularly during periods of rapid expansion. This is a crucial lesson that can be gleaned from their experience.

Transparency and Celebrating Successes: Using a transparent tracking system and celebrating milestones are effective ways to motivate teams and maintain enthusiasm.

User-Centric Approach: The emphasis on user feedback and continuous iteration is not just crucial; it's inspiring. It's a reminder that success is built on meeting the needs of your users, and it should motivate leaders to adopt a similar approach in their own organizations.

SUSTAINING MOMENTUM: KEEPING THE DRIVE ALIVE

If you think getting started is the hardest part, buckle up - keeping the energy going can be a whole new beast. Once the initial hype and adrenaline fade, your team might drift into autopilot or sink into complacency. But maintaining momentum isn't about cracking the whip 24/7. It's about creating an environment where consistent progress, adaptability, and celebration of wins come naturally.

SECTION 1: MONITORING PROGRESS – SETTING MILESTONES AND CELEBRATING ACHIEVEMENTS

Let's cut the crap: Everyone loves the feeling of achievement, but most organizations miss a huge opportunity by not systematically harnessing it. If you want your team to keep pushing, you need to make progress visible. We're talking about more than just a fancy dashboard or an occasional pat on the back; you need tangible mile markers that scream, "Hell yes, we're moving forward!"

1. **Setting Milestones** - A milestone isn't just a random deadline. It's a rallying point, a checkpoint where you stop, measure, reflect, and

recalibrate. Break your big objectives into smaller, digestible chunks - monthly revenue targets, weekly sprint goals, or feature rollouts. Why? Because reaching these micro-targets fuels motivation. People see tangible proof that they're inching closer to the larger vision. Think of it like climbing a mountain: each base camp reached is a mini-celebration, giving climbers the stamina to keep ascending.

2. **Celebrating Achievements** - Here's the unfiltered truth: if your team only hears from you when they miss a target, you're breeding resentment. Celebration isn't fluff. It's a potent reinforcer that shapes culture. When your people crush a goal - no matter how small - call it out. That doesn't mean you hand out participation trophies for breathing. But do something that stands out: shoutouts in Slack, a personalized note, or a brief "achievement spotlight" at the next team meeting. By regularly recognizing progress, you embed a sense of collective pride. That pride morphs into momentum, a forward-motion energy that propels the entire organization.

But let's be honest - milestones and celebrations aren't about coddling egos. They're about creating a rhythm that keeps everyone's eyes on the prize. They set a precedent for accountability: You commit to hitting certain goals by certain dates, and when you do, you get to revel in that success, fueling the next push.

SECTION 2: ADJUSTING COURSE WHEN NECESSARY - BEING FLEXIBLE AND RESPONSIVE TO FEEDBACK

The ability to pivot and adapt is powerful in sustaining momentum. It empowers leaders to take control of their organization's direction and respond effectively to changing circumstances.

Plot twists happen. Markets shift, technologies evolve, and sometimes your brilliant plan fizzles once reality sets in. Sustaining momentum demands that you're not just bulldozing forward blindly but keeping your ear to the ground for warning signs and opportunities to pivot.

1. **Listening to Internal and External Feedback** - Don't let your organization become an echo chamber. Yes, you set the vision, but your customers, partners, and even frontline employees see angles you can't. Make it easy for them to tell you what's not working or what could

be improved. That means quick surveys, open Q&A sessions, or designated feedback channels. Encourage radical candor: if someone sees a product flaw or a process bottleneck, they call it out before it grows into a crisis.

2. **Flexibility Over Rigidity** - Being a relentless visionary is great until you find yourself grinding toward a dead-end goal. Real leadership recognizes when a path isn't yielding results and it's time to switch gears. Adjusting course doesn't mean you lack conviction; it means you value results and are brave enough to shift to a more promising strategy. That agile mindset keeps the momentum alive because your team sees they're working toward a living, breathing goal that adapts to real-time conditions rather than a relic set in stone months or years ago.

3. **Fail Fast, Learn Faster** - Mistakes don't kill momentum - denial does. Own up to experiments that didn't pan out, glean the lessons, and pivot. This honesty fosters trust and keeps your foot on the gas pedal. If you hide or drag out failures, your team stays stuck in limbo, draining energy and morale.

Staying open to feedback and being unafraid to pivot means you keep your organization nimble. You can't sustain momentum by forcing a dead horse to run; you sustain it by shifting riders and direction when needed, ensuring the race goes on faster and stronger.

ACTION ITEMS

1. **"Momentum Tracker" Board**

   Set up a dedicated physical or digital board where milestones, progress updates, and celebratory wins are posted for everyone to see. Break down each primary goal into sub-goals, and let team members claim ownership over them. Update it weekly or bi-weekly. This public display ignites a friendly sense of urgency - nobody wants to see their name next to an incomplete task for weeks on end.

2. **"Pivot Drill" Workshops**

   Organize quarterly sessions where teams review what's going well and what needs to change. Encourage everyone to bring data, anecdotes, or user feedback that might suggest a need to pivot or refine the approach. The rule is that no idea is too ridiculous, and no critique is off-limits. Conclude with a short list of tangible experiments or changes. This normalizes adaptation and keeps momentum fresh by slashing bureaucratic inertia.

FINAL THOUGHTS

Momentum is the lifeblood of audacious goals, the difference between a flash-in-the-pan initiative and a lasting revolution. It's not just about firing the starting gun - it's about orchestrating a marathon, fueling runners with timely milestones, high-fives at each checkpoint, and unflinching adaptability. Run your team like an unstoppable force, and they'll move mountains faster than you can say "status quo."

As Muhammad Ali once said, "Don't count the days; make the days count." So step up, track your wins, pivot when you must, and never let the intensity wane. A leader who knows how to keep momentum alive can transform even the wildest vision into tomorrow's reality.

The Tides of Transition

LOW TIDE
(awareness)

Acknowledge the need for change and gather insights on potential reactions. This sets the foundation for effective communication.

RISING TIDE
(communication & engagement)

Roll out your vision clearly, addressing fears and highlighting benefits. The momentum starts picking up here.

HIGH TIDE
(overcoming resistance & implementation)

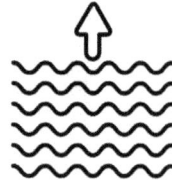

Tackle objections head-on. Provide the resources and support teams need to fully embrace new processes or structures.

EBB TIDE
(sustain & reflect)

Celebrate milestones, gather feedback, and refine your strategy. Don't let the momentum fizzle out - adjust course and prepare for the next wave of change if needed.

TOOL:
THE TIDES OF TRANSITION

Put your seatbelt on, and let's get one thing straight: Change isn't just inevitable - it's the fuel that'll push your business from "meh" to unstoppable. But you can't just drop significant changes on your team and hope for the best. You need a game plan.

That's where The Tides of Transition comes in: a straightforward, no-BS method to navigate the highs and lows of organizational change. When you embrace these "tides," you'll survive change and absolutely crush it.

Why It Works When You're Leading Through Change

The Dynamics of Change Management

- Phases of Change: The Tides of Transition outlines the emotional journey from initial shock to eventual acceptance, helping you address each phase head-on.

- Communicating Change: Just like the tide ebbs and flows, your communication strategy needs to rise at the right moments, ensuring nobody is left guessing or in the dark.

Overcoming Resistance

- Identifying Sources of Resistance: The Tides model encourages leaders to "check the currents" for underlying fears and objections before they swirl out of control.

- Strategies to Address Concerns: You can smoothly guide your team from resistance toward buy-in by timing your interventions (like the changing tide).

Sustaining Momentum

- Monitoring Progress: Just as you observe the tide's rise and fall, you regularly check in on milestones, celebrating small wins to keep morale afloat.

- Adjusting Course When Necessary: The Tides of Transition reminds you that change is rarely linear. You've got to stay flexible and pivot when new feedback rolls in.

What Is It?

Imagine four distinct stages that mirror the ocean's tides:

1. **Low Tide (Awareness)** - Acknowledge the need for change and gather insights on potential reactions. This sets the foundation for effective communication.

2. **Rising Tide (Communication & Engagement)** - Roll out your vision clearly, addressing fears and highlighting benefits. The momentum starts picking up here.

3. **High Tide (Overcoming Resistance & Implementation)** - Tackle objections head-on. Provide the resources and support teams need to fully embrace new processes or structures.

4. **Ebb Tide (Sustain & Reflect)** - Celebrate milestones, gather feedback, and refine your strategy. Don't let the momentum fizzle out - adjust course and prepare for the next wave of change if needed.

Each stage flows into the next, just like the ocean's tides.

How to Use It

In the Office

- Low Tide: Host a "state of the union" meeting to outline the need for change and invite questions.

- Rising Tide: Organize smaller breakout sessions or Q&As for teams to voice concerns and brainstorm solutions.

With Your Team

- High Tide: Provide clear frameworks, training, and real-time support as people adapt to new responsibilities or systems.

- Ebb Tide: Set up short debriefs and mini-celebrations after each successful milestone. Share lessons learned and highlight positive outcomes.

With Yourself

- Low Tide: Reflect privately on how you handle change. Are you resistant or eager? Understanding your own emotional triggers can help you lead with empathy.

- Ebb Tide: Keep a running journal of what worked, what didn't, and how you might improve next time. This helps you develop your personal "change leadership" style.

Change isn't something you endure; it's something you harness. The Tides of Transition gives you a simple, intuitive path to guide your team through the ups and downs of significant shifts.

When you manage each tide effectively - acknowledging the situation, engaging people, overcoming resistance, and sustaining the momentum - you transform chaotic transitions into stepping stones for growth. Now get out there and ride these tides to a bigger, better future!

LOOKING BEYOND THE PRESENT & INTO THE FUTURE

10

"DO YOU WANT TO LEAD
WITH AUTHENTICITY, BUILD
TRUST, AND UNLOCK YOUR
TEAM'S FULL POTENTIAL?"

SHAPING INDUSTRY FUTURES

Part One:
Becoming a Thought Leader

Part Two:
Collaborating Across Industries

Part Three:
Driving Industry Standards

"Don't wait for someone to call you a thought leader - make noise, share your insight, and let your bold ideas reshape the entire industry."

PART ONE:
BECOMING A THOUGHT LEADER

THOUGHT LEADERSHIP TO TRIUMPH:
HOW SHOPIFY BECAME THE GO-TO GURU FOR E-COMMERCE

When Shopify was just an idea among a small group of Canadian entrepreneurs, the team faced bigger, more established e-commerce competitors that seemed impossible to topple. Their platform began as a modest storefront for selling snowboards online - an experiment making digital retail more straightforward and personal. Investors weren't sold on yet another e-commerce tool, and many small retailers stuck to established channels like eBay or huge online marketplaces.

The founders realized they couldn't just offer a piece of software to stand out. They had to position themselves as the go-to authority on modern, scrappy entrepreneurship - championing that even the smallest business could hit a global scale with the right digital tools.

With that vision in mind, the co-founders started speaking at local tech events, penning blog articles on e-commerce trends, and hosting meetups for budding entrepreneurs. They didn't just discuss their platform; they addressed universal pain points: shipping logistics, branding, social media marketing, and online payment security.

They shared both the triumphs and failures they encountered, never shying away from the gritty realities of building an online business from scratch. Gradually, they became recognized voices in the digital retail space. Their insights appeared in business magazines, their presence was requested at more conferences, and their company - once overshadowed by established players - found itself leading the conversation on the future of e-commerce.

Over time, thousands of new merchants flocked to their platform, drawn not just by the software but by the authenticity and forward-thinking mindset they embodied. As a result, the company carved out a fiercely loyal following.

They rose from underdog status to a global powerhouse - spreading the gospel of entrepreneurship far and wide. What made this explosive growth possible wasn't just good code or slick marketing. It was thought leadership that resonated: a consistent voice that influenced an entire industry and built a thriving community around it.

TAKEAWAYS

Content Marketing as a Growth Strategy: Shopify's story demonstrates the effectiveness of content marketing and community building as a growth strategy, especially for startups competing in crowded markets.

Focus on a Specific Niche: By focusing on the needs of small businesses, Shopify carved out a distinct niche for itself.

Building Trust and Authenticity: The authentic and transparent approach taken by Shopify's founders wasn't just a strategy; it was a beacon of inspiration. Their honesty and openness helped build trust and credibility with their target audience, inspiring others to follow suit in their ventures.

THE WHY AND HOW OF THOUGHT LEADERSHIP

Let's get one thing straight: Thought leadership isn't about showing off. It's not about being famous or saying controversial things to get attention. Real thought leadership is about making a difference. You're sharing your ideas, knowledge, and unique perspective because you believe it can push your industry forward. You don't want to blend in with everyone else. You want to shape discussions, challenge old ways of thinking, and improve the whole industry.

In this chapter, we're diving into two main facets of thought leadership:

1. **Sharing Insights and Expertise** – Contributing meaningfully to industry discussions, seeding ideas that shift perspectives, and offering solutions to gnarly problems.

2. **Publishing and Speaking Engagements** – Cementing your credibility and influence by putting your name (and face) out there in front of the audiences that matter.

If you're rolling your eyes thinking, "I'm not a guru," or "I don't want the limelight," let's be blunt: If you have expertise - you're sitting on it and doing a disservice to your peers and field. People are hungry for authentic voices. They need leaders who can help them navigate an onslaught of change. That leader could be you - if you're willing to step up, speak out, and own your knowledge.

SECTION 1: SHARING INSIGHTS AND EXPERTISE – CONTRIBUTING TO INDUSTRY DISCUSSIONS

Why Your Voice Matters

You might assume everything worth saying has already been said. Wrong. The marketplace is evolving at breakneck speed - new technologies, demographic shifts, and changing consumer habits. Each shift opens a gap in collective understanding. Suppose you don't fill that gap with credible insights. In that case, someone else will - someone less qualified or pushing a narrow agenda. By sharing your expertise, you provide clarity in an environment often muddled by hype.

Finding Your Unique Angle

First, figure out what you bring to the table that's different. You've developed a unique marketing strategy or solved a problem in your industry that no one else has. Your expertise doesn't have to be groundbreaking. It just has to be real and helpful. The best way to find your unique angle is to ask yourself, 'What do people always ask me for advice about?' That's your unique perspective.

Active Participation in Industry Communities

Active Participation in Industry Communities: don't just lurk in LinkedIn groups or industry forums. Dive in. Answer questions. Pose your own thought-provoking queries. Attend or even host webinars. When you step into these discussions, do more than just repeat common knowledge - add value. Challenge assumptions, share real data or experiences, propose solutions, or poke at weaknesses in mainstream thinking. This active involvement is key to becoming a recognized voice in your industry, making you feel engaged and involved in the larger conversation.

Authenticity and Honesty

Authenticity and Honesty: look, everyone's allergic to corporate fluff. If your contributions sound like a press release, people tune out. Instead, be candid about struggles and lessons learned. Talk about that product launch that bombed and what it taught you or the pivot you made in your career that took you from floundering to flourishing. This vulnerability is what makes your insights compelling. It proves you're not parroting bullet points from a marketing deck but speaking from the trenches of real experience. This honesty and authenticity is what will earn you the trust and respect of your peers.

People start associating your name with quality knowledge when you consistently show up with fresh perspectives. They'll seek you out, quote you in their own discussions, and see your presence as a sign that something innovative is brewing. That's the heart of thought leadership - becoming a trusted reference point for others in your space.

SECTION 2: PUBLISHING AND SPEAKING ENGAGEMENTS – ESTABLISHING CREDIBILITY AND INFLUENCE

Why Going Public Matters

You can be the sharpest mind in your field, but if no one outside your immediate circle knows you exist, you're capping your impact. Publishing articles, speaking at conferences, or even hosting your own events magnifies your voice. It's the difference between influencing a handful of co-workers and shaping an entire sector's mindset. Plus, these avenues build intangible assets like credibility and trust - you become the figure people reference when they say, "I heard from so-and-so that...»

Choosing Your Medium

Whether it's a blog, a LinkedIn newsletter, a podcast, or a conference stage, pick channels that align with your audience's habits. If you're targeting a tech-savvy crowd, you may focus on social media and streaming webinars. Whitepapers or trade magazines hold more weight if you're in a more traditional industry. The key is consistency. You can't just drop one article and vanish. Keep a schedule - be it weekly, monthly, or quarterly - and stick to it. Over time, your consistent output signals reliability.

Building a Signature Style

Ever notice how some speakers just captivate the room from the moment they say "Hello"? Or how do certain writers have a voice so distinct that you'd recognize it without their byline? That's not an accident - it's cultivated. Aim for a signature style that reflects your personality. If you're irreverent, don't tame it; let that edge shine through your writing. If you're meticulous and data-driven, highlight the stats and logic others gloss over. People follow leaders who stand out, not those who fade into the backdrop of generic business jargon.

Networking Through Speaking

You're not just addressing attendees when you speak at an event - whether a panel or a keynote. You're connecting with fellow speakers, organizers, sponsors, and media outlets. These relationships can open doors for collaborations, co-authored articles, or future speaking gigs. Each stage becomes a networking hub, a chance to broaden your influence. Show up prepared, deliver value, and proactively connect with people afterward. That's how you transform a one-off talk into long-term relationships that amplify your message far beyond the event venue.

Turning Engagements into Momentum

Don't let your appearance or publication fade into oblivion. Repurpose that content. Got a conference talk? Convert its key points into a series of LinkedIn posts or a short e-book. Write a recap blog, embed the event video, and invite your audience to discuss the topic further. The real power of publishing or speaking isn't just the immediate impact - it's the ripple effect of continuing the conversation, building on the momentum, and driving deeper audience engagement.

So why does all this matter? Once recognized as a knowledgeable, original voice, you become a magnet for opportunities: brand collaborations, media interviews, and strategic partnerships. Instead of you always chasing down prospects or trying to prove your worth, people will come knocking on your door, eager to tap into your brain. That's the essence of being a thought leader - not for ego, but for expanding your platform so you can do bigger, better things that drive meaningful change.

TAKE ACTION

1. Develop a Content Calendar

It's time to get systematic. Brainstorm at least six topics you can speak or write about, tied to your domain expertise. These could be how-tos, trend analyses, or provocative opinions challenging the status quo. Plot them on a calendar - maybe one article every two weeks or one public speech per quarter. Block off writing and prep time so it doesn't get swallowed by daily tasks. If you can plan six months of content, you're miles ahead of the typical ad-hoc, last-minute scramble that kills momentum.

2. Embrace the "Pay-It-Forward" Rule

This is especially powerful for building your credibility. Identify two up-and-coming voices in your field - maybe they're junior professionals or lesser-known experts with something brilliant to say. Offer to co-author a piece or invite them to join you in a panel discussion. Elevating others doesn't steal your spotlight; it magnifies it. When you share your platform with promising talents, your brand gets an added dimension of generosity, and you foster goodwill that often circles back to you.

Final Thoughts

Don't wait for someone to anoint you, a "thought leader." The title is self-made, carved out by consistently showing up, speaking out, and delivering value that shifts how people see their world. If you're hoarding expertise, you're hoarding opportunity - not just for yourself but for everyone who could benefit from your vision. So stand up, grab the microphone (literal or metaphorical), and let the market hear your words.

As Ernest Hemingway famously wrote, "There is nothing noble in being superior to your fellow man; true nobility is being superior to your former self." Challenge yourself to share one more idea, spark one more conversation, and publish one more insight. In doing so, you evolve - and so does everyone you touch. That's how leaders become legends.

"They didn't just sign a rookie - they launched a cultural phenomenon and proved that cross-industry alliances can upend entire markets."

PART TWO:
COLLABORATING ACROSS INDUSTRIES

BETTING ON THE FUTURE: HOW NIKE TURNED A ROOKIE INTO A LEGEND (AND A BILLION-DOLLAR BRAND)

When Nike first ventured into the professional basketball scene, it was an audacious underdog in a market dominated by more prominent, entrenched athletic brands. Like David challenging Goliath, their bold move was not just about track and field gear but about stepping into the kingdom of bigger, flashier players with deep pockets and existing influence. This audacity, this willingness to take on the giants, is a lesson for all of us in the business world.

They found that opportunity in an up-and-coming rookie named Michael Jordan. He wasn't yet the global icon we know him as today - he was just a promising young athlete with raw talent and an electric style of play.

There were doubts on both sides: Would Jordan's star power be enough to make waves in the hyper-competitive footwear market? Would Nike be able to transfer its credibility from running to basketball? Some internal stakeholders at Nike were anxious about pouring resources into an unproven category, and Jordan had multiple offers from more established brands.

Yet both recognized the potential synergy - if they united, they could redefine the sneaker game, turning athletic shoes from practical sports gear into lifestyle must-haves.

They struck a bold partnership, birthing the Air Jordan line. Marketing campaigns spotlighted Jordan's acrobatic feats on the court. At the same time, design teams worked tirelessly to create performance-oriented and culturally disruptive shoes.

The collaboration wasn't just a corporate contract but a melding of brand DNA and personal flair. Jordan's on-court success and Nike's masterful marketing made Air Jordans a phenomenon. Within a few years, the footwear line spun off into its own brand extension, spawning legions of collectors and a global community of fans.

In the process, Nike didn't just capture the basketball market; it evolved into a cultural powerhouse, interwoven with music, fashion, and street culture worldwide. That massive success story sprang from one pivotal decision: to form a cross-industry (and cross-domain) alliance that leveraged a shared vision and complementary strengths.

BTW - Check out the 2023 movie 'Air' with Matt Damon, Ben Affleck, Jason Bateman, Marlon Wayans, Chris Messina, Chris Tucker, and Viola Davis.

TAKEAWAYS

Risk and Vision: Both Nike and Jordan demonstrated remarkable courage and vision. Nike took a significant risk by betting on a rookie, and Jordan made a bold choice by aligning with a company that wasn't a major player in basketball. However, their shared vision of what could be, their unwavering belief in their potential, and their courage to take on the challenge are truly inspiring.

Marketing Genius: Nike's marketing of the Air Jordan line was not just crucial, but also strategic and ingenious. They created a compelling narrative around Jordan and the shoes that deeply resonated with consumers, leaving a lasting impression and setting a new benchmark in the industry.

The 'Banned' Shoe: The Air Jordan 1, with its black and red color scheme, not only violated NBA uniform rules at the time but also sparked a revolution in the sneaker industry. This innovative design, which led to fines for Jordan every time he wore them, was famously turned into a marketing advantage by Nike with the 'Banned' campaign, leaving the audience fascinated and captivated by their boldness and creativity.

THE POWER OF COLLABORATION ACROSS INDUSTRIES

Here's the cold, hard truth: if you're staying locked in your own silo, you're leaving money on the table. No matter how innovative you think you are within your sector, you'll always be limited by the norms and constraints of that single environment. Collaboration across industries is like injecting fresh DNA into your bloodstream - it shakes up the status quo, introduces new perspectives, and fires up your capacity to innovate in ways you never imagined.

We're talking about forging alliances with companies, organizations, or individuals who aren't just outside your department - they're outside your entire industry's usual sphere. We're also talking about plugging into industry groups where you can rub shoulders with peers, adversaries, and future partners. Why does that matter?

In a world where technology is rewriting the rulebook at breakneck speed, the best ideas often emerge from the friction or fusion of multiple domains. Car manufacturers hooking up with software giants. Fashion labels pairing with tech startups. Banks forming strategic deals with fintech disruptors. The synergy possibilities are endless. For instance, the collaboration between Apple and Nike for the Apple Watch Nike+ is a great example of how two seemingly unrelated industries can come together to create a successful product. Another example is the partnership between Starbucks and Spotify, which brought music streaming to coffee shops, enhancing the customer experience.

In this chapter, we'll break it down into two sections:

1. **Partnerships and Alliances** – How to deliberately work with outside players to spark innovation.

2. **Participating in Industry Groups** – How to stay plugged into the networks, forums, and communities that shape your sector's future.

If you're still thinking, "We have enough internal talent; why collaborate?" let me give you a wake-up call: the speed of change today means no single organization has all the answers. Suppose you're not cross-pollinating ideas and solutions. In that case, you're sliding into irrelevance while your competitors are forging alliances that multiply their power. Don't let that be your legacy. However, it's important to note that cross-industry collaborations also come with their own set of challenges. These can include differences in organizational culture, conflicting priorities, and the need for effective communication and coordination. Understanding and addressing these challenges is crucial for the success of any cross-industry collaboration.

SECTION 1: PARTNERSHIPS AND ALLIANCES – WORKING WITH OTHERS TO DRIVE INNOVATION

Why Partnerships Matter

Think about this: every massive leap in the business world has come from bridging gaps. Hardware meets software. Content meets distribution. Physical retail meets e-commerce. By joining forces with a partner who excels where you're weak - or who has a foothold in a market you want to penetrate - you supercharge your efforts. It's like going from single-lane traffic to an express highway overnight.

But it's not just about plugging your gaps. It's also about cross-industry fertilization of ideas. This concept refers to the process of exchanging and combining ideas from different industries to create innovative solutions. An automotive company might team up with a green-energy startup to develop a new line of electric vehicles. A healthcare firm might join forces with a gaming company to design VR-based therapy programs. These collaborations don't just fill holes in each other's product lines; they spark brand-new innovations that no single player could've created alone.

Finding the Right Partners

Not every potential partnership will be a gold mine. The key is aligning on a few crucial elements:

1. **Shared Vision** - You don't have to agree on every detail, but your partnership is doomed before it starts if your strategic visions clash. Look for synergy: Do you both want to disrupt a stagnant industry? Are you both committed to sustainability or user-centric design? That common ground will serve as the glue that holds you together when inevitable challenges pop up.

2. **Complementary Strengths** - Partnerships should be about synergy, not redundancy. If you both bring identical skills to the table, what's the point? Instead, find a partner who excels in an area you lack, and vice versa. This interplay is where real breakthroughs happen.

3. **Cultural Fit** - Even if the strategic points line up, the alliance won't last if your cultures clash. If your organization thrives on openness and flat hierarchies, but your partner is a bureaucratic labyrinth, friction will kill momentum. You can't ignore cultural alignment.

Negotiating and Growing the Alliance

Sealing the deal is only the first step. Effective alliances evolve. You'll need to:

- **Set Clear Goals** - From the start, define what success looks like. Is it market share? A new product line? A proof-of-concept that can scale? Then, measure progress against these benchmarks.

- **Establish Transparent Communication** - Joint teams shared Slack channels or monthly face-to-face check-ins - whatever it takes to keep information flowing. Mistrust festers in the dark.

- **Adapt Over Time** - If the market changes or a better opportunity emerges, pivot. Partnerships can't be static. Evolve your objectives, add new projects, or even spin off a separate entity if that's what it takes to remain agile and innovative.

A well-managed partnership can turn ordinary efforts into extraordinary successes, driving massive leaps forward and forging new industry standards.

SECTION 2: PARTICIPATING IN INDUSTRY GROUPS - STAYING CONNECTED WITH PEERS AND TRENDS

The Value of Collective Wisdom

Isolation is the enemy of progress. Industry groups - be they associations, trade shows, conferences, or specialized forums - bring together the best minds (and sometimes the worst, but that's another story) to exchange ideas, debate trends, and shape policy. If you skip these gatherings, you're ignoring a massive, free resource that can keep you ahead of the curve.

Attending or even leading these forums puts you on the front lines of evolving tech and consumer behaviors. You'll discover new tools before they hit the mainstream, pick up on signals about where regulations might shift, and glean insights from peers tackling similar challenges. Nothing saves time and heartache, like learning from someone else's mistakes.

Building Your Network

Industry groups aren't just about absorbing information but about forging relationships. You might meet a competitor who's ironically the best collaborator for a side project. Or you might bump into a vendor who can solve a persistent supply-chain headache. The synergy from these spontaneous interactions often yields bigger breakthroughs than months of in-house R&D.

But remember: networking is a two-way street. Show up to give, not just take. Contribute your expertise, volunteer to lead panels, or offer mentorship in your domain. That generosity fuels your reputation, making people remember you as a go-to ally rather than just another face in the crowd.

Adapting to Industry Trends

Staying in these circles also means you can see the next wave of disruption. If you're plugged into relevant associations, you'll hear whispers of emerging technologies or shifting consumer sentiments. Instead of reacting late, you can pivot or double down early, positioning yourself as an industry leader rather than a laggard.

Plus, these groups often spark cross-industry alliances. You could connect with someone from a completely different sector who sees an angle you missed. That's how radical innovation is born. The friction or alignment of different perspectives can ignite game-changing ideas.

TAKE ACTION

Action Item 1: Mapping Potential Allies

Grab a whiteboard or a digital tool. Map out your entire ecosystem - vendors, competitors, complementary service providers, potential brand ambassadors, and thought leaders. Identify 2-3 entities you haven't considered partnering with that could bring massive value to your goals. Think outside your comfort zone. Then, create a short outreach plan: Who will contact them, what's the pitch, and what's the initial collaboration angle?

Action Item 2: Industry Immersion Calendar

Commit to a minimum of three significant industry events per year (conferences, expos, summits) and at least one specialized forum or association membership. Mark them on a calendar. Don't just attend passively - aim to speak, moderate a session, or lead a workshop. Post-event, schedule a debrief with your team to discuss new insights, potential alliances, or fresh ideas gleaned from the event. This ensures that conferences and trade groups become catalysts for action, not just boondoggles or academic outings.

FINAL THOUGHTS

Your next big leap won't come from barricading yourself in a conference room with your usual suspects. You need fresh energy, different perspectives, and audacious collisions of ideas. Partnerships across industries are like rocket fuel for your innovation engine, and participating in industry groups gives you a front-row seat to the next wave of disruption.

As Leonardo da Vinci famously said, "Everything connects to everything else." Embrace that connectivity. Let it shape your alliances, spark your creativity, and catapult you beyond the walls of your current market. Because if you're not forging new paths with unexpected partners, someone else will - while you're left asking, "Where did all my growth go?"

"Stop playing the game by everyone else's rules - be the one writing them."

PART THREE:
DRIVING INDUSTRY STANDARDS

THE $1 TRILLION LESSON: HOW CISCO BET ON OPEN STANDARDS AND WON

When Cisco was a scrappy networking startup in the late 1980s, the computing industry was a wild jungle of competing, often incompatible protocols. In large corporations, mainframes didn't talk nicely to PCs, different network hardware clashed, and IT staff spent countless hours bridging software gaps and debugging Frankenstein infrastructures. Cisco's core team saw a huge opportunity: if they could unify these scattered, conflicting standards under a cohesive framework, businesses worldwide would benefit from simpler, more reliable networking solutions - and Cisco would become a linchpin in the emerging internet era.

Early on, Cisco's founders realized that forging standards meant more than building a great router. They had to evangelize open protocols like TCP/IP, collaborate with hardware and software vendors, and even push back against well-entrenched, proprietary systems. This was not an easy task. Internally, some employees worried that aligning with open standards might undermine Cisco's ability to lock customers in with exclusive tech. Externally, established competitors fiercely guarded their closed ecosystems. The path to universal networking was paved with skepticism and fear of losing control. However, despite these challenges, Cisco remained steadfast in its commitment to open standards.

Still, Cisco went all-in. They joined industry working groups, hammered out specs with other tech firms, and argued relentlessly for solutions that would benefit the entire ecosystem - not just Cisco. They contributed engineers to standards bodies like the IETF (Internet Engineering Task Force), shaping the protocols that underpinned the modern internet. At times, forging consensus on these committees was like herding cats - everyone had their own agenda. However, Cisco stuck to the vision of making networks "just work" and persisted in championing common languages over proprietary dialects.

The outcome reshaped global computing. With consistent protocols, networks scaled seamlessly across campuses, countries, and eventually the world. Cisco evolved into a market leader, but it wasn't just about shipping more routers: the company became synonymous with stable, standardized connectivity. Thanks to this commitment to open standards and best practices, the entire tech industry advanced more quickly, fueling the rapid expansion of the Internet age. It all started with a decision: to look beyond Cisco's immediate business interests and lead a broad movement that set the benchmarks by which networks would be built.

TAKEAWAYS

Visionary Leadership: Cisco's founders, with their unwavering courage and determination, had a clear vision of the future of networking. Their strategic decisions, made in the face of skepticism and fear, not only benefited the entire industry but also inspired us all.

Long-Term Perspective: By prioritizing open standards over short-term gains, Cisco, with its clear vision and strategic decisions, positioned itself as a key player in the internet revolution. This long-term perspective reassures us about the company's commitment to the industry's future.

Importance of Collaboration: Cisco's active participation in standards bodies and collaboration with other companies was crucial to the success of this approach. This highlights the power of collective effort and the importance of collaboration in shaping the future of the industry.

INTRODUCTION: THE IMPERATIVE TO DRIVE INDUSTRY STANDARDS

Driving industry standards might sound like a job for big associations and government committees, but let's be clear: it can also be your ticket to significant influence and long-term market leadership. You're not just building a product or offering a service but shaping how an entire sector operates. That's a far cry from just hustling for the next sale. Establishing norms and benchmarks can unlock exponential growth. Why? Because a stable, predictable environment lets everyone innovate faster without reinventing the wheel.

There's a fundamental difference between simply "following" best practices and actually defining them. If you want to be a mere player in your industry, you can rely on other people's guidelines. But if you're itching to leave a dent in the universe, you step up and dictate the rules of the game. That can mean championing an open-source approach, setting certification criteria, or heavily contributing to policy discussions that steer entire markets. In fact, your active participation in these policy discussions can significantly influence the direction of your industry.

This chapter breaks down two vital elements of driving industry standards:

1. **Advocating for Best Practices** – The art of championing benchmarks that move the entire sector forward, not just your own bottom line.

2. **Influencing Policy and Regulation** – The power (and responsibility) of engaging in the legislative, regulatory, and broader governance processes that shape the future of your field.

In a world evolving at warp speed, the ones who lead the standards lead the industry. Full stop.

SECTION 1: ADVOCATING FOR BEST PRACTICES – LEADING INITIATIVES THAT SET BENCHMARKS

Why Best Practices Matter

People often talk about "best practices" like checklists or guidelines. But in reality, best practices can become the lifeblood of an industry. They define quality, ensure safety, and speed up adoption by reducing confusion and friction. The market benefits when everyone can align on specific baseline standards, from small startups to global titans. Products integrate more smoothly, consumers gain confidence, and innovations emerge faster.

By taking the initiative to articulate and push these standards, you become a recognized authority. Instead of competing on shady or ambiguous terms, you elevate the conversation to what genuinely benefits the sector's evolution. This positioning is not just altruism - it also cements your brand as synonymous with reliability and thought leadership. Moreover, advocating for best practices can lead to significant market benefits, such as smoother product integration, increased consumer confidence, and faster emergence of new innovations.

IDENTIFYING GAPS IN EXISTING NORMS

Where do you start? Begin by pinpointing the holes in your industry. Which processes are a constant headache for everyone? Where are consumers repeatedly burned by subpar products or misleading marketing? Which technologies remain partially incompatible because no one's hammered out a unified approach?

Scan online forums, talk to customers, and even chat with your so-called competitors. Usually, everyone complains about the same problems. If no recognized authority is addressing them, that's your golden chance. It's not about whining; it's about stepping in to define a new "gold standard."

CRAFTING AND DISSEMINATING YOUR FRAMEWORK

Once you've identified a gap, you can't just wave your hand and say, "We have new rules, follow them!" That's laughable. You must craft a credible framework or set of guidelines. That could be a whitepaper detailing recommended protocols, a certification program with strict criteria, or a user manual for safe, efficient deployment. Whatever form it takes, your solution must be:

1. **Evidence-Based** – Cite research, case studies, and pilot programs. Show you're not just guessing.

2. **Practical** – No one will adopt it if it's too complex or academic. Keep it actionable and user-friendly.

3. **Adaptable** – Expect iteration. The first version might not be perfect, so be open to revising as the industry's needs evolve.

Next, push it out to the world. Host webinars, speak at conferences, invite feedback, and refine. Don't be precious about it. The best standards are shaped by real-world input. The more inclusive you are, the more buy-in you'll get.

RALLYING ALLIES

No single company can unilaterally impose standards on an entire sector, no matter how big. You need allies. That means bringing on board key influencers - suppliers, major clients, adjacent technology partners, and even a few well-chosen rivals. If you can get a critical mass of the market aligned behind your framework, it gains a life of its own.

Keep an ear to the ground for new players or disruptive startups who might challenge or improve your guidelines. Fold them in if they propose meaningful enhancements rather than digging your heels in. Remember, the goal is driving universal acceptance, not hogging credit.

SECTION 2: INFLUENCING POLICY AND REGULATION - ENGAGING IN CONVERSATIONS THAT SHAPE THE FUTURE NAVIGATING THE POLICY ARENA

While best practices can emerge organically, full-blown industry standards often intersect with government or international bodies. That's where policy and regulation come in. Laws can make or break your industry's future. Suppose you leave legislation up to politicians with a surface understanding. In that case, you're rolling the dice on your business environment.

Stepping into policy discussions isn't for the timid. You'll deal with bureaucrats, regulators, and occasional hotheaded activists. But if you do it right - bringing data, reasoned arguments, and broad stakeholder support - you become a respected voice that shapes not just your corner of the market but the entire legislative framework around it.

BUILDING CREDIBILITY WITH REGULATORS

Regulators don't want to be duped. They're tasked with protecting public interest, ensuring fair competition, and avoiding crises. If you show up with a self-serving angle, they'll sniff it out in seconds. If you bring thorough research, highlight consumer benefits, and demonstrate that your proposed rules are balanced, you'll find open ears.

Case in point: If your sector faces concerns over environmental impact, proactively drafting guidelines for eco-friendly production or disposal can earn regulator trust. You basically save them the hassle of forming a committee to figure it out. The result? You get to shape the conversation, limiting unpredictable or draconian legislation that would stifle everyone.

COALITIONS AND LOBBYING

You don't have to do this alone. Form or join a coalition of businesses with overlapping interests. That's especially useful when tackling complex or controversial topics - privacy laws, environmental standards, or antitrust concerns. By uniting under a shared banner, your collective clout speaks louder than a single brand's voice.

Professional lobbyists can also be part of your toolbox - if used ethically. They understand the labyrinth of legislative processes and can help you target the right decision-makers with the right arguments. Just keep your moral compass intact: shady backroom deals might momentarily get you a win, but they erode trust and can explode into PR nightmares.

EVOLVING POLICY AS TECHNOLOGY SHIFTS

Nothing stands still, least of all technology. If you manage to pass or influence a key regulation, don't assume it's set in stone. Monitor the market's evolution, gather new data, and be ready to revisit the rules. By staying agile, you ensure the legislative environment remains a springboard for innovation rather than a straitjacket.

ACTION ITEMS

Action Item 1: Launch a "Standards Summit"

Organize a half-day or full-day summit featuring key players in your field - competitors, suppliers, academics, consumer advocates. The goal: identify the top three recurring pain points or inefficiencies that hamper your industry. Work through potential frameworks or guidelines in a structured workshop format. Document the outcomes, assign the following steps, and commit to a follow-up within 90 days.

This summit isn't a superficial networking event; it's a crucible for hashing out real solutions. If successful, you'll emerge with a rough blueprint for best practices and spark the creation of a new consortium or working group.

Action Item 2: Develop a Policy Playbook

If regulations in your industry are either outdated or nonexistent, take the lead by drafting a "Policy Playbook." Outline recommended guidelines for operations, consumer protections, or environmental standards - whatever the pressing issues are. Gather feedback from internal teams, external experts, and user groups. Then, present this playbook to relevant lawmakers, agency heads, or trade associations.

The key is to show how these guidelines benefit all stakeholders, not just your bottom line. Frame it as a common-sense approach to fostering innovation while safeguarding public interests. This approach positions you as a credible partner in future policy discussions, opening doors for deeper influence down the line.

FINAL THOUGHTS

Stop playing the game by everyone else's rules - be the one writing them. When you champion best practices, you rise above petty competition, building the very platforms on which future innovations stand. When you shape policy, you don't just profit - you mold the landscape for everyone who comes after you.

Or, as Benjamin Franklin once said, "If you would not be forgotten as soon as you are dead and rotten, either write things worth reading or do things worth writing." Go do both: pen the standards that will be read for decades and build the alliances that make your name worth remembering.

The Skyline Approach

PREVIEW THE HORIZON

Scan emerging trends, technologies, and market shifts. Publish your take - let the industry know you have eyes on what's next.

Scan Trends Share Insights

BRIDGE KEY ALLIANCES

Seek out complementary partners, even if they're outside your direct field. Cross-industry ideas often spark the biggest leaps.

Collaborate Across Sectors

SET THE STANDARD

Identify what "excellence" looks like. Advocate for best practices, propose frameworks, and step into policy discussions to shape how things get done.

Define Best Practices & Policies

ELEVATE THE FUTURE

Maintain momentum by continuously refining your approach. Keep feeding insights, alliances, and standards back into the pipeline so your industry doesn't stagnate.

Refine Innovate Stay Agile

TOOL:
THE SKYLINE APPROACH

Listen, if you're singularly focused on what's in front of you today, you will miss the bigger picture. The future belongs to leaders who scan the horizon, build game-changing collaborations, and step up to influence how entire industries evolve.

That's exactly what The Skyline Approach is all about - spotting those high-level vantage points, connecting with the right people, and shaping tomorrow's standards. So let's get you out of the weeds and onto the high ground. Ready? Let's roll!

Why It Works When You're Shaping Industry Futures

Becoming a Thought Leader

- Sharing Insights and Expertise: The Skyline Approach encourages you to "take the long view," which translates to publishing fresh perspectives and speaking confidently about where your industry is headed.

- Publishing and Speaking Engagements: Once you set your sights on the bigger picture, you naturally generate resonant content, making you the voice people look to for guidance.

Collaborating Across Industries

- Partnerships and Alliances: Like a skyline brings multiple buildings together, this method helps you align with different sectors, fueling innovation and fresh ideas.

- Participating in Industry Groups: By actively engaging in these communities, you stay connected to the trends shaping your skyline - and help paint a better view for everyone.

Driving Industry Standards

- Advocating for Best Practices: From that elevated vantage point, you can spot what's working (and what's not), then push for policies and practices that level up the entire playing field.

- Influencing Policy and Regulation: With the Skyline Approach, you're not just reacting to changes - you're up there with the people who write the rules, shaping the future firsthand.

What Is It? The Skyline Approach

Think of it as four key steps, each representing a natural progression toward industry leadership:

1. **Preview the Horizon** - Scan emerging trends, technologies, and market shifts. Publish your take - let the industry know you have eyes on what's next.

2. **Bridge Key Alliances** - Seek out complementary partners, even if they're outside your direct field. Cross-industry ideas often spark the biggest leaps.

3. **Set the Standard** - Identify what "excellence" looks like. Advocate for best practices, propose frameworks, and step into policy discussions to shape how things get done.

4. **Elevate the Future** - Maintain momentum by continuously refining your approach. Keep feeding insights, alliances, and standards back into the pipeline so your industry doesn't stagnate.

Each step feeds into the next, forming a continuous cycle of forward momentum and industry leadership.

How to Use It

In the Office

- Preview the Horizon: Kick off Monday meetings with a quick review of upcoming trends or events. Encourage team members to share articles, insights, or new tech they've discovered.

- Bridge Key Alliances: Organize monthly "external expert" sessions. Invite someone from a different industry to speak, sparking ideas you can adapt to your own field.

With Your Team

- Set the Standard: Facilitate workshops where the team brainstorms best practices. Present these ideas to industry groups or publish them in a white paper - adding credibility to your collective voice.

- Elevate the Future: Run quarterly retrospectives. Ask, "Where did we lead the pack, and where did we lag?" Then, fine-tune your forward strategy based on real-world learnings.

With Yourself

- Preview the Horizon: Commit to reading one industry-forward article or research paper daily. Keep a notebook reflecting on how these trends intersect with your leadership goals.

- Elevate the Future: Revisit your personal brand strategy every six months. Are you pushing yourself to speak, write, and engage at the right level to shape your industry's skyline truly?

Look, if you want to be more than just another player in your market, you've got to step up and shape what comes next. The Skyline Approach puts you on the fast track to authentic thought leadership, meaningful partnerships, and tangible impact on the standards that define your industry.

It's about raising the bar for everyone - and having a blast while you do it. So get out there, preview that horizon, build the right bridges, set the standard, and elevate the future.

11

"ARE YOU READY TO
UNLOCK YOUR LEADERSHIP
POTENTIAL, EMPOWER
YOUR TEAM, AND CREATE A
LEGACY THAT LASTS?"

THE PATH FORWARD

Part One:
Personal Leadership Development

Part Two:
Leading Your Team's Transformation

Part Three:
Sustaining Catalyst Leadership

"He walked the aisles every day, turning real-world feedback into a blueprint for unstoppable growth - proving that true leadership starts on the ground floor."

PART ONE:
PERSONAL LEADERSHIP DEVELOPMENT

LEADERSHIP BY EXAMPLE: SAM WALTON'S BLUEPRINT FOR SUCCESS

When Sam Walton embarked on the journey of opening his first Walmart store in Arkansas, he was met with formidable challenges. The retail landscape was dominated by big-city chains with superior resources, brand recognition, and streamlined supply chains.

Walton's fledgling operation faced skepticism from suppliers who saw more potential in big-city opportunities. Even his own team sometimes questioned the viability of a discount retail model in rural America. Despite these daunting odds, Walton remained steadfast in his vision: to provide unbeatable value to everyday folks and foster a people-first workplace culture.

Walton understood early on that his leadership would be the linchpin of his venture's success. He meticulously crafted a personal plan to evolve as a leader who was both hands-on and forward-thinking. He didn't just read every book on retail operations and management, but he also walked the aisles of his store daily, engaging with employees and customers.

This direct contact constantly challenged him to improve. He would observe which displays were ineffective, seek staff feedback, and refine his communication style to ensure everyone felt invested in the store's success. These small leadership experiments over time evolved into a blueprint for scaling Walmart. He introduced morning team rallies to keep employees informed and inspired, implemented cost-saving measures that his staff understood and championed, and set ambitious expansion milestones that gave everyone a stake in the store's forward momentum.

The results were staggering. Walmart expanded from a single location to a national powerhouse, revolutionizing the discount retail industry. But beyond the sales figures and the national footprint, Walton's most significant achievement was building a culture rooted in empathy, transparency, and relentless curiosity about what worked and what didn't.

His personal leadership plan didn't just transform him from a small-town retailer into a visionary CEO; it created an entire generation of future leaders at Walmart who echoed his ground-level approach: staying close to the operation, listening to employees, and never resting on yesterday's success.

TAKEAWAYS

Customer Focus: Walton's unwavering focus on providing value to customers was a key driver of Walmart's success.

Employee Empowerment: He believed in empowering his employees and giving them a stake in the company's success.

Continuous Improvement: Walton's relentless pursuit of improvement was a driving force behind Walmart's success. He never settled for the status quo, always seeking ways to enhance the business and encouraging his employees to do the same. This dedication to growth and progress is a powerful inspiration for leaders at all levels.

INTRODUCTION: CRAFTING YOUR LEADERSHIP GROWTH

If you think leadership is an innate trait some people are born with, you're missing the bigger picture. It's not about having a certain gene or a special personality quirk - it's about deliberate development. You can't just coast on your natural charisma or your track record of wins. If you're complacent, the market will outgrow you, your skills will become stale, and your team will stagnate.

This is the final chapter for a reason: Everything we've discussed so far - igniting innovation, navigating technological transformations, fostering emotional intelligence, driving industry standards - means nothing if you, the leader, aren't growing alongside it. Leadership is never a static role; it's a living, breathing process. You need a systematic plan to elevate your capabilities and a willingness to invite feedback (even the kind that stings) if you want to reach your next level of impact. Having a structured plan in place will keep you organized and prepared for the journey ahead.

SECTION 1: CREATING A LEADERSHIP PLAN – SETTING GOALS FOR GROWTH AND IMPROVEMENT

Let's be brutally honest: The moment you think you've "arrived" as a leader, you've already started falling behind. The marketplace evolves too fast. Your team's expectations grow, too. If you're not actively honing your leadership acumen - learning new strategies, refining your emotional intelligence, or expanding your network - you're sending a message to your people that good enough is good enough.

What is a Leadership Plan, Exactly?

Think of it like a personal development roadmap. Sure, you have strategic plans for your company, but do you have one for your leadership journey? It outlines:

1. **Core Skills to Master** – Maybe you're a visionary strategist but a clumsy communicator. Or you're great with one-on-ones but struggle to inspire crowds at town halls. Identify the skills that will most impact your organization's future.

2. **Milestones and Timelines** – Don't just say, "I want to be better at public speaking." Specify, "Within three months, I'll deliver a keynote at a local industry meetup." Tie your skill-building efforts to actual deadlines so it doesn't become a vague aspiration.

3. **Resources and Learning Approaches** – Books, online courses, podcasts, executive coaches - whatever. Lay out what you'll use and how often. For instance, "Attend a monthly workshop on advanced negotiation techniques" or "Complete one leadership-focused audiobook per week."

4. **Accountability Mechanisms** – You can't rely on your motivation. Commit to a system - maybe you'll share your goals with a peer or get periodic check-ins with a mentor. This keeps you honest and prevents your aspirations from falling by the wayside.

Why Goals Matter

Setting clear, actionable goals is a crucial aspect of a leadership plan. Without specific targets, your personal leadership growth remains a vague idea that you might get to 'someday.' Goals force you to confront your weaknesses head-on, rather than just pay lip service to the notion of self-improvement. They also provide a sense of momentum - each milestone you hit affirms that you're on the right track.

Customization is Key

Don't blindly copy someone else's plan. Your organization, team dynamic, and personal style are unique variables. Adapt best practices to fit your reality. For example, suppose your company thrives on flat hierarchy and collaboration. In that case, your leadership growth might focus on mastering facilitation skills rather than top-down directives. If your environment is fast-paced and cutthroat, you may need to sharpen your decisive action-taking.

Self-Awareness: The Core Ingredient

Before you even start setting your goals, it's crucial to conduct a thorough self-assessment of your strengths and weaknesses. Are you prone to micromanagement? Do you struggle under pressure? Are you too quick to take on tasks that should be delegated? This honest self-audit, aided by some of the feedback methods we'll discuss later, ensures your plan targets the right areas for growth.

SECTION 2: SEEKING FEEDBACK AND MENTORSHIP - LEARNING FROM OTHERS TO ENHANCE SKILLS

You can read all the leadership books in the world - still, there's no substitute for external perspective - especially from people who've been there, done that, or observed you in action. Feedback and mentorship provide that outside vantage point that often reveals your blind spots.

The Role of Feedback

We humans are notoriously bad at evaluating ourselves. We rationalize or downplay our weaknesses. That's why real-time, honest feedback is like gold. It tells you how your decisions affect others, which parts of your communication style are confusing, and where your emotional intelligence might be faltering.

But feedback isn't always served on a silver platter. Sometimes, you have to dig for it. Ask direct questions: "What's one thing I could do differently to make our meetings more effective?" or "If you were me, what would you change about my management style?" Normalizing these questions creates a culture where your team isn't afraid to speak up.

Mentorship: The Shortcut to Growth

A mentor is someone who's navigated the path you're on, or at least one with parallels. They know the pitfalls, make the mistakes, and glean insights that could save you from learning everything the hard way. Sure, you can find tidbits of wisdom in podcasts and books, but a one-on-one mentorship relationship is a game-changer. A mentor can tailor advice to your specific challenges, hold you accountable, and expand your network by introducing you to the right people.

Finding the Right Mentors

Don't assume your mentor has to be older or from the same industry. Some of the best mentorships come from lateral industries where leadership principles overlap, but the context is fresh. The key is that they have the expertise or perspective you lack and are willing to invest time in your growth. When approaching a potential mentor, be prepared: know what you want to learn, show that you respect their schedule, and highlight mutual benefit, whether it's your fresh viewpoint or your network.

Being Coachable

The world's feedback and mentorship won't help if you're defensive or dismissive. Coachability is a mindset. You must be ready to accept critiques and suggestions even when they feel uncomfortable. Mentors aren't there to coddle you - they're there to challenge you so you can transform. That's the price of leveling up: you have to let go of your ego and trade comfort for relentless self-improvement.

TAKE ACTION

1. **Draft a 90-Day Leadership Plan**

- Start by listing 2-3 leadership competencies you want to improve or acquire (e.g., strategic storytelling, conflict resolution, advanced delegation).

- Assign each competency at least one measurable goal (e.g., "I'll resolve three team disputes using a structured process within the next two months").

- Identify resources (books, courses, or workshops) and people (potential mentors or peer coaches) who can accelerate your progress.

- Schedule monthly check-ins with yourself or a colleague to track achievements and roadblocks.

2. **Establish a Personal "Feedback Loop"**

- Handpick 3-5 individuals - could be direct reports, peers, or even clients - whose opinions you value.

- Invite them to provide candid input on your leadership behaviors monthly or quarterly. Encourage them to highlight both strengths and areas for improvement.

- Make sure to respond graciously. A simple "Thank you for sharing that. Can you give an example?" shows you're not just mining for praise but actively searching for growth cues.

- Integrate their feedback into your leadership plan, adjusting or refining your goals as necessary.

Tool: Rich's "Coaching Matrix"

My Coaching Matrix is a simple yet powerful tool for planning and tracking your personal leadership growth (I use it with all of my clients):

Creating a Leadership Plan:

- **Goal Setting:** Use the matrix to categorize development goals, plotting them in the "Technical Skills" or "Soft Skills" rows, and under "Immediate Goals" or "Long-Term Goals," creating clarity around your development priorities.

- **Categorize each goal into the appropriate quadrant:**

  - **Technical Skills + Immediate Goals**: For example, "Learn how to use new project management software" or "Become more efficient in creating budget reports."

  - **Technical Skills + Long-Term Goals:** For example, "Master advanced data analytics," "Obtain a specific industry certification," or "Deepen knowledge of our business operations."

  - **Soft Skills + Immediate Goals:** For example, "Improve meeting facilitation skills," "Give more effective feedback," or "Improve active listening skills."

  - **Soft Skills + Long-Term Goals:** For example, "Develop stronger strategic leadership," "Improve conflict resolution," or "Become a more effective communicator."

- **Balanced Development:** It helps you consider immediate and long-term goals across different skill sets, ensuring your leadership plan is well-rounded.

- **Actionable Plan:** The matrix helps break down development goals into clear, actionable steps.

- **Visual Prioritization:** It provides a clear overview of your development priorities and opportunities.

Seeking Feedback and Mentorship:

- **Identifies Gaps:** The matrix highlights areas where you might need external help, feedback, and guidance, showing where mentorship would be most valuable.

- **Targeted Mentorship:** Use the matrix to clarify the type of mentorship needed and match areas of need (e.g., seek a mentor to improve technical skills or seek mentorship for strategic leadership).

- **Feedback-Driven Growth:** It encourages reflection on your current strengths and weaknesses in order to seek valuable, specific feedback.

- **Progress Tracking:** Revisit the matrix regularly to track your progress in all quadrants, which helps identify areas for continued development or any shifts in focus.

By using my Coaching Matrix, you create a roadmap for personal leadership development, actively identifying opportunities for growth, seeking guidance, and tracking progress.

FINAL THOUGHTS

You've made it this far - good. But knowledge without execution is just a pipe dream. It's time to raise the stakes for yourself. Write your leadership plan like it's your next blockbuster product launch. Seek mentors as if your future depends on it - because it does.

As Bruce Lee once said, "Knowing is not enough, we must apply. Willing is not enough; we must do." So, turn these pages into a springboard, not a mere memory. Commit to your growth. Attack your weaknesses. Multiply your strengths. If you're bold enough to transform yourself, you'll ignite a chain reaction that transforms your team and the very industry you serve.

"He shattered the cheap-carnival mindset by pouring everything into cleanliness, courtesy, and magic - proving the guest-first ethos could spark an entire revolution in family entertainment."

PART TWO:
LEADING YOUR TEAM'S TRANSFORMATION

THE GUEST EXPERIENCE IS KING: HOW WALT DISNEY REDEFINED FAMILY ENTERTAINMENT

When Walt Disney first envisioned building a world-class theme park - what would become Disneyland - he didn't just face budget shortfalls and skeptical investors; he confronted an entire entertainment industry that thought he was crazy. His courage and determination in creating an immersive, family-focused amusement experience with staff meticulously trained in customer satisfaction was unprecedented.

He was told that amusements were supposed to be cheaply built, quickly forgotten, and run by employees who cared more about punching a clock than delighting a crowd. Investors balked at his insistence on cleanliness, staff courtesy, and constant innovation. They believed he was inflating costs and overcomplicating a simple business model.

Refusing to be swayed, Disney poured his personal finances into the project. He partnered with television networks, striking deals that funneled publicity and partial funding for the construction of Disneyland. He hammered out new operational guidelines, training manuals, and a performance ethos emphasizing an almost theatrical approach to guest services.

Engineers, designers, and park staff were all challenged to think beyond the norms of the day - actively encouraged to point out inefficiencies or potential enhancements in real-time. This environment became a testing ground for new technologies like animatronics and advanced ride systems.

In the end, Disneyland opened to overwhelming fanfare. Sure, there were hiccups: plumbing issues, insufficient rides for the initial demand, and staff exhaustion from the grueling ramp-up. However, the positive response to the overarching concept - an immersive, clean, guest-first amusement park - validated Disney's vision.

He'd effectively reshaped theme parks and the entire leisure and hospitality sector. Families raved about the experience; engineers found fertile ground for creative expansions, and rival parks scrambled to copy and catch up. Walt Disney didn't just build a place - he catalyzed a cultural shift, setting higher standards for what a "park" could offer and reorienting the entire industry around guest satisfaction.

KEY TAKEAWAYS:

Visionary Leadership: Walt Disney's unwavering vision and determination were not just essential, but they were the driving force behind the creation of Disneyland. His ability to see beyond the present and envision a future that others couldn't even imagine is a testament to the power of visionary leadership.

Focus on the Guest Experience: The emphasis on creating a magical and immersive experience for guests was a key factor in Disneyland's success.

Innovation and Technology: Disney's willingness to embrace new technologies and push the boundaries of what was possible in theme park design and operation was also crucial.

INTRODUCTION: LEADING THE FINAL CHARGE

We've traveled a long road - discussing emotional intelligence, technological transformations, collaboration, and forging industry standards. But none of that matters if you can't bring your team along for the ride. Ultimately, you stand at a crossroads: either you implement these catalyst principles and spark real transformation, or you file them away as "nice ideas" and watch the status quo remain unchallenged.

This is your last chapter - not just in this book but in the sense of your final directive: leading your team's transformation. Because you can't do it solo. As a leader, you have the power to initiate and guide this transformation. You need a groundswell of commitment from the people who will execute the big ideas, champion the new initiatives, and embody the cultural shifts daily.

So let's break it down:

1. **Implementing Catalyst Principles** – Taking the conceptual frameworks we've discussed - vision, innovation, empathy, resilience - and weaving them into everyday team operations.

2. **Measuring Impact** – Evaluating whether all these changes work or are just lip service. Because if you're not tracking effectiveness, you're shooting in the dark.

This chapter is the brass tacks of transformation. You've got the knowledge; it's time to deploy it with a vengeance and verify the results. This is the path forward, the final baton pass that ensures your entire crew is not just on board but sprinting across the finish line with you. But what happens when you hit a roadblock? When a project fails, or a team member struggles? Planning for these moments is crucial to keep the momentum going and not let a setback derail your progress. We'll discuss this in the next section.

SECTION 1: IMPLEMENTING CATALYST PRINCIPLES – APPLYING CONCEPTS LEARNED TO YOUR TEAM

Let's get one thing straight: Telling your team, "We're going to be more innovative!" isn't enough. You have to embed these catalyst principles into your team's operational DNA. That means rewriting processes, setting new cultural norms, and holding people - especially yourself - accountable for exemplifying the change. For instance, if you want to foster a more innovative culture, you could implement a monthly hackathon where employees can pitch and prototype new features. Provide small budgets and time blocks explicitly dedicated to these hackathons. Let them fail, iterate, and share learnings. This is just one example of how to embed the catalyst principles into your team's operations.

TRANSLATING VISION INTO ACTION

You might have a grand vision - maybe it's revolutionizing your product category or shifting your organization's culture from complacent to fearless. But it'll remain abstract if your team doesn't see how this vision impacts their day-to-day tasks. Break it down into tangible projects, milestones, and mini-experiments.

Example: If you want a more "innovation-friendly" culture, implement a monthly hackathon where employees can pitch and prototype new features. Provide small budgets and time blocks explicitly dedicated to these hackathons. Let them fail, iterate, and share learnings.

EMPOWERING THE TEAM, NOT JUST "MANAGING" THEM

True catalysts don't micromanage; they empower. Ask your team for ideas, solutions, and critiques. Give them autonomy to make decisions in their domains. You've already lost if someone's afraid to step up because they fear retribution for mistakes. Shift your management style from "command and control" to "guide and energize." This demands trust on your part and clarity on theirs - they need to know what's expected, how success is measured, and the boundaries within which they can operate freely.

Key Move: Incorporate "failure reviews" as a standard agenda item in team meetings. Instead of blame, treat mistakes as data. This normalizes risk-taking and breaks down fear-driven inertia.

REINFORCING EMOTIONAL INTELLIGENCE

We covered emotional intelligence earlier, but let's reiterate that empathy, self-awareness, and adaptability are non-negotiable for a catalytic team. Every hire, every leadership style, and every policy you create should reflect these values. Suppose your team sees you blow up in a meeting or disregard feedback. In that case, they'll assume all that emotional intelligence talk was just hot air.

Practical Step: Introduce short, monthly EI skill sessions - maybe a 15-minute segment in staff meetings - where you discuss real scenarios of conflict or communication breakdowns. Let the team weigh in on how better emotional management could have changed the outcome.

ALIGNING INCENTIVES WITH CATALYST GOALS

Talk is cheap if your reward structures push people to do the opposite of what you're preaching. If you want collaboration, but your performance metrics reward siloed heroics, guess what? People will cling to silos. If you want risk-taking, but your bonus system punishes errors, you'll get safety over innovation. Make sure your recognition and compensation reflect the new principles.

Concrete Example: If you want more cross-team synergy, set a portion of each person's bonus on company-wide metrics rather than just departmental. Or offer a "collaboration award" that specifically highlights cross-functional accomplishments.

SECTION 2: MEASURING IMPACT – EVALUATING THE EFFECTIVENESS OF CHANGES

Without measurement, you're just guessing. Implementation feels great now - everyone's excited about new goals, processes, and energy - but you must confirm that these changes deliver results.

DEFINING KEY METRICS

Not everything can be neatly distilled into a single KPI. However, you can still define relevant metrics for each transformation area:

- **Innovation:** Number of new product ideas generated, prototypes developed, or the ratio of new features launched to total features.

- **Culture:** Employee engagement scores, feedback from 360 reviews, retention rates - particularly of high performers.

- **Collaboration:** Cross-functional project success rates, frequency of joint initiatives, or the time it takes to deliver a project with multiple departments involved.

- **Customer Impact:** Net Promoter Score (NPS), customer churn, or growth in user engagement post-innovation rollouts.

These metrics aren't just a scoreboard; they're a diagnostic tool. If the numbers aren't moving as expected, you investigate and iterate. The point is not to pass or fail but to glean insights and refine your approach.

THE FEEDBACK LOOP

Monitoring is only half the story. The other half is acting on the data you gather:

1. **Collect** – Set regular intervals for measuring your chosen metrics. It could be monthly, quarterly, or after significant initiatives.

2. **Analyze** – Ask why. Why did that metric spike? Why did it tank? Avoid superficial answers - dig for root causes.

3. **Adjust** – Tweak your processes, resources, or cultural levers based on what the data says. If collaboration is still lacking, maybe you need new cross-team tools or restructured incentives.

4. **Communicate** – Update your team on findings. Celebrate gains, own shortfalls, and clarify any new action steps.

This cyclical approach ensures you're never coasting. Continuous improvement becomes the norm, not a buzzword in a mission statement.

ACCOUNTABILITY CHECKPOINTS

Don't rely on rosy progress reports. Implement accountability checkpoints. Every quarter, you have a leadership roundtable where managers present the catalyst metrics for which they're responsible. Or you can hold public "town hall" sessions where employees can ask tough questions. The transparency and regularity of these sessions keep people from slacking or papering over issues.

TAKE ACTION

1. Catalyst Implementation Scoreboard

- Collaborate with your team to pick 3-5 metrics that represent your catalyst principles - innovation, emotional intelligence, collaboration, etc.

- Use a simple, highly visible scoreboard (online dashboard, physical board, weekly email) to track progress on these metrics.

- Update it monthly. In each update session, ask: "What's driving our progress? Where are we slipping? What new experiment or pivot is needed?"

- The scoreboard isn't just data; it's a narrative of your transformation. People see, in real-time, how their efforts contribute.

2. "Pulse Check Interviews"

- Every quarter, pick 10-15 employees at random from across departments - no hierarchy limitations - and schedule brief, confidential chats.

- Ask them about the changes implemented: Do they see tangible benefits? Are they encountering new obstacles? Which initiatives have fizzled?

- Summarize these insights to the broader leadership or the entire team, depending on scope. This direct, unfiltered feedback can reveal hidden issues your official metrics might miss.

FINAL THOUGHTS

You hold the spark, but your team is the tinder that ignites the wildfire of transformation. Implement the catalyst principles relentlessly. Measure every outcome with brutal honesty. Iterate till it sticks. Don't settle for shallow commitments and half-baked follow-through. Refuse to let your vision die in the realm of "could have, should have."

As Amelia Earhart said, "The most difficult thing is the decision to act; the rest is merely tenacity." Light the match, fan the flames, and lead your team into a future only you have the guts to imagine. Now burn bright.

"A true catalyst leader doesn't just build success - they build successors. If your impact dies when you step away, you weren't leading - you were just holding the reins."

PART THREE:
SUSTAINING CATALYST LEADERSHIP

HUSTLE & HEART: HAIER'S STORY OF GRIT AND GLOBAL GROWTH

They told the founders of Haier, a struggling refrigerator factory in Qingdao, China, that turning the company around would be near-impossible. In the 1980s, the company had inherited backward manufacturing processes, abysmal quality control, and a demoralized workforce used to poor standards. Competitors from abroad were flooding the market with cheaper, more advanced appliances. Even local consumers weren't sure whether Haier products were worth their dwindling savings.

The new leadership, however, refused to accept that fate. They embarked on a radical journey of continuous improvement and rigorous standards. Early on, they discovered an entire batch of defective refrigerators - units that might still have been serviceable with some post-sale repairs.

Instead of patching and shipping them out, the CEO famously had employees line them up and smash them with sledgehammers, demonstrating that zero tolerance for subpar product quality was the new norm. People thought it was wasteful, maybe even insane. But the message was clear: This company would not compromise on excellence.

That singular act of destruction became a catalyst for Haier's larger cultural shift. Employees got the memo: If you want to be taken seriously, you'd better adapt, improve, and hold yourself to higher standards than your competition.

Over the next few years, Haier relentlessly updated production systems launched cross-functional improvement projects and opened up lines of communication so that every worker - from machine operator to sales rep - had a voice in refining processes. The company didn't stop at refrigerators.

With time, they ventured into washers and air conditioners and eventually expanded globally with advanced smart-home appliances.

They didn't do it by coasting on initial successes; they kept pushing, iterating, and challenging employees to evolve. Haier went from a local joke to one of the world's most reputable appliance brands. These outlasting rivals once dominated the space.

TAKEAWAYS:

Symbolic Leadership: The sledgehammer incident is a powerful example of symbolic leadership. It sent a clear message to employees, customers, and competitors about Haier's new priorities.

Cultural Transformation: The incident was a catalyst for a broader cultural transformation within the company, emphasizing quality, continuous improvement, and employee involvement.

Long-Term Vision: Haier's success is a testament to its long-term vision and commitment to building a strong brand based on quality and innovation.

INTRODUCTION: THE ENDGAME OF CATALYST LEADERSHIP

This is the final section, where all the concepts - from emotional intelligence to forging industry alliances, from transforming your team to driving industry standards - come together. And it boils down to two final, critical pieces:

1. Continuous Adaptation – Because the second you stop moving, you start dying.

2. Legacy and Succession Planning – Because if your catalytic impact ends when you step aside, you've only done half the job.

If you've made it this far, you're not interested in quick wins or surface-level changes. You're here to create sustained momentum that lifts not just you but your team and, ultimately, your entire industry. So, let's break it down into actionable steps that ensure your leadership doesn't peak and fade like a flash in the pan.

SECTION 1: CONTINUOUS ADAPTATION – REMAINING AGILE IN THE FACE OF NEW CHALLENGES THE MINDSET OF ETERNAL EVOLUTION

It's easy to go into autopilot once you've hit some big milestones. You've achieved market share, the brand is recognized, or the team's morale is high. This sense of "we've made it" is the exact moment you become vulnerable to disruption. The marketplace shifts, technology evolves, and new generations of talent bring fresh expectations. If you're not living in a constant state of readiness to pivot, you'll be that leader who clings to the old ways while your competition surges ahead.

Continuous adaptation isn't about sporadic bursts of innovation - it's about building an organizational "immune system" that automatically adjusts whenever external or internal changes arise. Think of it like this: your company is a living organism, and adaptation is the evolutionary trait that keeps it healthy and thriving in changing habitats.

WHAT ADAPTATION DEMANDS FROM LEADERS

1. **Relentless Curiosity** - Curiosity is the fuel that drives adaptation. As a leader, you should be the most curious person in the room. Ask unconventional questions, read widely (even outside your industry), and build cross-functional think tanks where people can propose wild ideas without the fear of immediate shutdown.

2. **Calculated Risk-Taking** - Playing it safe is the fastest route to irrelevance. You don't want reckless gambles but need a structured way to experiment. That might involve a portion of your budget or resources earmarked for new initiatives - an "INNOVATION Space" where you can test prototypes, market approaches, or organizational changes before rolling them out at scale.

3. **Structured Decentralization** - You want every level of the organization to feel empowered to propose changes. If every decision needs your green light, you become the bottleneck. Instead, set guiding principles and let teams adapt them to their contexts. This fosters a culture where adaptation isn't top-down - it's woven into daily work.

THE REWARDS AND PITFALLS

Rewards: You remain on the cutting edge, attracting top-tier talent who crave dynamic environments. Your company is known for agility and resilience, which wins over customers tired of stagnant brands. You're more likely to spot new revenue streams before they go mainstream.

Pitfalls: You may chase every shiny object if you can't differentiate between actual trends and hype. That's why structure matters - so you can quickly test viability without overcommitting. Another pitfall is "change fatigue," where employees get overwhelmed by constant pivots. The solution? Communicate the purpose behind every change and offer support for the transition.

SECTION 2: LEGACY AND SUCCESSION PLANNING - PREPARING THE NEXT GENERATION OF CATALYST LEADERS THE BIGGER PICTURE: WHY LEGACY MATTERS

If your leadership prowess evaporates the day you step away, you've squandered a massive opportunity. True legacy isn't about your name on a building or your face on the company website; it's about creating an ecosystem that outlives you. It's about ensuring that the spark of innovation you ignited keeps burning in the hearts of future leaders.

Look at the biggest shifts in history - whether it's social movements, technological revolutions, or corporate giants that endure decades. They all hinge on one fact: the baton passed, and each successor built upon the foundation before them.

IDENTIFYING FUTURE TORCHBEARERS

1. **Spotting Talent Early** - Future catalyst leaders might not have the perfect resume. Still, they exhibit insatiable curiosity, a willingness to take calculated risks, and genuine concern for team well-being. Don't just look at performance metrics; look at how they solve problems and how they rally peers.

2. **Mentoring and Coaching** - Once you spot the right people, invest in them. Mentorship is about sharing your knowledge, your network, and

your perspective. Put them on the front lines of big projects, expose them to the complexity of leadership decisions, and then step back. Let them learn by doing, and don't swoop in to fix every mistake.

3. **Public Recognition** - It's not about hogging the spotlight. Give up-and-coming leaders roles in public-facing opportunities - industry panels, high-profile client meetings, or internal summits. That's how they build credibility and confidence, and it signals to the whole organization that leadership development is woven into your culture.

BUILDING INSTITUTIONAL CONTINUITY

Creating a legacy requires more than just grooming individual successors. It's about ingraining your guiding principles - innovation, emotional intelligence, adaptability - into the very DNA of your organization. Document best practices, ritualize certain cultural behaviors (like open idea pitching or monthly reflection sessions), and embed them in policies and job descriptions. This ensures that the blueprint for catalytic action remains even if key personalities depart.

BALANCING EGO WITH IMPACT

It's easy for leaders to get attached to being the face of everything. However, a true catalyst leader recognizes that the ego can become a barrier. If you're hoarding power because you secretly fear losing relevance, you're stifling the pipeline of future leaders. Let them shine. When the next generation sees you're willing to share the stage, they'll be more confident stepping up - and your collective impact multiplies.

TAKE ACTION

1. **Agility Sprints**

• At least once a quarter, run an "Agility Sprint." Pick an aspect of your operation - product development, marketing, or internal HR processes.

- Task a small cross-department team to propose improvements or new approaches in two weeks. Provide minimal constraints but a clear outcome (e.g., a small-scale demo or pilot).

- Follow up with a public debrief on successes, failures, and lessons. This normalizes the rapid test-and-learn cycle, ensuring that continuous adaptation becomes part of your organizational muscle memory.

2. **Succession Mentorship Circles**

- Form small mentorship circles pairing experienced leaders with two to three high-potential employees. Focus on real projects - assign them tough deliverables that matter to the company's future.

- Mentors guide but don't micromanage. Encourage mentees to present in executive forums or town halls so they can hone their communication and leadership presence.

- Cycle these groups every six to nine months, allowing more employees to step into the spotlight and fostering a broad pool of next-gen talent.

FINAL THOUGHTS

This is where the road forks: you can either collapse under your success - let it turn you stagnant - or carry the torch into a future filled with reinvention. The catalyst leader doesn't dwell on past glories; they crave the next challenge. They don't hoard power; they cultivate armies of innovators. The final question isn't about how far you've come - it's about how far your leadership legacy will reach after you're gone.

As Beethoven said, "Recommend virtue to your children; it alone, not money, can make them happy. I speak from experience." Swap "virtue" with "catalyst leadership," and you've got your mantra. Pass this torch. Build an ever-evolving culture where the seeds you've planted grow forests beyond your horizon. That's the end game - and it's only the beginning.

The Evolution Spiral

A dynamic, four-stage cycle that repeats itself to keep you, your team, and your entire organization always moving forward.

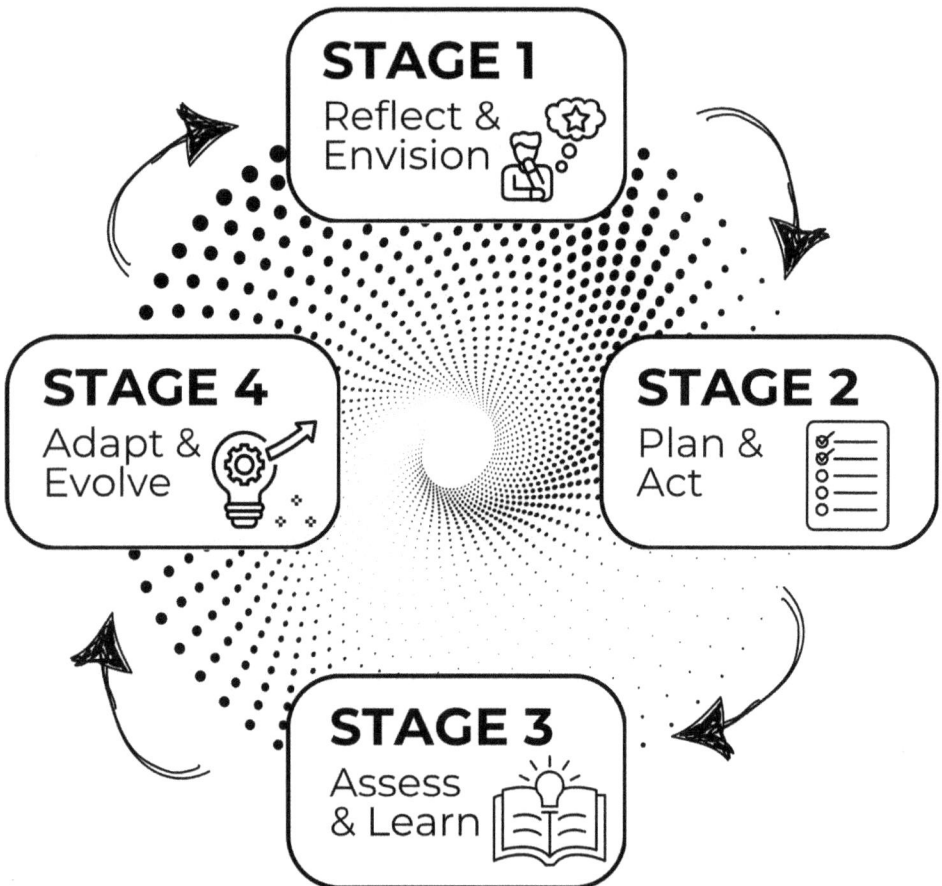

STAGE 1
Reflect & Envision

STAGE 2
Plan & Act

STAGE 3
Assess & Learn

STAGE 4
Adapt & Evolve

TOOL:
THE EVOLUTION SPIRAL

Listen up: You don't become a legendary leader by accident - you evolve. And you don't just evolve once; you keep doing it, again and again. That's where The Evolution Spiral comes in. It's all about stepping up your personal leadership game, guiding your team's transformation, and then making sure it sticks for the long haul.

Bottom line: If you're serious about taking your leadership to the next level - and leaving a legacy while you're at it - you need this. Let's go!

Why It Works When You're Mapping The Path Forward

Personal Leadership Development

- Creating a Leadership Plan: The Spiral kicks off with self-reflection and goal-setting, making sure you've got a clear roadmap for your own growth.

- Seeking Feedback and Mentorship: Each loop of the Spiral pushes you to incorporate external insights, so you're constantly sharpening your skills.

Leading Your Team's Transformation

- Implementing Catalyst Principles: Once you've leveled up personally, the Spiral naturally flows into applying what you've learned to your team.

- Measuring Impact: The Spiral includes a feedback mechanism where you assess how well your new ideas are working. If something's off, you pivot quickly.

Sustaining Catalyst Leadership

- Continuous Adaptation: The Spiral isn't linear - it loops. That means you're always ready to face new challenges head-on.

- Legacy and Succession Planning: A true leader lifts others up. By repeating the cycle with emerging talent, you ensure the Catalyst approach lives on even after you've moved on.

What Is It? The Evolution Spiral

Think of it as a dynamic, four-stage cycle that repeats itself to keep you, your team, and your entire organization always moving forward:

1. **Reflect & Envision** - Know your strengths, weaknesses, and leadership goals. Then, envision where you want to be - both personally and team-wide.

2. **Plan & Act** - Draft a clear action plan: what changes you'll make, how you'll involve your team, and what metrics matter. Then, execute with purpose.

3. **Assess & Learn** - Measure the impact of your actions. What's working? What's not? Gather feedback from mentors, peers, and especially your team.

4. **Adapt & Evolve** - Tweak your strategy, refine your leadership style, and prepare to loop back to reflection again. This is how you sustain progress long-term.

This cyclical structure ensures you're always building upon previous insights - never stagnating.

How To Use It

In the Office

- Reflect & Envision: Kick off each quarter with a leadership audit - what have you done well, and where are your pain points? Set clear targets for growth.

- Plan & Act: Involve your team in creating an action plan. Assign roles, establish deadlines, and define success metrics together.

With Your Team

- Assess & Learn: Hold an all-hands review session after a big project or initiative. Gather feedback on what worked, what didn't, and what you can improve next time.

- Adapt & Evolve: Use the insights to adjust processes or communication strategies. Then, loop back to the reflection, setting new goals for the next cycle.

With Yourself

- Reflect & Envision: Start each morning by journaling one leadership trait you want to improve. Over time, you'll spot patterns where you excel and need more work.

- Adapt & Evolve: Incorporate your growth lessons into your larger life plan - whether that's taking a course, finding a new mentor, or embracing a fresh approach to leadership.

Here's the real talk: You never "arrive" at perfect leadership - it's a continuous journey of leveling up. The Evolution Spiral gives you a powerful, repeating cycle for ongoing growth - both for you and the teams that depend on your vision.

Embrace this process, and you won't just create progress - you'll become the catalyst leader everyone wants to follow. Game on!

NEXT STEPS: IGNITE YOUR CATALYST

"ARE YOU READY TO BLAZE
A NEW TRAIL IN YOUR
INDUSTRY?"

"Catalyst leaders don't wait for permission - they ignite action, disrupt complacency, and rewrite the rules. Stop playing small. Step up, light the fire, and lead the charge."

NEXT STEPS:
IGNITE YOUR CATALYST

Look, you didn't spend precious hours devouring these chapters just to close the book and carry on like nothing's changed. You came here because some force in you yells, "I'm done messing around—I want to blow the doors off my potential and unleash my team's hidden brilliance."

Here's the deal: **Catalyst Leadership** isn't some passing buzzword—it's how bold leaders in volatile times crush mediocrity. Every story in this book—whether it's Netflix's reinvention or Slack's pivot—shouts one thing loud and clear: you must dare, innovate, and invest in your people, or you'll get buried by the next wave.

WHY CATALYST LEADERSHIP RULES

We're in an era where entire industries can flip overnight due to a single disruptive idea. Gone are the days you could skate by on a legacy brand or incremental improvements. If you're not scanning future trends, forging daring paths, and firing up your team to innovate alongside you, guess what? Someone else will. **Catalyst Leadership** isn't about playing it safe. It's about igniting your organization with a hardcore vision, relentless agility, and the guts to risk failing forward.

Catalyst leaders tear down excuses and champion the future. They treat rapid shifts—like AI or new consumer demands—as an open playground. They see global expansion not as a headache but as a shot at exponential impact. And they never, ever tolerate complacency. Because if you're coasting, you're already behind.

Need proof? Look at Blockbuster's downfall, Tesla's boldness, Slack's resurrection from a failed game, or Starbucks 'unwavering focus on team training. They all hammered home one truth: either you embrace a catalytic mindset or you get smoked by unstoppable competition. Catalyst Leadership doesn't just keep you afloat; it turbo-charges you forward, rewriting your entire field's playbook.

USE THIS STUFF DAILY

I'm not here to give you a temporary dopamine rush that fades by Monday morning. You've just inherited a blueprint of real company wins and fails, along with practical steps to reprogram your team's culture, creative triggers, and synergy. Don't treat these tools as trophies for your shelf. Treat them like daily weapons in your leadership arsenal.

- **Stories:** Whenever you feel stalled, recall how Netflix broke past DVDs or how Starbucks bet on barista training when others slashed budgets. That's real possibility, not theory.

- **Learnings:** We covered emotional intelligence, cross-functional brilliance, AI-driven reinvention—this is your skill set for a world that doesn't wait for you to catch up.

- **Actions:** No one built a billion-dollar empire by passively reading. Implement the concepts relentlessly. Whether it's hosting Momentum Sprints, using the Priority Ladder to nuke busywork, or launching a Team Growth Map initiative, you must take consistent, bold steps to reshape your environment.

- **New Tools:** We replaced the old frameworks with hardcore Catalyst methods—from the Orchestra Alignment Canvas (to unify cross-functional teams) to Innovation Hubs (for unstoppable creativity). Each one systematically busts silos, slays busy excuses, and unleashes unstoppable synergy.

WHEN YOU'RE STUMPED, STUCK, OR LOST: OPEN THIS TOOLKIT

Let's be real: you will face chaos. Some new competitor, a crisis, or just personal burnout might push you to the brink. That's exactly why you should keep this resource handy. Each chapter tackles a unique piece of the Catalyst puzzle—emotional intelligence for tough convos, bridging departmental gaps for big leaps, or forging forward visions that dodge stagnation. Face unknown disruptions? Revisit strategic foresight. Running into massive turnover? Flip back to team development. This is your Catalyst Swiss Army knife, right here to bail you out of any slump.

Don't rely on memory alone. Real life can blindside you. Keep these sections bookmarked so that when the moment hits—when your instincts fail and panic rises—you can flip to the solution faster than your competition can say, "We're doomed."

READY FOR MORE? REACH OUT

If you're fired up to launch your Catalyst revolution but need deeper support, I'm your guy. My name's Rich Gee, and I transform good leaders into unstoppable catalysts.

Through dynamic speaking, interactive workshops, and no-BS executive coaching, I deliver strategies that weld Catalyst thinking into your leadership DNA.

We skip the fluff and plunge into your challenges, leveling up your assertiveness, creativity, and influence. If you're an executive aiming to reignite your team or a business owner bracing for your next pivot, I've got the playbook and the push.

Reach out at **www.richgee.com** to set up an intro demo. Sometimes an external catalyst is exactly the jolt you need.

A FINAL KICK IN THE ASS

So here's the moment: use what you've learned or let it slip away. Don't let fear of failing or pushback from your team stifle your ambition. Dial up your clarity, step into uncomfortable territory, and cultivate an environment where risk is embraced, collaboration is fierce, and results blow the roof off expectations.

As Winston Churchill once growled, "Difficulties mastered are opportunities won." Embrace that. Difficulties? They're not your enemy—they're your chance to prove Catalyst Leadership is more than hype. The baton's in your hand, the stage is yours, and the crowd awaits. Go bring the house down.

Catalysts, Onward and Upward!

WAIT—WE'RE JUST GETTING STARTED

Look, if you made it to this point in Catalyst Leadership, I already know something about you:

You're not here to just read about transformation — you're here to lead it.

But this book? This is just Step One.

Behind the scenes, I'm building out an entire arsenal of bonus chapters, bite-sized insights, private YouTube drops, exclusive interviews, deep-dive toolkits, and yeah — even group coaching experiences designed for high-performers like you who want to go from "great" to absolutely unstoppable.

I'm talking about:

- **Extra strategies** I couldn't fit in the book (the legal team said "cut it," I said "fine, I'll just release it later.")

- **Video trainings** that break down the exact systems and habits my clients use to dominate in their fields.

- **Behind-the-scenes** breakdowns of what real Catalyst Leaders are doing right now — no fluff, just impact.

- **First dibs** on upcoming live coaching sessions, masterminds, and new projects I'm testing.

It's not all built yet — but it's coming.

And I want you in from the ground floor.

Head over to **RichGee.com/Catalyst** and throw in your name and info. That's it.

I'll keep you in the loop as this evolves, and when something new drops, you'll be the first to get it — no spam, no fluff, just value.

We're building a movement of leaders who don't wait for permission.

If that's you, let's keep going.

See you on the inside,

Rich Gee Executive Coaching
www.richgee.com